CW01391309

Field of Dreams

150 Years at The County Ground, Hove

Patrick Ferriday & James Mettyear

First published in Great Britain by
VON KRUMM PUBLISHING
31 Highcroft Villas
Brighton BN1 5PS

www.vonkrummpublishing.co.uk

Copyright 2022 Patrick Ferriday & James Mettyear

All rights reserved. No part of this publication may be reproduced, stored in a retrieval system, or transmitted, in any form or by any means without the prior written permission of the publisher, nor be otherwise circulated in any form of binding or cover other than that in which it is published and without a similar condition being imposed on the subsequent purchaser.

The right of Patrick Ferriday & James Mettyear to be identified as the Authors of the Work has been asserted by them in accordance with the Copyright, Designs and Patents Act 1998.

A CIP record of this book is available from the British Library.

Cover and all interior graphic design by Josh Robinson & Patrick Ferriday.

Printed and Bound in King's Lynn by Biddles

ISBN 978-0-9567321-9-4

Contents

Place

1. Towards Cricket   1

2. Play!   9
   WG at Hove // Lord Sheffield and William Murdoch //
   Cricket Weeks // Cardus, Fry and Ranji at Hove //
   A Tragedy of the Cricket Field // Alletson's Innings //
   World War I

3. Between the Wars   51
   Maurice Tate // A Cricketer in Retirement //
   Cricket Weeks Again // Women's Cricket at Hove //
   World War II

4. 1946-1971   81
   Big Hits at Hove // The Gilligan Stand

5. 1972-2002   106
   Women's Cricket Continued // Hove at the Centre
   of World Cricket // The View from the Away
   Dressing-Room // Spen Cama // The Groundsmen //
   The 300 Club

6. Champions, At Last   140

People

Jim Parks

Nigel Russell

Michael Simkins

Tim Burges

Brenda Lower

Sam Wheeler

Paul Weaver

Michael Wilkinson

Laurie Marshall

Peter Graves

Frances Low

Holly Colvin

Don McCrickard

John Spencer

Jon Filby

Paul Parker

Hayden Brunsdon

Leigh Latham

Alec Keith

Rob Steen

Clare Rogers

Springhar Shinwari

John Barclay

Georgia Adams

Foreword

My year as MCC President began in October 2021 and the timing could not have been better as cricket, and women's cricket in particular, continues to grow around the world. In August, we will see cricket included in the Commonwealth Games for the first time, whilst the record-breaking crowds that attended The Hundred last year have created new levels of interest in the game across the country.

A happy coincidence is that this year also sees the 150th anniversary of cricket at the Eaton Road ground. I am delighted to have been invited to write the foreword to this book and to send my congratulations to all at Hove as we celebrate the role of the ground in the life of the people of Brighton and Hove, the counties of East and West Sussex and to cricket lovers across the world.

My own love for this special place started as a very young girl when I came to matches with my nan and grandad and their friends. We sat in the north-west corner and enjoyed wonderful picnics and equally wonderful cricket chat throughout the day. It was there, amongst the deckchairs, watching players like Paul Parker, the Wells brothers and Ian Gould, that my passion for cricket first grew. My grandad, who followed 'the cricket' throughout his life, was to live to the ripe old age of 98. It is very special to me that his ashes are interred just inside the boundary in front of the committee room.

The importance of the ground in my cricket development was immense. I was soon invited to join the junior Sussex Boys squads and trained with great coaches like Pat Cale and Stuart Storey, who treated me no differently to any of the boys. I started in the Chalet where the low net stopped me getting all of the loop I wanted on my bowling, but soon moved to the Gilligan Stand where flight was unimpeded and finally to the new Indoor School built close to where I used to sit with my grandparents.

I fondly remember two of the most important games in my career, both played at the ground. Firstly in 2004, when Hove hosted the first ever T20 International in this country and I captained England against New Zealand in a team which included another home-grown Sussex player in Rosalie Birch, and then, in 2005 when another Sussex cricketer, Holly Colvin, made her debut in the Ashes Test against Australia. We drew that game but went on to win the Ashes for the first time in 42 years at Worcester. Occasions never to forget!

Since retiring from playing, Hove has continued to play an important part both in the growth of Women's Cricket, and in my own life and career. I was delighted to join the Board of Sussex County Cricket Club in 2009 and served as a board member for four years where I learned a huge amount about governance and how to influence at board level, all of which complemented the work that I had just started on the ICC Cricket Committee. Hove has also continued to be the venue of choice for many women's internationals and was the prefect home to three of four Kia Super League Finals, the precursor to the development of The Hundred. I will certainly never forget the sell-out crowd for the Ashes T20 International against Australia in 2015.

The ground at Hove is such a special place to me. From my first visits as a little girl, the warm welcome and encouragement I received as a developing player, a home Test Match, my first steps into the boardroom, and now continuing a rich Sussex tradition in the role of President of the MCC, following such greats of Sussex Cricket as Johnny Barclay, Mike Griffith, Robin Marlar, Christopher Martin-Jenkins and Hubert Doggart.

It is truly wonderful to celebrate 150 years of the ground, to see the Tate Residences rising at the sea end and to know that the redevelopment plans will enable the ground to continue to play a huge part in the life of the city and to provide a venue for cricket and so much more to be enjoyed by so many. Here's to the next 150 years!

Clare Connor – Lord's, October 2021

Preface

The seed for this book had been germinating for the best part of half a century; it took root at the end of July 2018 when the authors attended the second day of the pink-ball day-night game against Glamorgan. Our usual basecamp is on the deck chairs in the north-east corner, where space is usually sufficient for nattering out of earshot of fellow spectators. You can gaze across the ground and talk of how the sea used to form its southern horizon and other important matters of the day.

Each to their own. Some seek solitude, solitude in a lightly-salted crowd to the slight accompaniment of athletic endeavour. Others bring scorebooks and pencils or read the paper cover-to-cover with an occasional glance over the top to see what the flannelled fools are up to. Young parents discover that the sound of leather and willow acts as a sleeping draught to their baby – they'll be back. Children on holiday, eager for intervals in order to stretch their restless limbs on the grass. It's both congenial and inclusive. Live and let live. The ground itself has been there for 150 years, originally isolated and now surrounded but still beating back the tide of urbanisation. It offers so much, and you choose which bit draws you in according to mood, company, weather, and the nature of the game being played out before you.

On that hot, crystal-clear July day, we took up our seats in the Shark Stand. John Arlott once wrote that it was Neville Cardus who taught him to watch cricket rather than merely see it and this, we sensed, was a day for watching. After all, how often in these days of central contracts do you get the chance to see Jofra Archer, Chris Jordan and Ollie Robinson in harness for the home side in a Championship game?

Sussex had been bowled out at the end of the first day for 327 which did not tell of demons in the pitch, but there was something in the air. We didn't have much trouble finding two seats in our favoured location – half-way up, just high enough to take the slope out of the equation, but close enough to the gangway to make unobtrusive trips to the bar followed by concomitant visits to the gents. But the stand was full enough to obscure the 'SHARK' lettering from the sight of those lounging in the deckchairs at the northern end.

In the event, there were but few trips to the Tony Greig café. We were right about it being a watching day. It started with a bang. It wasn't just that Jofra Archer removed both openers and Usman Khawaja in his first three overs, it was how he did it. It's well-nigh impossible with the naked eye to tell what the ball is doing – nipping around, swinging or perhaps it's going straight on? What you can see is bounce and the batter's reaction. On this evidence, Archer was bowling extremely quickly. Within 30 overs, the first innings was done and dusted. In the break, pickup games sprouted on the outfield. We watched a man near our own vintage getting peppered by 10-year-olds with a wind ball – less competitive-dad, more game-grandad. He caught our appreciative eye as he fended off another throat ball and grinned back in acknowledgement; such small, unspoken interchanges are part of what make a day at the cricket such a precious thing.

Looking towards the Cromwell Road end, the crowd had grown by the time the Glamorgan openers took to the field for the follow-on, and as the visitors again folded in short order, even the north-east corner filled further with the after-work crowd. They didn't get to see much. Twenty wickets in less than a day, all over before they even had a chance to turn the lights on. One of us saw all of them, the other, with the weaker bladder, got caught in the gangway mid-over and missed a run-out, the view obscured by the broad back of Paul Farbrace, perhaps down to watch his stepson Ollie pick up four for 44. You can spend hours, days, seasons, a lifetime even, not seeing such arresting bowling live. Fittingly, we spotted John Snow, still as lithe as in his pomp, witnessing the final knockings from the same gangway.

It was fitting too, that it was this exceptional day's play, viewed from the from the unfamiliar vantage point of the ground's newest addition, that sealed a joint commitment to do something to celebrate it.

The book is divided into two sections:

Place

Even though this book is emphatically not another history of Sussex cricket, but rather the story of the ground itself and some of those who people it, the game itself inevitably forms part of the narrative. Cricket and money. Finances will be a recurrent topic over the following pages. Without money there is no development and no cricket, without money there is no field of dreams, no stage for Fry, Ranji, Tate, Parks, Greig, Snow, Mushtaq Ahmed and many others on which to strut their stuff.

Right from the outset, themes are unearthed which echo throughout the next 150 years: the need to attract punters, to diversify income, to avoid the covetous eyes of property developers and to attract benefactors. All are perennial problems a succession of administrators has grappled with. That they have managed to keep the County Ground in the heart of the town, and to somehow keep its essential character alive, is testament both to many of those involved, but also perhaps to the indomitable magic held within the old perimeter wall's embrace. Long may that remain.

Six main chapters will tell the story of the 'place'. Short vignettes after most chapters will evoke particular instances or themes that would distort the main narrative but are crucial to an understanding of what has happened at Eaton Road in the last 150 years.

People

My first visit to Eaton Road was in 1966. We sat on the south-east terrace not far from a long-haired man with thick pebble glasses who, with pocket-set and professional looking timer, played speed chess with himself throughout the day. Since that first day, I've always been as fascinated by the people at the County Ground, as I have by the game played within it. And I've always thought the Hove crowd to be a much broader church than the standard stereotype of the county cricket follower. It has been a real pleasure to confirm that belief.

The 24 people who have here generously shared how and why the ground is stitched into the fabric of their lives, are not deemed to be in any way representative. When it comes to what makes the place special, common threads emerge, but just as with everyone who has ever walked through the Tate Gates, they are all individuals, with their own stories.

We had originally planned for there to be more than a couple of dozen voices captured here, but Covid restricted things more than a little. We worried particularly that our youth policy was grievously under-developed, but then reflected that, as one of those we talked to breezily reminded us, "Don't worry, today's youth will get their turn when the club celebrates the 200th anniversary. Now it's our go. Before it's too late".

Acknowledgements

The authors have been fortunate enough to receive encouragement and help at every step of the way in writing Part One of this book. The Hove ground is blessed by the hard work of the members of the Sussex Cricket Museum under Jon Filby. This has been our first port of call.

David Jeater and Nicholas Sharp read early drafts and offered guidance and advice on all manner of subjects. Nicholas has been a regular at Eaton Road for over 70 years and there is little he doesn't know. Also Trevor Burton, Norman Epps, and David Stoner gave useful information and pointers in their own fields of expertise. Phil Barnes quickly became the go-to man for all pictures and supplied a steady flow to meet every need.

Special thanks to James Cory-Wright – like his father before him, his wit and selection of exotic snacks have enlivened many a day at The County Ground.

Outside the ground we would like to thank the patience and help of staff at The Keep in Falmer, and for questions answered by the supreme local historian Judy Middleton.

Thanks are also due to Clare Connor for her heartfelt foreword and to Rob Andrew for his afterword.

Part Two is somewhat simpler. Twenty-four people gave of their time and their reflections. A huge thank-you to all of them.

Image Credits:

Sussex Cricket Museum and Educational Trust: 11, 21, 39, 48, 57, 61, 70, 74, 79, 90, 92, 94, 99, 107, 110, 114, 130, 132, 143, 145, 147, 151

Roger Mann: 14, 28, 31, 56

Trevor Burton: 141

All other images are from the authors. If any is perceived to be in infringement of copyright, please contact the publisher.

Part I

PLACE

-One-

Towards Cricket

From the first Bronze Age settlements to the arrival of raffishness, Brighton survived any number of upheavals. Sandwiched between the more significant towns of Lewes and Shoreham, storms, raids from across the channel, fire and the gradual disappearance of the River Wellesbourne was a combination that might have crushed a less hardy, or foolhardy, gathering of people.

With the motley array of dwellings teetering on the brink of desolation by the mid-eighteenth century, a certain Dr Richard Russell of Lewes rode to the rescue with the 1752 publication of his *Dissertation on the Use of Sea Water in the Disease of the Glands*. The moneyed classes of London took note and were happy to make the journey south to 'Dr Brighton's' treatment centre at Russell House. These visitors brought money, which naturally begat expansion and prosperity – bathing machines dotted the shingle beach while those of a less sturdy disposition avoided the worst of the elements in hot and cold seawater baths. With watering places such as Buxton and Harrogate experiencing transformative injections of cash, Hove now joined the act via the 'remarkable health-giving properties' of St Ann's Well.

Just as it seemed that this fad might be a boom-and-bust phenomenon, Brighton's second saviour, the Duke of Cumberland (George III's brother), brought his profligate ways and coterie of dubious acquaintances to Brighton, well away from the prying eyes and wagging tongues of the capital city. The first priorities were a racecourse and suitable social, gambling and carousing rooms for which the now-vacated Russell House was deemed ideal. George, Prince of Wales and later King George IV, was impressed and became an ever-more frequent visitor, and then inhabitant, of a town now widely known as Brighton (the name became official in 1810) on the cusp of a new epoch.

These were the Regency Years. Fashionable town-house enclaves appeared – Royal Crescent, Bedford Square and Regency Square – in quick succession. The Chain Pier opened in 1823, complete with a steam packet to Dieppe. Libraries, theatres, assembly rooms, pleasure gardens and, the jewel in the crown, the Royal Pavilion. Taverns, shops and lesser accommodation were required for the tradespeople who flocked in on the back of this building boom and the infrastructure, such as it was, overhauled with new streets, sewage systems and the laying of gas pipes from the new works at Black Rock. With a veritable army of domestic servants, livery workers and such like required to support these wealthy incomers, Brighton became a place to be and a place to be seen. With this came inevitable urban expansion, particularly along the coast, as outlying smaller settlements were drawn into the new metropolis.

HRH 'Prinny' also liked a game of cricket. The ground at The Level flourished under his patronage, but wilted when he decided to give up the game on ascending to the throne in 1820. James Ireland stepped into the breach and opened his Gardens and Cricket Ground in 1823 just north of The Level where Park Crescent now stands. The new venue incorporated assembly rooms, refreshments, a grotto, an aviary and a ladies' bowling green. Cricket in Brighton had been firmly established, proof of which was no less than six matches between Sussex and England between 1827 and 1834, including experimenting with the new-fangled round-arm bowling.

But with the King now frequently absent, decline set in across the town. Building projects failed and it seemed that this man-made construct with few natural advantages had overstretched itself and was now set for an alarming slump. The third saviour of Brighton was a spitting, smoking, roaring son of the Industrial Revolution.

The burgeoning railway construction industry had brought six companies into competition in 1835 to lay a direct line from London to Brighton. Royal assent was given in 1837. The chosen route, proposed by Sir John Rennie, would be as direct as possible and pay little heed to natural barriers. Furthermore, branch lines to Lewes, Shoreham and Newhaven (the latter pair with natural harbours) would put Brighton at the epicentre of a transport revolution in the heart of Sussex.

The project was vast, but Victorian engineers lacked nothing in either ingenuity or ambition. They also had the huge advantage of patient investors with deep pockets as well as almost limitless cheap labour. And this vast workforce was sorely tested. A huge encampment appeared at Pyecombe for workers on the Clayton Tunnel through the South Downs. Nearly 4000 men were employed, carving out the route to, and then the building of, Brighton Station. The line opened in 1841 and with seven trains a day and a journey of two hours Brighton took its first steps to becoming a satellite of London. Day trips, weekends away and retirement by the sea became possible, and holiday and service industries grew in parallel to cater for them.

The lack of any serious heavy industry was rectified by the opening of the locomotive works in 1852 to service the newly formed London, Brighton and South Coast Railway Company. Some 4000 skilled and semi-skilled jobs were thus created. Local lines quickly joined the network as its tentacles spread east and west to Kent and Hampshire.

With cricket becoming an increasingly popular spectator sport across the land and the failure of James Ireland's grand, too grand, project, a new venue was required on the coast. The first attempt was Lillywhite's Ground which is now the home of Montpelier Crescent, but with the formation of Sussex Cricket Club in 1839 presaging the beginning of inter-county competition and ultimately the County Championship, something better was needed. If this could be found, there was no telling what effect the railways might have on attendances with a day-trip from across the county now a viable option.

Charles Gausden was the man behind the Royal Brunswick Ground, situated between Third and Fourth Avenues and a six-hit from the sea. It opened in 1848; one of the gentler developments in a turbulent year for Europe. Gausden soon ran into financial trouble and the lease was bought by local brewers Vallance & Catt who then wasted no time in opening *The Brunswick Cricket Ground Hotel*, which was to prove a lucrative venture. This was now a ground, complete with thatched pavilion, run as a business and for profit. Sussex were blessed with players to take on the best in the country, who were only too pleased to visit the ground and the town with its already notorious reputation as a playground by the sea.

Cricket on the Brunswick Ground, down by the sea.

Faithful servant Tom Box, the family Lillywhite and John Wisden were amongst those who enabled Sussex to match allcomers, be it the Australian Aborigines, Marylebone Cricket Club or Nottinghamshire. Despite the advantages of ground and players, interest began to wane until Bridger Stent breathed life back into the club.

A meeting was called in July 1857 at which 'leading and influential Gentlemen of the County' foregathered for the purpose of forming a County Cricket Club. Viscount Pevensey (later Lord Sheffield) was elected president, with the tireless Stent as secretary. The main ambition was to make the side more inclusive and attract a wider variety of players and spectators. Stent's success was indisputable, but he had no control over a new threat: the owners of the Brunswick ground were uneasy. An attempt to acquire the leasehold in 1862 foundered through lack of funds and the rent spiralled by 150 per cent in a decade.

Great and historic deeds had been recorded at the Brunswick ground, not the least of which was HG Wells' father taking four wickets in four balls, but the success of Brighton and the demand for sea-view residences meant that the playing field was now an 'eligible plot'. The owner, Stanford Estate, was keen to cash in.

A notice to quit was issued in 1869 and arrangements urgently set in motion to find a new home for the nascent Sussex CCC. The committee did not have to look far, and Stanford Estate, particularly Ellen Stanford, was instrumental in procuring an admirable new home. Ellen had inherited the estate at the age of five in 1854, but no official guardian had been appointed to protect her interests, leaving the trustees and executors with a free hand to conduct business as they saw fit. The estate itself consisted of land in Wiltshire and Surrey as well as some 376 acres in Hove stretching from Preston Manor to the sea. In 1869 Ellen Stanford celebrated her 21st birthday and was finally able to take full control.

Moving Inland

Stanford Estate had plenty of land to go round and half-a-mile from the old ground almost due north, a perfect 10-acre plot was identified. Whether or not the move was entirely altruistic is uncertain, it certainly gave Stanford Estate prestige as landlord to the county side as well as adding value to the adjacent land. The new site was more accessible by public transport than the old. The original Hove Station situated hard by the Palmeira pub had opened in 1840, halfway between Brighton and Cliftonville (the current Hove station) with short journeys to the mid-Sussex heartland of Burgess Hill and Haywards Heath. Though the pub remains, the original Hove Station was superseded by Cliftonville in 1865 and closed within a decade. No matter for the club, the new Hove station was just a leisurely 15-minute stroll from the new arena.

The club had been in informal discussions with Ellen Stanford prior to approaching the Estate trustees in July 1871. The wording of the proposal is highly illuminating as to the aims and ambitions of those representing the interests of cricket. This was not merely a question of finding a green field on which to play county games:

It is vitally important to the numerous boys' schools in the town that they should have some ground for cricket and other recreations to which their pupils may resort, and it is also of consequence to the well-being of the town that it should not be deprived of the cricket ground, as the opportunities of recreation are few, and cricket is among the most popular of them.

In modern parlance, a community sports arena was envisioned. The advantages were obvious. Variety would bring in a broader spectrum of visitors, school involvement would be an investment in the future and, most important of all, the new ground would become an integral part of the community and town life. In these senses the club could be regarded as 'forward-thinking'. Their plans would be even more far-reaching than initially described.

The 10 acres 'between Mr Rigden's farm and the railway station at Cliftonville' were duly secured and leased for 21 years, at an annual rent of £100. The success of the hotel at the old ground had not been forgotten. A sum of £1924 was expended by Stanford Estate on a public house, in turn they would charge the club £50 annual rent. Again, as secretary Mr GW King's report showed, the club trustees were looking to the future. The fact that his report didn't tally with the final ownership of the hotel is indication that the initial arrangements were far from simple:

> The new inn has been planned in such a manner as to provide a very spacious and handsome room for dining, and its other arrangements cannot fail to meet the tastes and wishes of the public. As the inn will be the property of the club, the trustees are negotiating a mortgage upon advantageous terms to cover the cost of its erection, and in a few years it will become a valuable piece of property.

As it transpired, it took half a century to acquire the hotel and pay off the mortgage. In the immediate term, there was pressing work to be done if the ground was to be fit for play a mere eight months later.

First up the barley crop had to be harvested, and then there was a slight problem with the gradient. Quite simply the plot wasn't flat (and still isn't) and needed serious levelling. On the positive side, however, was the nature of the soil, a chalky slurry overlaying deeper chalk formations which allowed for good drainage. While vast amounts of soil were being deposited and compacted, the ground was being encircled by a six-foot brick wall. Built in six layers, this remarkable and hardy edifice still surrounds the majority of the ground. At a cost of £1200, the treasured turf was stripped from the Royal Brunswick Ground and laboriously transported up the hill to be transplanted onto its new bed. A concrete running track encircled this new green oasis, tennis courts and croquet lawns prepared at the north end, a skating rink/boating pond (measuring 130 ft by 35ft and containing 200,000 gallons of water) to the south. On the west side, a hive of activity saw the tavern and pavilion emerging throughout the autumn and winter of 1871. A swathe of young trees was less successful, a local flock of sheep nibbling the saplings beyond repair. The speed and scale of the achievement was astounding, and by spring 1872 the new home of Sussex County Cricket Club was ready to receive players, guests and spectators.

There was a financial burden to be borne. A subscription list to enable outright purchase had failed and club funds of £860 were insufficient to meet the requirements set out. Stanford Estate came to the rescue with a loan of £1500 as well as meeting the building costs for the tavern. Enough was cobbled together to get the ground ready for the new season.

Despite this upfront support, the lack of ready funds and the repayment of loans put the whole enterprise on a somewhat precarious footing right from the outset. The attractive potential needed to be converted into hard cash if the Stanford loan was to be repaid in a rapid 10-year stint beginning in 1874. There was a danger even before a ball had been bowled in anger that the club had overstretched itself.

The club's annual meeting on March 21 1872, held at Brighton Town Hall, was 'very largely and influentially attended', and all were pleased to hear a letter from John Lillywhite, thanking the club, not only for his benefit, 'but for the uniform kindness he had received at the hands of the club and its officers'. It was estimated that his benefit must have raised around £700 (in excess of £80,000 at today's value). This was all well and good, more alarming though was the news that following the considerable outgoings of the previous year the club's balance in hand was a meagre £5 7s 3d.

The old ground had been much loved by those it touched but there was an acceptance of the inevitability of progress and the town was said to be supportive of the new venture

But who exactly was 'touched' by cricket in 1871? The preceding 50 years had seen a considerable increase in the fortunes of the game, but despite the appearance of professional players, it was still essentially the property of the leisured classes and reliant on their money. For the purse-holders, the game was the thing; a game not to be sullied by anything as vulgar as a County Championship. The working class could hardly afford either the time or money to attend a full day's play, especially as the Sabbath still reigned supreme.

But Brighton had a growing middle class. Those enfranchised by the 1867

Reform Act felt themselves promoted. It was the need to attract these new patrons, while keeping the patronage of the upper classes, that would be the route to survival and even, perhaps, prosperity. Accordingly the strict restrictions applied to membership applications were eased and the price doubled to two guineas. The thrup'nny cheap seats were still to be invented.

Haygarth's *Scores and Biographies* introduced the wider world to the new developments in Hove:

> The new Sussex County Cricket Ground is situated about half a mile from the sea, almost direct north of the old Brunswick Ground, and is approached by a good wide carriage drive and footpath from the south. There is only one entrance, and it would be desirable and convenient to make another – or, at any rate a means of exit by a turnstile – at the north-east corner, which is scarcely 100 yards from the Hove Railway Station. The ground is ten acres in extent, and round it, inside a six-foot concrete wall, is planted a belt of young trees. There is also a good level running-path all around the ground which is almost square. The turf has been taken up from the old ground, and so favourable has been the weather for transplanting, that even now it looks playable. The ground is not quite level, but the rise from south to north is scarcely perceptible. At the south end of the ground a cemented-bottom reservoir is being constructed, large enough to be used as a skating ground in the winter. Close to the entrance gates will be the tavern, now about half built; and on the west side a pavilion. The ground is better sheltered from the south-west than was the old ground, to which in many other respects it will probably prove greatly superior.

A strong endorsement, but a major question still remained. Did Sussex still have a strong enough side to attract visiting teams of the calibre that would entice crowds and thus enable the club to service its debts? And if there was a wet summer, the club would be plunged into a crisis. The ice was thin.

A detail from the original ground lease dated February 1873, now held at The Keep in Falmer.

Two

Play!

The two local newspapers, the weekly *Herald* and thrice-weekly *Gazette* provided regular updates on the progress of works. By the time spring arrived, a fixture list had been prepared and a rather muted 'grand opening' was reported on 11 May:

> The opening match in the new County Cricket Ground is fixed to take place on Monday and Tuesday the 20th and 21st of May. The match promises to be a most interesting one. It will be between "Ten Gentlemen and Three Players" and "Twelve young Players with a Captain."

A week later the 'ten Gentlemen' had become 11 and the captain of the young players was announced as William Napper, who had first represented the county in 1842. The *Herald* was cautiously optimistic:

> The ground is now in capital order, and should the Fluvial deities withhold their favours a goodly attendance may be safely anticipated.

The rain did indeed stay away, and the Gentlemen strolled to an innings victory. The *Herald* took the opportunity to both praise and criticise:

> We can endorse everything that has been said in respect of the superiority, as to the convenience and appearance possessed by the new over the old ground. But we think one or two improvements and additions might be made. We are perfectly aware that it was a difficult piece of ground to deal with, its natural fall from north to south being very great; and that great pains and skill displayed in bringing it into its present condition. We can only come to the conclusion that the hollows which are here and there seen have been caused by the sinking of the made ground. The excellent condition of the ground itself, considering that it was last autumn covered with agricultural crops, is really surprising, but it requires raising in places to make it level. One or two other matters require attention – such as more seats and shelter from sun and wind as well as rain…we allude to it now lest the receipts of the Club should suffer from an oversight or from a spirit of false economy.

The *Gazette's* reporter took his brief very seriously indeed. He had a real scout around the ground and provided a detailed description of what awaited visitors:

The old ground by the sea, or at least a portion, has been removed northward in the shape of the turf to form the match ground of the new enclosure which is situated about 200 yards from the main road to Cliftonville, a little to the west of Palmeira Square. At the south-west corner are the entrance gates with the hotel, or tavern, from the design of Mr Woodward. It has a neat appearance from the exterior. On the north side, facing the ground, is a bar for dispensing the necessary refreshments, it is under a kind of piazza and has a shifting glazed front. The dining room is approached by a flight of steps to the westward; it is a room 45ft by 30ft with windows opening down to the floor and is calculated to seat 100 persons comfortably, that great desideratum, ventilation, forming a prominent feature; outside is a small balcony. There are also lavatories and every comfort for visitors and players. The inner man has not been forgotten. On the ground floor we find a range fit to roast a sheep whole, if requisite, with hotplate for cooking those necessary adjuncts in the shape of trimmings or cementing the jellies or boiled custards so dear to the 'Stubber' of departed times – may he find the corn cakes of our American brethren as much to his taste. But we digress. Following the passage we come to the back yard with coach-houses and stabling, and if we may suggest to the "powers that be" – a stall or loose box would be an acquisition to the stabling department. A difficulty between the Gas Company and the County Club has delayed the laying of gas mains until the present time, but we trust matters may be speedily arranged. On leaving the Hotel we find the old pavilion, one part of which is set aside for the Press representatives and the other for professional players; to the north is the pavilion proper, a spacious building erected by Messrs Nash from designs by Mr Woodward. It has a frontage of 60 feet, and is raised considerably from the ground, allowing room for cellarage beneath. In the centre is a large compartment measuring 30ft by 15ft, the walls are battened with stained deal with ceiling to match, the windows opening to the floor and overlooking the ground, the view of the Furze Hill Estate adding materially to the beauty of the scene. On the north side is the Club room fitted with lockers with lavatories etc in the rear. To the south side is the Committee room, with special accommodation for ladies attached, approached by a secluded staircase in the rear. A number of step seats lead from the ground to the pavilion but we think a little more knee room and more seats would have added materially to the comfort of the visitors. A platform, sheltered by a verandah, connects the pavilion with the step seats the whole being enclosed with posts and rails. The next to attract our notice is a small pavilion erected by the Brunswick Club, from the designs of Mr John Davey jnr. It is light and elegant and has a dressing room attached, fitted with every requisite. On the east side we find the scorer's box of which Mr GF Salter has so long had the occupancy.

WG Grace batting at the Cromwell Road end during the initial first-class fixture at Hove, 1872. Open field beyond with a sight of the gasworks chimney.

The real test of all these amenities would follow in June:

> The first grand match in the New County Ground will be played…between Sussex and Gloucestershire. Sussex will send to the field a capital team and among the Gloucestershire players are the Brothers Grace.

The brothers Grace meant the appearance of *the* great cricketer. The only current equivalent might be Virat Kohli appearing at the inauguration of a new ground in small-town India. There is, of course, no record of any money changing hands to ensure this was the first big match, but with WG's record it is unlikely that he made the journey back to Cheltenham out of pocket. This was the opportunity to flood the ground with visitors, boost the two-guinea membership fund, truly entrench the new ground as part of the town's fabric and advertise the pleasures of cricket by the sea (if not right next to it anymore) through the national press.

Unfortunately, Mother Nature remained unaware of the need for dry weather and all three days were blighted to the extent that just four hours of play were possible. On 15 June the *Herald* put events into perspective:

The result of the match inflicted serious loss on the Sussex Club. Unusual interest had been felt in the contest, and extra arrangements were made for an additional number of visitors; but, owing to the unpropitious state of the elements, the receipts did not amount to £10. What adds to the misfortune of the Club is that an extra match between the same teams cannot be made this year to compensate for the loss; because, at the end of the season, the Messrs Grace cross the Atlantic, the Marylebone Club having made arrangements for some matches with our American cousins. It is also very doubtful if the inhabitants of this part of the country will ever have the opportunity of seeing these "giants of cricket" play again; for we believe that we are correct in stating that, at the termination of their present engagements, they resume their professional studies.

Even at the best of times being denied the opportunity to exploit the presence of WG would be a serious setback, but this was a ruinous blow. At least the *Herald* was somewhat wide of the mark in its predictions as to the future plans of the great cricketer. Far from retiring, he was still scoring 1000 runs in May and playing Test cricket over two decades later. One significant feature of the game was that the home side fielded an unusual nine professionals, the visitors had none.

The June rain had severely dented the club's already parlous finances, but better fortunes awaited. With only a handful of county games possible, social fixtures remained the staple fare of any cricket ground and Hove had its fair share. The Gentlemen of Sussex took on The Anomalies and The Grasshoppers while the Gentlemen of Brighton entertained The Butterflies. The armed forces also made a grand showing as The Artillery locked horns with The Rifles, and the Brighton Club played host to The Officers of the 19th Hussars. Sussex's fixture against Kent was mired in controversy – the visitors were prevented from fielding a professional Nottingham ringer and were then trounced, to the satisfaction of no-one, as the *Gazette* recorded:

> We are informed that Sussex now seeks foeman more worthy of her steel; and there being in the County a strong revival of interest in the national game, as well as a vast improvement in the quality of the Sussex players, the Kent matches will, in all probability, be dropped for more important ones with the stronger Northern Counties.

There were some grounds for taking this stance, but Sussex weren't perhaps quite as strong as they thought. They were thoroughly reliant on just two bowlers, the James's Lillywhite and Southerton: the batting, led by Henry Charlwood, whose

105 against Surrey was the first century on the new ground, could sometimes prove fragile.

On the upside, the family nature of the county side was coming to the fore. The Hides, Jesse and Arthur, and wicket-keeper Harry Phillips (reputed to be the first gloveman to dispense with a long-stop) and his brother James were precursors of the family names that would resonate throughout the next 150 years – Cox, Relf, Gilligan, Tate, Langridge, Parks, Buss, Greig, Wells and Lenham to name but a few. Hove also had its oddities in its first season; Bennett of Kent was given out 'handled ball' and Charlwood managed to be out 'hit ball twice' against Surrey. The umpire who adjudicated this contentious issue was the Godalming born, ex-Surrey and England player, Julius Caesar.

As the September evenings drew in, despite the inauspicious start, the club and committee could reflect on a job well done. The reaction to the new ground was largely positive; the playing surface had knitted well and was a worthy replacement for the old ground. The Sussex side was just about strong enough to take on the very best and, despite some setbacks, the town was fully aware of this new development and was likely to support it.

On the downside, much of the work had been financed with borrowed money. It would need repaying and the playing strength was about to be severely diminished as new regulations on registration forced star bowler Southerton to make a choice. His choice was Surrey. The next decade would not be an easy one. Times had changed but there was absolutely no guarantee that the new county ground wouldn't go the same way as James Ireland's ambitions 50 years earlier.

Bedding In

All in all, a promising start but with a future freighted with some uncertainty. The creation of the new ground had been something of an engineering wonder in terms of the speed and end product, but matters on the field hardly reflected this triumph. There was little doubt that Eaton Road, Hove was now a place to be listed amongst the social centres of the area for the right class of person. Wisely, the club recognised that cricket alone wouldn't cover ongoing running costs, let alone repay the considerable debt. Croquet, lawn tennis, ice skating and dining would all have to play their part.

Most lucrative of all was likely to be the hotel in the south-west corner by the main entrance. The land was conveyed to the club trustees 'in consideration of £260' and within two months a mortgage of £2000 had been negotiated and building work begun. With just £860 credit remaining from the management of the old ground, the Stanford Estate loaned the club a further £1500. But repayments of £150 per year were to begin almost immediately and continue until 1884, at which point it was hoped the club would be in a position to purchase the ground outright.

Cricket remained the financial centrepiece, with the county side the flagbearer. Without any formal inter-county competition at that point the pressure to succeed was less than it would later become, but great players and teams could hardly be expected to make the long trek to the South Coast just to roll over a bunch of second-raters.

Despite their withering assessment of Kent's abilities in 1872, the fact was that Sussex themselves were in danger of trying to punch above their weight. Being bowled out for 19 by Nottinghamshire in 1873 hardly smacked of a top-class side. Equally embarrassing was the scorecard that noted 'Phillips (absent – missed the train)'. The loss of James Southerton to Surrey was grievous, his bowling skills allied to those of James Lillywhite were crucial to any chance of competing against the northern or London counties. These new rules on residence did, however, lay the foundations of the County Championship. Sides became more settled, fixtures increased in regularity and newspapers increasingly compared the performances of the big eight sides and considered which might be the best team.

It was a slow process. At Lord's there was no great appetite for the vulgarity of averages, statistics or league tables and it would require MCC to sanction

The pavilion in its original form taken in the early 1880s.

14

and organise an official inter-county competition. That didn't stop others from making unofficial observations, particularly in Nottinghamshire. A wide variety of 'champions' emerged, depending on the method of assessment adopted. *Bailey's Magazine* and *Cricketer's Companion* had already begun announcing a champion county in the 1860s. After 1873, when the counties agreed on simple rules about who could play for which county, various other publications found the element of season-long competition irresistible, even if there remained disputes as to which sides were actually first class. Not that this interrupted the flow of non-county matches. These were useful in terms of earnings and establishing Eaton Road as a sporting, social and cultural hub. The Gentlemen of Sussex were the most frequent guests in the early years, although Jockeys v Sporting Press attracted interest in 1879, before increasingly the county team took over residency.

Sussex itself had already become something of a breeding ground for cricket publishing. John Wisden represented the county 82 times before establishing his famous yearly almanack, while James and John Lillywhite's rival output included their *Guide to Cricketers* and *Companion*.

Finally, in 1890, the counties agreed a system of establishing who would be where in the table at the end of the season. Eight counties participated in the inaugural season, Somerset joined the following year and in 1895 five new counties were admitted and MCC, finally, formally recognised the County Championship.

Sussex were first class from the outset, though often in name only. Apart from 1875 they floundered at or near the foot of every table. In 1880 they failed to beat another county and then repeated the trick the following year. The first year of true Championship cricket, 1890, saw Sussex bottom of the table with just one victory and 11 defeats.

The reason for this was simple: the players were not good enough. The northern counties were better organised, attracted bigger crowds that crossed class divides and were simply more professional. Gloucestershire had Grace and the London counties had the resources and geography to attract talent from both amateur and professional ranks. That left Sussex and Kent as the minnows.

During the 1870s the boat was largely kept afloat by the efforts of James Lillywhite and his new bowling partner Richard Fillery, aided and abetted by the Hide brothers, with the reliable Harry Phillips behind the wicket. One tribute Hove did receive was to be visited by the Gentlemen versus Players fixture in 1881, and a remarkable game it was too. The teams tied on first innings and the Players eventually won by one run, though later still an error was found in the scorebook and the result should have been a tie.

As players came and went through the next decade, Sussex managed little more than maintain a level of mediocrity. Charles Aubrey Smith was a shining light and added a touch of glamour, while Billy Newham emerged as a faithful and prolific servant over 25 years. But when a representative team was required to compete in new-fangled Test matches only Lillywhite and, briefly, Henry Charlwood and Aubrey Smith played any part from Sussex.

The first visit from down-under came in August 1878 and, despite unseasonable weather, brought considerable interest. Five thousand attended the first day and 3000 were at the storm-ravished ground on the second and final day when the visitors completed a victory and then agreed to stay on for an exhibition match against eighteen Gentlemen of Sussex.

Australian player Tom Horan's diary gives a clue as to why – 'We liked Brighton well, and our only regret was that we had so short a time to pass in such a handsome and fashionable town.' And it was not just the town. Horan reported the ground to be 'as good as any…the playing area is about 500 yards round [with] capital accommodation' in both pavilions and 'a spacious room for representatives of the press'. What is unclear is who used which dressing-rooms. It seems unlikely that the egalitarian Australians would have exiled their two professionals, the Bannerman brothers, to the smaller space. No doubt this conundrum caused some discussion behind the scenes. At the very least Hove was an attractive venue and the Australians had attracted good crowds.

Financially, with the generous assistance of Lord Sheffield, the wolves were kept from the door and the initial loans repaid. But the actual purchase of the ground would be no simple matter. A subscription list failed, perhaps hampered by the lack of success on the field. Complex and expensive negotiations between Stanford Estate and Sussex trustees Henry Campion of Danny, Hurstpierpoint, Charles Smith of Whaphams, Henfield and Messers Bevan, Hardy and Beard along with solicitors Verrall & Borlase then ensued. Somewhat farcically there were disputes over fees, a refusal to allow legal firm Day & Cather scrutiny of an original document and even the loss of the original lease to the ground.

Matters were finally brought to a successful conclusion in 1886 with a loan of £10,000 at 4% interest from Stanford Estate and a further £3500 from the Old Bank in Lewes. For a total sum of £13,500, the ground was purchased at last. The presence of RA Bevan of Union Bank (and later Barclays, who took over the mortgage) amongst the five club trustees, and the influence of Lord Sheffield, certainly helped smooth financial negotiations. The purchase would leave the coffers dangerously bare, with an annual interest payment of £540. Moreover, the conditions of sale meant that Stanford Estate still held considerable influence over development and would continue to do so until 1935. For example, the club could not build any houses on any part of the purchased land – if they were to do so then the entirety of the ground must be offered back to Stanford Estate for £12,000 rising to £13,500 after 15 years.

This wasn't unreasonable; the parcel of land had been conveyed as a cricket and recreation ground pure and simple. In the event of the club going bankrupt, the original owners were ensuring that an increasingly valuable piece of real estate would revert back to them. The stipulations were not universally popular, however. One correspondent from Wilbury Road wrote:

> One would have thought that the trustees of the Stanford Estate had made enough money out of the land in this town without imposing on the club the arrangements you speak of as to getting back the ground under certain eventualities.

Despite this indication of support, the cricketing show the public witnessed was still less than satisfactory. If an example were needed of what could happen, it came from along the coast when Hampshire lost their first-class status for eight years.

The bi-annual Australian visits through the 1880s did, however, bring welcome distraction and star-quality to Hove, and Sussex were inclined to acquit themselves half decently. In 1880 a rain-affected draw saw Australia struggle with the lob bowling of Walter Humphreys. Two years later the respective merits of the two sides were more evident, William Murdoch's unbeaten 286 and George Palmer's 14-110 ensured a crushing victory for the visitors. In 1884 and 1886 Australia just about survived with a draw with Humphrey's lobs again causing consternation as he repeated his hat-trick of 1880 in the former game. The crowning achievement of the decade was a 58-run victory against the might of Ferris, Turner, Giffen, Trott and the rest – Arthur Hide and Humphreys taking full advantage of a devilish wicket by out-bowling Ferris and Turner and collecting 17 wickets for 84 runs. But these interludes could scarcely hide the fact that Sussex were struggling on the field, and as the club arrived at its 50th birthday, *Wisden* penned an unwelcome article of advice:

> The Sussex eleven had a thoroughly unsatisfactory and dispiriting season… and in match after match played a spiritless, hopeless sort of game…and unless some recruits are found, home grown or imported [their] position will become untenable. The men who do most of the work for Sussex are not likely to improve, but are, on the other hand, getting past their best…We have thought it well to state clearly and uncompromisingly the unfortunate position of Sussex and we

should say that the best remedy is to import some young professionals from Nottinghamshire or Yorkshire.

The authorities at Hove took notice. Overtures were made to bring Charles 'The Terror' Turner and then Ernie Jones into the fold from Australia. Money proved an insurmountable stumbling block. Certainly something was needed: in 1890 Sussex played 12 Championship matches and 10 were lost by an innings.

Another Australian, William Murdoch, was a different matter. He'd developed a liking for the Hove wicket and Brighton life on a number of previous visits and agreed to take on the captaincy in 1893. With the arrival of Fred Tate's slow-medium-paced control, Ernest Killick's batting (almost uniquely he played in spectacles) and the skill of new wicket-keeper Harry Butt, there was a strengthening of the team, especially on the professional side. Even so, it was deemed necessary to tempt the 52-year-old Alfred Shaw back into the first-class game from his position at Sheffield Park, where he was tasked with finding and honing new talent for the county. He proved to be still one of the best bowlers in the country before Murdoch, who made no allowances for age, bowled him into the ground and out of the team in a season.

There was also the question of the Quaife brothers. Walter was a decent batsman and had headed the county averages in 1890, but mid-way through the following season he refused to answer the committee's enquiries as to whether he was qualifying for Warwickshire and was dropped. He did indeed move to Edgbaston where he continued to perform adequately. More injurious was the fact that he took his younger brother, Willie, with him. Willie was still playing for Warwickshire in 1928 and blessed his new county with 33,862 runs. Their departure led to an 'unholy row' as to who was to blame and how it could have been avoided.

It's no coincidence that the three highest team scores by visitors to Hove date from these years, or at least they did so before Middlesex joined them in 2021. In 1890 Cambridge University trailed by 91 on first innings but won by 455 runs having sprinted to 703-9 declared in their second innings. In 1893 there was no sprinting from Nottinghamshire in their patient compilation of 674 over 254.4 overs before Murdoch's two half centuries saved the game and the visitors left Hove without a single point. In 1895, with 651 including a century by young opening batsman, Charles Fry, it was the turn of Oxford University. Sussex eked out a draw thanks to a century of their own from qualifying player KS Ranjitsinhji. What Sussex really lacked was star quality; a Richardson or a Shrewsbury, a Stoddart or a Briggs – preferably bowlers. Within two years they had two – both batsmen.

The last six years of the century saw the total transformation of the Sussex team. George Cox, Bert Relf and Joe Vine came into the side and were all still playing in the 1920s, amassing 2530 games for Sussex between them. Cyril Bland burnt brightly over four seasons, while all were dwarfed by the achievements of their amateur team-mates CB Fry and Kumar Sri Ranjitsinhji.

The Golden Age

Now, for the first time, Sussex could compete with the very best and even harbour ambitions of winning a County Championship. Not that they were above being picked off by exotic tourists such as the Gentlemen of Philadelphia, whose astonishing swerve bowler Bart King found the sea air conducive to his methods to the tune of 13-105, including Ranji for a duck.

With the expansion of the County Championship, from nine to 14 sides, in 1895, came an inevitable increase in county fixtures. Initially only two more matches were played, but the club came under increasing pressure to be a real *county* rather than merely Hove-based, particularly as committee members were elected by districts. In July 1895 Sussex entertained Yorkshire at Hastings' Central Recreation Ground, a move long overdue considering how well the ground had been used over the previous decade for high-profile September festival games. Two years later The Saffrons in Eastbourne became the third county venue.

Charles Fry arrived in 1894 as captain at Oxford and a renowned all-round athlete. He was no natural cricketing genius. Hard work and a calculating brain were his greatest assets and it took seasons of thoughtful toil before he flourished. The same was true of Ranji – there was a unique skill and approach to batting, but this hadn't been immediately evident through long hours of practising and perfecting it while at Cambridge. Fortunately for Sussex, the two men had become good friends and when Ranji thought of county cricket, Hove offered three great advantages – he would be playing with Fry, he would be helping a weak team and he would be living in Brighton.

In his biography of Ranji, Alan Ross draws a vivid picture of the town and the allure it held for the Indian prince:

> It was still a place where people – the gentry and the riff-raff, equally with east Enders – went to have a good time. It had vitality and style, the eighteenth century not lost to view under modern development. Moreover, there has always been a whiff of the Orient about Brighton, not only about the Pavilion, but about the town as a whole, its pleasure gardens and parades.

To the young Ranjitsinhji the domes and balconies of Brighton must have conjured up visions of India, an India momentarily lost to him, but there in memory, not beyond recall. In its piers and bathing-machines, the bulging bow windows and verandahs of its lodging houses, its fish markets and steep streets, its palatial hotels and ordered crescents, there was that mingling of the grand and the earthy, the dashing and the classic, which was part of Ranjitsinhji's own make-up. Its element of pure fantasy was akin to his own.

Not that the town, or his version of it, didn't hold the same beguiling attraction for Ross himself when he was resident in the 1950s – in 'Cricket at Brighton' he wrote of 'Regency Squares, the Pavilion, oysters and mussels and gin.'

For the next decade, though, due to their lack of bowling resources they rarely seemed likely to challenge for the Championship, particularly as Lord Hawke had assembled a team of all talents in Yorkshire. But Sussex became a very difficult side to beat.

If Fry had any illusions about helping out with his own bowling, he was disillusioned in 1898 when 'Dimboola Jim' Phillips called him for chucking in the game against Oxford University. It was hardly news, any professional with the same action would long since have been drummed out of the game. But Fry was so 'completely disgusted' that he finished the over bowling underarm lobs. Butch White of Hampshire was to be a similar transgressor at Hove in 1960.

In 1899 Ranji became the first cricketer to pass 3000 runs in a season. In 1901 Fry followed suit. Attendance records set in 1899 – the daily total against Gloucestershire and the match total of 15,500 against Australia – were broken again in 1901 as 19,000 came along to watch county champions Yorkshire.

Hove saw the best of the majestic duo. Half of Fry's 1901 run of six successive centuries were at Hove and nine of his 16 double centuries. Ranji's golden years between 1899 and 1901 featured 29 centuries (eight doubles), all bar two were made for Sussex and 13 were at Hove. Little wonder that easy chairs had been purchased for the Pavilion during the pair's heyday. The 1896 accounts show an expenditure of £147 13s and 5d for this new amenity, needed 'because the members had to get accustomed to sitting long hours while Fry and Ranji made their hundreds.'

Fred Tate joined the bonanza with a record benefit that was well deserved for a skilful bowler who spent much of his time wheeling away on Hove's flat pitches with its invitingly short boundaries. Despite Tate's efforts, the first year of the new century exposed the paucity of bowling; only two defeats in 24 games but only four victories and all against weak opposition. In July, Fry entered the record books when taking a century and double-century off Surrey (including Tom Richardson and Bill Lockwood) at Hove, a feat never before achieved in first-class cricket. Needless to say, the match ended in a draw. As if in response, the following week Ranji hit a double-century off Middlesex's Albert Trott and JT Hearne on a wet wicket in yet another drawn game. In August 1901 Fry scored 1116 runs, still a record for a calendar month.

The ground given over to tennis around the turn of the century.

The near misses of 1902 and 1903 were the highpoints of this era – Fry and Ranji breaking further records, and with Tate working through the opposition, Sussex were good enough to beat all bar one. In the first of these two years Yorkshire were runaway winners and the Sussex cause was hardly helped when the captain, Ranji, brought low by Test-match failure and eager creditors, deserted the ship for the last part of the season complaining of 'a monstrously selfish spirit prevalent in the team…some of them are getting distinctly above themselves.'

No better illustration of the bowling shortcomings was the tour match of 1902 in which Warwick Armstrong and Monty Noble put on a record 428 for the sixth wicket, forcing even Fry (carefully) and Ranji to turn over their arms.

The following year Sussex were somewhat unlucky – 14 draws in 24 games was as much due to the poor weather as the lack of bowling resources. Fry had a brilliant season (including 1679 runs at Hove alone), though the batting performance of the year at Hove came from Gilbert Jessop. His 286 from 381 scored while he was at the crease took less than three hours, and this when the ball had to be hit out of the ground to count as a 'sixer'.

The upturn in cricketing form improved finances which would allow for some significant developments within the ground. Back in 1890 a mere £735 had come to the club through membership. With mortgage payments of £434 and with most games unlikely to generate any significant profit, the requirement to maximise the revenue from the ground itself was paramount. The Rink brought in £353, football £145 and the hotel £250. Proceeds from allowing clubs and schools to use the ground logged a further £110 in the credit column. Somehow the club returned a profit of £110.

However, with no investment in the ground or in young players, the club risked treading water. Fortunately, Sussex had Fry and Ranji. By 1896 membership was bringing in £1248, rising to £1428 in 1900. The total income of £3004 in 1890 almost doubled within 10 years. The club indicated awareness of the value of its prize assets by granting £190 for Ranji's 1896 'testimonial' when he had only just started playing for the team; perhaps as much a bribe to join the club as a 'thank-you' for doing so. Either way, it was a sound investment. When Ranji was largely absent in 1898, the committee reported that 'His loss has been a severe blow to the exchequer.'

Much later, in 1930, the club would receive a payback in the form of a £1000 donation from their former golden ticket, and elected him president. Thanks mainly to the exploits of the two friends, the club was able to grant benefits to five men – Fillery, Charlwood, Humphreys, Jesse Hide and Bean.

Facilities for both players and spectators required improvement. In 1898 local architect FT Cawthorn submitted plans for additions and alterations to the pavilion as well as a new stand and players' room, with committee member, and later president, Harry De Paravicini representing the interests of the club.

Not only had the changing-rooms for the professionals been a hurried construction back in 1872, but also the status of these men had increased – not enormously, but significantly enough; a fact that was reflected in a staggeringly increased wage bill, partly explained by the increase in fixtures with professionals paid 'per-match'. In 1890 the bill for 'ground bowlers' (as the professionals were described) was a mere £56; only six years later it had risen to £397 and then on to £559 and £779 in 1898 and 1900. There was no question of the growing ranks of professionals mixing with their betters in the pavilion, but they would henceforth be housed in a smart new building measuring 54 by 14 feet (16.5 x 4.2m) and raised six feet to accommodate storage underneath and provide better viewing and privacy. There would still be no shower or bath. Some spectators were slightly less than complimentary about the building:

…the 'players'…were tucked away in a sort of loft with steps leading up to it. I can remember seeing them waiting inside the doorway, occasionally peeping out to see whether the 'gentlemen' had left the pavilion. If they had gone the 'players' would emerge and follow them on to the field at a respectful distance.

Cawthorn's architectural mark is still present throughout the local area from Barclays Bank on Boundary Road to the St Agnes Church in Hove. Both he and Paravicini would work together again in 1927 on the major extension to the pavilion, the club's biggest building project of the twentieth century.

The club's diamond jubilee was 'celebrated' in 1899 though the event appears to have passed unnoticed according to an incandescent Alfred Taylor in the *Brighton Gazette*:

> Was a great meeting called and touching speeches delivered on the merits of Sussex in the days gone by? Did we even arrange a match in celebration of the event? Alas no! Our committee were silent – were even ignorant of the fact. Could the greensward speak it would pour maledictions upon our governing body for their negligence.

The committee was perhaps more concerned with the future than the past. It was time to consider the spectators beyond the pavilion. A first stand was called for and at the southern end, the 'Cowshed' was erected. Fully 170 feet in length with five concrete steps and seating covered by a galvanised iron roof, it stood directly in front of the Ice Rink which was then serving as the open-air Hove Tennis Ground.

This lowly and rather unpicturesque edifice would finally be demolished in the early 1970s to make way for the Gilligan Stand. Ugly it might have been, but it afforded a particularly good view of play from directly behind the bowler's arm in the days when sightscreens were considered a luxury and one per ground the norm, even at Test venues.

With these two major projects taxing the county coffers to the tune of £882, the pavilion was afforded only minor improvements – the ladies lavatories and the bar receiving particular attention. A bill of £570 indicates that high standards of workmanship were expected in the members' area. What these projects indicated above all was optimism for the future and a belief that Eaton Road would not be disappearing to residential development.

County finances had stabilised and the club was now just about paying its way. There were no grounds for complacency though, as emphasised in 1902 when

Stanford Estate, while suggesting a partial payment 'might stave off the evil day', expressed a desire to call in the mortgage.

Their impatience was understandable. Only 25% of the original 1886 mortgage had been paid off in 16 years and clearly another financial institution would be required to take on this loan. The 'two-way street' of Sussex finances was never better illustrated when, in 1904, CB Fry opened a bazaar which eventually raised £900 for the club. In return, in recognition of his outstanding batting, he was presented with an eight-horse power Clément by the members in which he could travel to London in two hours. It might all have ended badly when Fry knocked Admiral Moresby off his bicycle in Fareham a few months later, but the 74-year-old was made of stern stuff and lived to 92. Fry, for his part, soon upgraded to a 20hp Clément-Talbot.

One complaint that emerged in these years was voiced by the *Sussex Evening Times*:

> It is generally known that the two-guinea subscribers are privileged to have a turn at the nets, but surely some little consideration should be shown those on whom the success of the county team rests. Only those who witness the subscribers putting in an appearance every morning and afternoon with alarming punctuality, and demanding the bowling services of the staff, will realise what I mean. Surely our rising amateurs, after being fed by the best professional trundling, could take a turn with the ball instead of scooting to the pavilion.

This was, of course, the 'Golden Age' where amateur cricketers such as Jackson, Jessop, Foster and Palairet garnered the plaudits, while professionals of the class of Rhodes, Hirst, Blythe and Tyldesley did the donkey work. It was supposedly the age of 'chivalry' and 'fair play' where the game was the thing. Tests mattered (but not *that* much) and averages were somehow a bit mucky and degenerate.

Chivalry and fair play were little more than skin-deep; bickering and undermining each other was common among the amateurs and AC MacLaren of Lancashire was often at the heart of it with CB Fry a worthy opponent, as the two demonstrated in July 1905.

The pitch at Hove was flat, the sky blue and Lancashire amassed 601-8 declared, so infuriating Fry that he brought on two non-bowlers with underarm 'daisy cutters'. Sussex replied with a meagre 383 but MacLaren, knowing a draw to be sufficient for his Championship ambitions, elected not to enforce the follow-on. Lancashire went back in and batted and batted and the game finished with Sussex wicket-keeper Harry Butt bowling. A thoroughly unedifying spectacle.

Poetic justice was served when Lancashire ended up losing the Championship to Yorkshire.

The Australian tourists at Eaton Road in 1905. Monty Noble scored 267 and the visitors won by an innings.

The Hove ground and its Royal Brunswick turf had garnered a country-wide reputation as a place to make hay when the sun shone. Not that the sun always did. The proximity to the sea could cause conditions to vary rapidly and the damp air, prevalent breeze and state of the tide could often affect the behaviour of the ball. Given reasonable weather, the pitches were largely reliable as the run-gorging of Fry and Ranji showed. They could get wet and spiteful, but the outfield was adept at self-draining. Rendzina soils developed over calcium-rich rock such as chalk had been ideal for barley cultivation before 1872 and proved equally suited to preparing dry, true wickets. The incline further aided this natural drainage although that could lead to problems at the south end. As late as the 1960s, Michael Wilkinson, a member of 50 years standing, remembers sitting in the baking sun for two sessions while puddles slowly shrank in front of the Cowshed.

By 1906 the two stellar names were rarely to be seen. Fry suffered a bad injury and soon decided to continue his career in Hampshire, while Ranji became increasingly preoccupied with his title and its responsibilities. This actually opened out the county by allowing other players more freedom of expression, and seemingly led to a more harmonious atmosphere amongst the team. One of Sussex's brightest shooting stars emerged briefly: John Elicius Benedict Bernard Placid Quirk

Carrington Dwyer, who followed 9-35 against Derbyshire (still a Championship debut record) with 16-98 against Middlesex. To this day these remain Hove's best in an innings and a match for a home bowler. Sadly, the elaborately-named Dwyer was virtually lost to the game within 12 months and died six years later.

No More Ranji, No More Fry

With the Championship now enlarged, Sussex found relatively easy pickings amongst counties such as Northants and Leicestershire. But they could only cast envious eyes eastwards, where Kent's Tonbridge Nursery had uncovered and tutored a new generation of professionals good enough to beat Yorkshire and the rest. To this end, an investment in the future was made with the appointment of Arthur Millward as coach for three years. In the event, he didn't see out the contract and the following year was standing as a Test umpire.

There was also still work to done in getting the whole town and wider county to support their cricket side, either as spectators or participants. The use of 'sandwichmen' in the town's streets was deemed a fit and proper method to encourage potential future players to try their hands

While Millward and the sandwichmen might reap future dividends, the absence of Fry and Ranji had the expected sobering effect on attendances. Solid professionals and unreliable amateurs were never likely to keep the county near the top of the table and draw in the crowds. Experiments such as scrapping the tea interval 'to attract afternoon spectators' had little impact and the decline in income was exacerbated by seven of the nine fixtures failing to last beyond luncheon on day three. Reform of the various membership schemes saw life members now paying £25 (for gentlemen) or £10 (for ladies) with two guineas securing annual membership and the right to practice with the professionals. Improvement in income was marginal. As the 1906 end-of season report noted:

> Sussex had to get through the season as best they could without the help of either of their two great batsmen. Small wonder under the circumstances that the general result was unsatisfactory.

Despite faltering revenues, however, 1906 saw the club finally acquire something which had long been desired – a second entrance at the north-east corner of the ground to accommodate those arriving by train. With Palmeira Avenue becoming a road rather than a track at the turn of the century, access had become more pressing than ever. A strip of land 13 feet 3 inches wide connecting the new avenue and the ground was duly conveyed by Mr D'Avigdor Goldsmid to Reverend David Davies and then on to the cricket ground trustees. Various provisos were attached: that land not to be used for 'sport which is habitually attended or likely to be attended by a noisy or unruly crowd', i.e. football or rugby. It should be lit by two lamps at the extremities and that 'substantial posts' were to be erected to ensure entrance only for pedestrians, bicycles and bath chairs. The new entrance now provided access for spectators travelling to the ground from the Holland Road Halt station, which served the single-carriage railmotor service between 1905 and 1951.

Access secured, getting the populace to use it remained the challenge; improvement in the playing side deemed key to meeting this challenge. Results did pick up within two seasons but only enough to ensure upper mid-table positions. The Relf brothers and Joe Vine were proving to be consistent county stalwarts and new names started to appear such as Vallance Jupp, Percy Fender, Ted Bowley and Maurice Tate, four players who would rise to the top following the Great War. Sadly for Sussex, the first two named would enhance their reputations for other counties. Jupp was tempted to Northants by the offer of the secretaryship which allowed him to play as an amateur. Fender moved back to London to play for Surrey and work at his father's wholesale stationery firm, though as testament to the strength of the amateur fraternity, he was still awarded a Sussex county cap 15 years later by Arthur Gilligan.

The Struggle for Survival

As the first decade of the new century drew to a close, a long period of relative national prosperity was on the wane. German and American industry was challenging British hegemony, even British naval strength was under threat. The far-ranging reforms of Asquith's Liberal government were providing much needed security for the working class and those too old to work, but a recession was causing hardships that harked back 50 years and led to labour unrest and an increasing shift towards the new Labour party.

This was largely at odds with what had been happening in Brighton and Hove. The arrival of the railway works back in 1852 had brought with it a 40% rise in Brighton's population in a decade. While this rate was not sustained, growth continued to be significant – 77,693 in 1861 became 131,237 in 1911. Hove's population boom was even more startling: 113.3% in the 1870s alone.

For Sussex County Cricket Club this should have represented something of a bonanza. A huge rise in potential customers from exactly the kind of people who might want to spend a day at the cricket. Semi-skilled and skilled manual workers enjoying increased leisure time, day trippers and holiday-makers down from London and upper middle-class gentlemen with time on their hands who filled the stately detached properties that began to rise just a gentle stroll from Eaton Road. A glance at the town maps of the period shows that what had been an isolated sporting green in 1872 had become enclosed by housing on three sides by 1892 (see page 50). The question remained as to whether the club had taken full advantage of this growth in potential customers.

Match in progress. Note the Hencoop before it was moved across the ground from west to east.

Cricket's popularity had boomed in the late nineteenth century with the advent of the County Championship, the birth of international cricket and the deeds of WG. Against that, there was also a significant rise in alternative attractions and Brighton was well endowed in this department; more so than almost any town of a similar size in the country.

The club had weathered the storms of moving home, a poor team and increasing costs over 40 years despite occasionally lurching towards insolvency. On the plus side there had been generous benefactors, star players, a better team and hard-working, sometimes inspired, administrators. Many counties could only really exist by being predominantly amateur while the metropolitan giants of Yorkshire and Surrey had advantages that would never exist in Sussex by the sea.

One comparable county that had prospered was Kent. Their investment in the Tonbridge Nursery continued to pay dividends that other counties could only wonder at. With Frank Woolley, Colin Blythe and Arthur Fielder, they were the most consistent side in the country in the decade before 1914. Sussex were not blind to this unwelcome upsurge in the fortunes of their neighbours. The reasons for it were easy enough to understand but did not make it any easier to replicate. In 1909 an appeal for funds to establish a nursery was issued, with Ranji pitching in for three years at £150 per annum on condition that the remaining required funds were found. The fact that Eaton Road was a strain on the exchequer through its mortgage and development was certainly one factor counting against greater investment in finding and training talent. But Eaton Road was home, and for the long-term security of the club it was essential that it was a home that spectators and opposing teams would wish to visit and where local players would want to play. If that were to remain the case then updating and modernising would be required.

In 1908 a tea bar was established which would become known as The Chalet. The last major works on the ground before 1914 saw the players' changing-room equipped with a viewing balcony and a railed enclosure. Despite these enhancements, four consecutive wet summers saw the club struggling again in 1910. One man who certainly suffered was Ernest Relf, as his application for payment for a month's illness was rejected. Perhaps he had hoped the fact that his two older brothers were county regulars would count in his favour. It didn't.

A 20,000 shilling fund was launched in order to 'put the club on a sound and satisfactory basis'. The Duke of Devonshire led the way with a 500s donation and the great and good of Sussex stepped forward. But all the collections and appeals in the world only masked the lack of regular income through the turnstiles. Sussex were a good all-round side but without the star quality of Ranji and Fry attendances were down. In 1910 the biggest single paying crowd was under 3000, leading one newspaper to refer to the 'apathy of the Sussex people'.

The two buildings within the ground expected to bring in a steady income were also proving less than reliable. The club had bought the hotel and stables behind it in 1906 for £2000, a sum raised by mortgage which was transferred in 1912 to committee members Lord Leconfield and David Reuben Sassoon. It had been a hardy annual for the club exchequer for many years although relations between the owner and tenant had not always been cordial. Increasing the rent from £250 to £350 in 1899 hardly smacks of generosity, even given that takings had presumably been rising steadily with the fortunes of the club over the previous decade. In August 1911 the hotel license was put out to tender and won by local brewery Tamplins who installed Mr J Piggott as landlord. The tender process must have been interesting given that various brewing companies were represented on the committee.

With this license came the operation of the 'beer shed' in the south-east corner and the newly opened tea rooms. It proved anything but a sound investment on either side. Within a year Tamplins were successfully petitioning to have their rent reduced from £275 to £200; a further reduction followed two years later.

The issues with the Rink were more complex still. Ice skating had soon lost favour to the new American fad of roller skating; a craze which also proved to be short lived. Meanwhile there were questions of ownership. Although the Rink had been bought with the rest of the ground outright from Stanford Estate back in 1886, a portion of it, amounting to approximately 25%, still remained in the ownership of Goldsmid Estates. It wasn't until May 1914 that a legacy from Lt Col Shaft allowed for a full purchase, with the increased rent being earmarked for young players in the club nursery.

Both club and local entrepreneurs had been wrestling with how to turn a profit from what was little more than a large concrete void. In 1901 the local Volunteer Artillery rented part of the space to practice stripping and assembling – presumably in response to the war in South Africa. Over the next decade, tennis was introduced and then, in 1909, the Hove Brighton Skating Rink Company made a disastrous decision to lease the land and put a roof over it at the cost of £3000. Disastrous for the new tenants, because neighbours obtained an injunction for 'creating a nuisance' and the company immediately filed for bankruptcy. A Mr Dott took over the lease in 1911 on the proviso that he could rip up the wooden floor, to what purpose is unclear. In March 1914 the club paid the sum of £317 10s for vacant possession and all fixtures and fittings. The following years of war provided an immediate solution as to usage.

By 1911 the financial situation had reached a critical level. The maximum overdraft level of £1000 had been reached, partly due to expenditure on the new tennis grounds (with permanent water supply) at the north end of the ground. Despite cost cutting on all fronts and charitable efforts from such as Miss Chester, who pledged 40% of the takings from her theatrical performances on the Palace Pier, the wolves were well and truly at the door.

In 1913 the financial sub-committee deemed it 'advisable to call a County Meeting to decide whether the Club is to be carried on and how it shall be managed'. The previous year had seen the ill-starred Triangular Test tournament and also record-breaking rainfall – Sussex were considered fortunate to have emerged with an operating loss of only £46. But they were also carrying a balance-sheet deficit of £1158 (£127,400 at today's value) and an outstanding mortgage of £7450 (£820,000). A debenture scheme to clear the mortgage was proposed but found little favour and Sussex returned to scrimping and saving.

Cricket, a Weekly Record of the Game divided the counties into three financial divisions – 'prosperous', 'struggling' and 'desperately struggling'. With an average gate return of £89 per match in 1913, Sussex were firmly in the desperate camp. One victim was faithful old servant William Newham whose pay was cut by £100 as he was shuffled from the position of assistant manager to nursery coach.

The first ball of the Indian tourists game at Hove in 1911, Salam-ud-din to Bob Relf.

The following year, with the clouds of a more extensive war than the 'skirmish' with the Boers gathering inexorably, the club with sudden generosity voted to grant Newham an annual pension of £100 'as long as the club lasts'. Less generously, a begging letter from the debt-laden Worcestershire club for a survival loan of £20 was rejected.

On 12 February a 'gathering of the clans' at the Brighton Dome heard that the president, Viscount Hythe, had gifted the club £500 which then inspired various other wealthy members to contribute lesser sums. There was still a shortfall, but the debt had been reduced to £250. Less good news was that the ground's gross value in February 1914 was assessed at £12,100, not the £13,500 previously reported. The club's prize asset had not appreciated in value over the first 42 years of its existence. The final financial loss, was the cancellation of the last match of the 1914 season, and the second match of Hove cricket week, against Surrey, due to the outbreak of the Great War.

WG at Hove

IT WAS CERTAINLY no coincidence that the first 'big match' arranged for the new county ground at Hove was against Gloucestershire. Gloucestershire meant the brothers Grace, and especially William Gilbert.

Now in his mid-twenties, WG Grace was transforming the game of cricket. In no particular order of achievement, he had proved the batting could involve forward and back play, he had shown the ability of one man to bring huge crowds into a cricket ground and he had re-established parity between the sides in Gentlemen versus Players fixtures. He dominated batting in the way that Don Bradman would do 60 years later. As a bowler he was amongst the best in the country. He showed the commercial possibilities of cricket and, perhaps less laudably, he could play fast and loose with the rule book.

Grace had already shown a great liking for the sea air of the Royal Brunswick ground. At 15, playing for the touring South Wales Club, he hit his first century in a serious match and scored 226 for once out. This was the arrival of 'The Great Player'. He later recalled being lonely and out of sorts due to the absence of his brother, EM Grace, but his chanceless century proved to all present, not least WG himself, that here was a batsman as had never been seen before. In his *Reminiscences,* Grace did not forget the significance of that day: 'I cannot remember ever again being really nervous, although on many occasions I have felt anxious to do well.'

One of these 'occasions' was certainly on the same ground eight years later. John Lillywhite of Sussex had been accorded the rare honour of a Gentlemen-versus-Players benefit match in Brighton, only the third time in its history that the game had been played outside London. Grace was the big draw and he obliged with a golden duck in the first innings. Lillywhite chose to gee Grace on by giving him two sovereigns before his second dig with the caveat that Grace should return sixpence for each run he scored. Curiously, Grace saw this as 'the greatest compliment I have ever had paid to my batting skill.' How this was a compliment it is hard to imagine as Grace would start to lose sixpence a run once he'd got to 80.

By close of play the score was 353-3 and WG was unbeaten on 200, having totally forgotten his financial obligations. The tale twists at this point as Grace recalled giving Lillywhite five pounds but demanded to be let off the rest of the bet which had left him pounds down. He went on to score 217, the highest score recorded at the ground to that time.

It certainly didn't pass by the Sussex Committee that this game had attracted a crowd of 10,000 and raised £700. This was exactly the kind of rapid cash injection that the new ground needed and WG Grace was the only cricketer capable of attracting that kind of interest. Hence Gloucestershire in June 1872.

Although rain ruined the big day, WG took the first ever first-class wicket on the new ground and managed to stamp his mark on the game by dismissing the Gloucestershire substitute fielder, the Sussex player George Humphreys, from the field after he had dropped his own brother Walter. The implication that he had cheated was clear enough; doubtless an amateur would have been treated differently if, by some odd chance, he'd been in the same position.

Grace was a regular visitor over the next 25 years, as at every first-class ground in England; years which saw the advent of Test cricket, the birth of the County Championship and cricket established as an institution for all classes. He always brought the crowds in as well. In 1899 for the Whit Monday fixture, the *Hove Gazette* reported a crowd of 11,000 for the first day. In those 25 years WG earned a fortune and made himself the most recognisable Englishman alive. At Hove he recorded four centuries, the last of which, in 1896, was an unbeaten 243.

But more important than his deeds was his presence, as crowds flocked for a glimpse of the great man. All through the 1890s the gate receipts at Hove for the matches against Gloucestershire dwarfed all others. In fine weather Kent or Surrey would bring in just over £100 over three days, Yorkshire or Lancashire might generate £150, the Australians could be relied on for £200, Grace's Gloucestershire averaged over £300. All the greats of the decade from Jessop to Giffen and Briggs to Lohmann were mere sideshows – *the* great cricketer indeed.

Lord Sheffield and William Murdoch

OF THE GREAT Lords at the dawn of county cricket's golden age, most are aware of Harris and Hawke. Sheffield comes a distant third. Perhaps because he had played just once, as Viscount Pevensey, maybe because his name is not so readily associated with his county and probably because he never sought a leading role within MCC and the administration of the game. But Lord Sheffield had his beloved Sheffield Park in Sussex and his name is still associated with cricket in Australia every summer.

Sheffield Park may have been the first love and concern for Henry North Holroyd, 3rd Earl Sheffield, but his largesse extended 25 miles south to Eaton Road over some 30 years. It is fair to say that without him Sussex CCC might have disappeared into financial oblivion before Queen Victoria's reign was over. As Sussex president for 31 years over three terms, his influence and money guided the county club through crises aplenty that, at times, seemed likely to overwhelm the team and threaten the ground.

The most significant of these three reigns was the second, between 1879 and 1896, particularly as Sussex had managed just one victory in two seasons prior to his election. Although strictly 'hands-off' in terms of personal contact, Sheffield's influence was felt immediately by the appointment of William Mycroft of Derbyshire, one of the country's best bowlers, to coach at Sheffield Park. He was, in turn, followed by Alfred Shaw of Nottinghamshire. The not inconsiderable wages of both men were paid in full by their patron even when Shaw returned to first-class cricket for the county for two seasons.

During the 1880s, Sheffield's greatest contribution came in the form of hard cash. In 1881, even for a wealthy man he undertook an astonishing guarantee. He would make up any shortfall where expenditure outweighed receipts at the end of the season. Somewhat surprisingly, this pledge was made public with all the dangers that entailed, but the cricket men and women of Sussex followed his lead rather than hide behind it and subscriptions rose by some 20%.

Despite this, Lord Sheffield needed to stump up £370 and a further £1300 over the next five years, to allow for day-to-day functioning. On top of this, there was the little matter of buying the ground from the Benett-Stanford family under the terms of the lease signed back in 1872. The sum of £13,500 was required which was achieved in 1886 through a mortgage and a 'ground purchase fund' endowed to the tune of £600 by his Lordship.

As head of the sub-committee responsible for organising the funding and completion of the purchase, Sheffield was keen to find other, more permanent, methods of raising revenue. The doubling of fees for local club privileges at Eaton Road was met with resistance from sides such as Brighton Brunswick, Early Risers, Stanford, West Hove and District Teachers before Sheffield threatened to withdraw his £600 and a compromise was reached. Sussex now owned their own ground, albeit, with a £10,000 debt.

Cricket clubs needed patrons and Sussex were lucky to have one of the best. His fixtures against the Australians on five successive tours brought the cream of players to Fletching. Ernie Jones parted the Doctor's beard and Giffen, Jackson, Hill, Fry and Ranji displayed their talents and in so doing undoubtedly made the Sussex county side a more attractive proposition than many others. Sheffield was largely responsible for recruiting the erstwhile captain of Australia, William Murdoch, and his presence was certainly a consideration when both Fry and Ranji were deciding where to play their county cricket.

Notwithstanding Lord Sheffield's patronage, that debt needed attending to, and a combination of belt-tightening, fund raisers and local support saw it steadily whittled down over the next 10 years. A bazaar at the Hotel Metropole in 1894 alone raised £750, a large part of which was due to Lord Sheffield's generosity in parting with various mementoes of his travels and cricketing life.

Also involved in the 1894 bazaar was Billy Murdoch, one of Australia's first great batsmen, now in the evening of his career. A veteran and captain on four English tours, he had been a rock for his national side. But a rock that needed to earn a living. His wife came from a wealthy family but had done poorly from her father's last will; the Murdoch's still aspired to 'comfortable living'.

Cricket was Murdoch's trade (along with fighting for a greater share of his father-in-law's estate) and England offered greater possibilities. He settled on Sussex and moved to Burgess Hill for his two-year residency qualification. Why Sussex? The ground held a certain allure – he was the holder of the highest score recorded there, until Victor Trumper trumped him. Sussex had an attraction for a man who enjoyed the life of a country gentleman, albeit a poor one, and when he later moved to 37 St Aubyns in Hove with his five young children, Brighton provided plenty of diverting entertainment. Most important of all was the generosity of Lord Sheffield who was responsible for the £300 retainer, although Mr WL Murdoch was, of course, an amateur.

On paper Murdoch's batting for Sussex was something of a reflection of the trajectory of his career over seven seasons. An average of 24.68 reads moderately but his influence was considerable. Having an ex-Australian captain at the helm certainly gave Sussex considerable county kudos and his first season saw better form from the side together with a great improvement in gate receipts, which served to reduce Lord Sheffield's guarantor bill.

Murdoch also threw himself into Sussex's fight for financial viability, aided by his star batsmen who gave the side the sparkle that made the turnstiles click and kept the boat afloat. Another who might have done was the exotic Crowborough-born Brazilian player Leonidas de Toledo Marcondes de Montezuma. Sadly he played for less than one season, form and mental instability barring his further progress.

Cricket Weeks

LIKE ALMOST EVERY first-class county, Sussex's exchequer was highly reliant on the 'cricket weeks'. The grandest of these was held in the last week of August at Hove and featured, after WG had stopped stepping out for Gloucester, the biggest county draw, Yorkshire, along with the touring team when available.

A special committee sat each year to ensure that the week went off without a hitch and the gathered throng could eat, drink and make merry to their hearts' content. This was a time for the club to not only raise revenue but also to place cricket firmly at the centre of town and county life. If enough well-heeled gentlefolk could be persuaded to spend six days by the sea, then the hotels, places of entertainment and all manner of other local enterprises would benefit which could only, reflect well on the cricket club.

AJ Gaston, 'Leather Hunter' of the *Sussex Daily News*, described the scene around the turn of the century:

> Tents engaged by members and friends and local clubs on either side of the pavilion…The Colours of the popular Brighton Brunswick club and its younger brother, the Sussex Martlets, fluttered in the breeze, while the special reserved county enclosure looked most entertaining, the decorations blending beautifully. [Music was provided by the Brighton Municipal Orchestra] the enthusiasm of the musicians at different incidents in the game was exceedingly stimulating.

Gaston was a hugely popular and influential figure around the ground over three decades. As journalist, unofficial publicity agent and friend to many players he became synonymous with the club in the way that Alfred Pullin had done in Yorkshire. In 1924 he published *Sussex County Cricket 1728-1923*.

In 1908 the cricket week sub-committee pulled out all the stops to involve the whole town. Both piers and the *Alhambra* and *Hippodrome* theatres were approached in order 'to help in booming the cricket week'. An illuminated motor boat procession, promenade concerts in Brighton Pavilion and appearances at the ground of the Hove Lawns Band and Brighton Corporation Band were all designed to encourage and engage a wider audience. The highpoint of the festivities was a Saturday evening military tattoo with full 'illumination' costing the club 10 guineas.

During play a transformation would take place with marquees and stalls erected on all vacant spaces and local tradespeople vying for the opportunity to display their wares. Music and entertainment would fill all intervals and crowds then enticed back in the evening for spectacular musical and theatrical performances.

The one element that could not, as ever, be controlled was the weather and Hove had its fair share of misfortune. A prime example was 1908. Two attractive fixtures against Gloucestershire and Yorkshire had brought the usual numbers in from London, the Sussex countryside and beyond but a week of squally weather ensured that a carnival atmosphere was completely lacking. A total of only 252 overs were bowled across both games. For those brave souls that stuck it out, things only got worse. A storm blew down trees, took the roof off St Matthew's Church in Kemptown, blew a steamer ashore at Shoreham and was then followed by a day of incessant rain. The ground itself was devastated with all the marquees blown down and a large number damaged. As if after all that anyone still cared, the final day's play was a washout.

Light entertainment during the interval, a feature of cricket week.

The following year offered welcome recompense and encapsulated everything a cricket week should be. The game against Yorkshire was hard fought but, ultimately, the blameless pitch was the victor with Wilfred Rhodes showing uncharacteristic laxity in being dismissed for 199. Astonishingly, 60 years later and in his 93rd year, Rhodes was still hurt by this dismissal, especially as his partner, Schofield Haigh, had just run one short.

It was the second game, however, that had the town buzzing. As the *Herald* reported:

From station to cricket ground the electric light and tramway standards were gay with lines of streamers; and on the balconies outside the shops were shields and ensigns; in fact so bright was the scene on Thursday that the very sun was shamed out of its seclusion and laughed down on the gay picture…At the Dispensary at the top of North Road a fine opportunity was taken to display a welcome to the visiting team in black letter on a white background…From the Clock Tower a number of ropes were run to adjoining premises, making a miniature triumphal arch.

Massed banks of spectators for the visit of Australia in 1909, in the background the professionals' dressing-room. Australia sneaked home by one wicket.

The visitors were the Australians, fresh from a 2-1 Ashes victory and boasting such shining lights as Victor Trumper, Tibby Cotter and Charlie Macartney. Despite these luminaries, Sussex gave them a right scare; the visitors eventually prevailing after a stand of 19 for the 10th wicket. But perhaps the most dramatic entertainment took place on the evening of the first day and was then forensically reported in the *Brighton Gazette*:

The whole stretch of the ground had been prettily illuminated with festoons of Chinese and Japanese lanterns; while the pavilion, the covered stand and the enclosures were brilliant in their array of lanterns and fairy lights.

A huge 'mimic naval battle' – 'The sharp fusillade of musketry rang out in a fierce rattle that was almost continuous, punctuated at intervals by the heavy boom of exploding bombs, representing the bursting of shells from the big guns. In fact, there was so furious a banging and booming that people in the distance might well have imagined that the gallant city of Hove was being bombarded. Now and again a flash of light from a rifle would stab the darkness and bring into fleeting revelation the face of the man behind the trigger. Rockets hurtling into the air acted as signals and threw a momentary light onto the battlefield.

There were, however, two luridly picturesque moments. These came when two of the guns were supposed to be blown to smithereens – a maxim on one side and a 12 pounder on the other. The blaze of light which shot up when the guns went crashing asunder coloured the clouds of smoke with a crimson hue. Through this lurid mist the sailors could be seen darting hither and thither like weird figures in a colossal phantasmagoria conceived by Doré.

While the naval fight had been carried out under the pall of darkness… the military tattoo rejoined the people with a splendid view. The blazing torches carried by the troops lit up the whole ground with brilliant effect, and gave a fantastic touch to the movements of the men as they paraded up and down and to and fro in almost every conceivable formation…At one point the torch bearers formed a Union Jack; at others they swept around the ground in a double line of flashing light. Sometimes they would concentrate into squares, then form into separate bodies, advance upon each other and then retreat. For all these movements there was a never-ceasing accompaniment of music. Familiar calls were sounded by the trumpeters, a bugle march played its battery of piercing sound upon your ear; more exhilarating still were the lively marches played by the bands of the 4th Dragoon Guards, then of the Royal Field Artillery, and sometimes the two bands would unite their forces whereat there was a more imposing volume of sound than ever.

One can easily imagine committee men and money men thanking providence that they had been delivered from the rain.

A flavour of the scene can be found on the British Film Institute website. Although shot at Horsham, it gives a picture-perfect cameo of the Cricket Week of 1913 and footage of the Sussex team emerging from their dressing-room.

Cardus, Fry and Ranji at Hove

THE GOLDEN AGE of cricket is not the invention of Neville Cardus, but he is certainly its most famous chronicler. His lyrical evocations of Archie MacLaren, Victor Trumper, Gilbert Jessop and a host of other Edwardian giants, remain the defining words of the years when Players and Gentlemen were evenly matched; the years when the game was the thing and the sun always shone. This world died in 1914 and could never return but, even now, there remains a curious nostalgia for an era frozen in time despite being unremembered by any living being.

Consider Cardus at Hove:

> When Fry was seen in his heyday at one end of the wicket and Kumar Shri Ranjitsinhji at the other, on a June day at Brighton long long ago, imagination beheld visions of Oriental conjurations in contrast to a Spartan austerity of exercise. Fry batted by the book of arithmetic and, while 'Ranji' seemed to toss runs over the field like largesse in silk purses, Fry acquired them – no, not as a miser his hoard but as a connoisseur his collection.

Has there ever been a better description or could there ever be? Not that Cardus was there, mind. Born in 1888, he didn't visit Hove until the 1920s and he may, at most, have seen Fry or Ranji bat once or twice at Old Trafford. Does it matter?

Ted Wainwright of Yorkshire described the annual Hove trip to Cardus:

> Aye, Ranji and Fry at Brighton on a plumb wicket. It were t'same tale every year. We'allus lost t' toss at Brighton in hot weather. Every year it were t' same tale. Sussex 20 for 1 at half-past twelve, Vine out. Then Sussex 43 for 2 at one o'clock. Aye we told oursel's, every blessed year, we're doin' reight well, Yorkshire! Sussex 43 for 2! But, bless your soul, we knowed there were nowt in it.

True enough, in 1896 Ranji scored two centuries in a day; in 1898 Fry carried his bat for 179; in 1901 Fry put on 349 (with Killick) and in 1904 Fry hit another double-century – all against Yorkshire. Cardus's words, attributed to Wainwright, may have no relation to the actual truth but are perhaps much better than factual verisimilitude in catching the essence. This tampering may be dangerous in journalism, but cricket writing would be poorer without it.

It certainly must have seemed to many a county bowler around the turn of the century, that there was literally 'nowt in it'. Between 1899 and 1904, excluding

1902, Fry and Ranji headed the averages every year for players who scored 1000 first-class runs. They didn't just head them, they dominated them. The pair was 13 runs clear of the next best in 1901 and eight clear in 1903 and 1904. The lowest seasonal average by either man was 56.58. Just shy of 20,000 runs were accumulated by the two of them in those five seasons.

Little wonder then that the image of the Hove of these years is of bowlers toiling in the sun while hay was made at both ends. Did the Sussex bowlers really go down to the sea for a swim if their captain won the toss and chose to bat? Or was it the opposition taking a dip if *they* won the toss?

Cardus always looked for more, he wanted to see inside the man. 'To go to a cricket match for nothing but cricket is as though a man were to go into an inn for nothing but drink.' He could marvel at the quantity of runs flowing from the bats of Ranji and Fry, but it is his evocations of the qualities that bring back those images of 'a June day at Brighton long long ago'. Can we really believe Cardus' account of SF Barnes bowling to Ranji on a treacherous pitch at Hove and Ranji thanking the bowler for exercising his skill so adroitly? Sadly we shouldn't, it didn't happen. But perhaps that doesn't matter

Statistics only tell part of the story. Through assiduous practice and sheer hard work both men had honed their styles and all but eliminated errors. Fry's scientific on-driving and Ranji's artistic leg-glancing were revolutionary. Their footwork astounding: Fry, Gene Kelly to Ranji's Fred Astaire. Fry's biographer

*Sussex's handsome and golden
pair pose together.*

Ian Wilton goes so far as to claim 'they can be regarded as the men who invented modern batting'. It is hard to envisage a more charismatic and prolific pair of batsman paired in the same county team – only Compton and Edrich and Greenidge and Barry Richards come close.

For the club it was a godsend. Although the lack of bowling and the strength of Yorkshire precluded a Championship title, Sussex could boast an enviable record around the turn of the century and were a side the public would pay good money to see. 'At Brighton long, long ago' they brought the in the crowds and opened up a new era in the history of Sussex cricket.

A Tragedy of the Cricket Field
Brighton Herald – July 1910

THERE WAS A real calamity at the Hove Cricket Ground yesterday. The cat was killed. We would have called it a catastrophe but the subject is too serious for a joke. Poor old puss, black where she wasn't any other colour, she was as familiar at a county cricket match as the captain of the eleven. She would lie just in front of the pavilion and bask contentedly in the sunshine while the boundary hits went whizzing past her. At exciting moments, when spectators could hardly breathe in their suspense, she would saunter out on to the field of play and leisurely perform her toilet.

A day or two ago she brought out two young kittens to show them the best place for viewing the game. She earned her place, for she waged relentless war on the dogs who ventured into the sacred arena. She knew that dogs had no business there. The dog is not content with being a passive spectator; he is so convinced that the ball is hit his way for him to fetch it. Many a dog has fled in terror before puss's menacing hiss and scarifying claw. At a recent match she absolutely 'chivvied' a dog all the way down the field. It didn't want to go and wouldn't run; but puss followed it as a policeman moves on an obstructing hawker, giving it a push – and a scratch – every time it stopped.

Yesterday puss sauntered across the cinder path to tell her kittens Sussex were beating Leicestershire when a great blundering motor-car swooped round a corner and crushed out every one of her nine lives.

Alletson's Innings

TED ALLETSON WAS what we might now call a 'bits and pieces cricketer'. A powerfully built man, he could bat correctly in the lower-middle order and bowl a bit when required. He played for Nottinghamshire for nine seasons before war finished his career. In that time, he appeared in 118 first-class matches scoring 3217 runs and took 33 wickets at 19. He was easily dropped when team-mates returned from Test duty or an amateur fancied a run-out on a fine day. Alletson was not a moaner, he was a good team man in a good team and made the most of what he had without ever considering finding a weaker county. His best friend was a much better player: John Gunn made 23,000 runs, took 1000 wickets and played six Tests:

> He was a good chap, Ted, and a real trier; you would not call him a great player, but once or twice a season he would hit harder than anyone else I've seen. He had only one real stroke – the drive. Hitting was his game and he had so little bowling to do it became his job. He was not consistent with it, of course, but he had a good eye and when he got going he could win a match in an hour.

George Gunn, 31,000 runs and 15 Tests, echoed his brother's words:

> He has the hardest hitter I ever saw. When the ball was coming onto his bat he drove harder than Jessop.

Jessop himself said, in 1910:

> Of all English hitters at the present moment for pure distance Alletson of Nottingham deserves to be placed first. It is not necessary for him to make his best hit to clear the majority of our grounds.

He once had the temerity to hit Wilfred Rhodes for three consecutive sixes (he was out next ball) and when taking umbrage at a disparaging comment, he dispatched the speaker for four sixes in two overs. Two went right out of Trent Bridge and one carried 150 yards. But nothing matched his day of days, his perfect storm, at Hove on 20 May 1911.

Nottinghamshire travelled south for two fixtures with just 12 players, two of whom were injured. Alletson's sprained wrist was deemed the less severe of the two and he was selected in place of Tom Wass. The first two days went in favour of the home county. With a first-innings lead of 176 and the visitors six wickets down and still behind at stumps, Sussex could reasonably hope for a victory by lunchtime on a grey and blustery final day.

Hoping to ease his wrist, Alletson took an early dip in the inhospitable sea, but soon found himself walking down the steps of the players' room carrying his featherlight 2lb 3oz bat equipped with extra rubber grip to accommodate his large hands. Nine runs behind and just three wickets in hand, an early train back to Nottingham seemed likely.

Nottinghamshire took the game beyond the lunch interval, but only just. Two more wickets fell and Alletson was missed twice in scoring 47 – a lead of just 84 with one wicket to fall on a dank afternoon; not a scenario designed to bring spectators to the ground. The few hundred hardy souls that were present would never forget what happened in the next 40 minutes.

The final pair of Alletson and Riley added 152, of which Alletson's share was 142. In 12.2 overs of mayhem, the ball flew to and over the boundary time and time again. It was not scientific, it was brutal. Fielders were not a consideration; if the ball was hit hard enough or high enough they became an irrelevance. Ernest Killick made the mistake of bowling two no balls and was dispatched for 34 in one over, a record that stood till Garry Sobers hit six sixes off Malcolm Nash at Swansea in 1968. Both the scorebooks became a blurred mess and it was only the assiduous forensic work of PC John Arlott and Roy Webber that rescued definitive details for posterity. Not just that, they collected witness statements. Bob Relf was an astounded fielder:

> He just hit firm-footed. He made no attempt to get to the pitch of the ball, but, unless it was right up to him, hit under it straight off the middle of the bat... My chief memory is that shower of cricket balls going over the boundary and

the crowd mad with delight. Of course it cost us a match we were winning, but I don't think anybody minded about that – it was such an experience to watch it.

As George Gunn recalls, there was both damage to the ground and fear in the field:

> Ted cut one ball over point that smashed the pavilion window and wrecked the bar. He sent his drives skimming; you could hear them hum…Ted drove several at the Relf brothers and the ball fizzed through them as if they were ghosts…It was not a case of it being hard to set a field to him, but one of those drives would have smashed a man's hand.

The bespectacled Killick was the chief sufferer:

> …Ernie was almost frightened to bowl at him. I do not think he minded his bowling being hit so much as he was worried Ted might hit one back at him.

One account has a ball embedded in the wooden fascia of the new Cowshed stand, one through the pavilion clock, balls on the roof of the Ice Rink and in the streets beyond – 15 sixes in all. Forty minutes of carnage.

The innings finished in some controversy when he was caught by opposing captain, Charles Smith, who was clearly leaning against the stand. But Alletson didn't care; time was tight, there was still a match to win and Notts almost pulled it off. Sussex gave it a go and were eight down at end of play.

It had long been said that the Duke of Portland, on whose estate Alletson was born, had promised him a cheque for £100 should he ever hit a century for the county. Hopefully he was as good as his word. Alletson was reportedly at least rewarded with a home-fed ham.

In truth the facts and figures have been slightly diminished by the big bats, short boundaries and innovations of the modern one-day game. Hove has seen some mighty hitting, centuries before lunch by Jessop, Tate, Parks, Duleepsinhji and Paynter; a century in 48 minutes by Arthur Carr and a double-century in two hours by Jessop. All of these men played for England, Ted Alletson never came close, but surely nothing has ever matched the sheer unadulterated simplicity and brutality of his striking that day.

World War I

FOLLOWING THE ASSASSINATION of Archduke Franz Ferdinand in Sarajevo on 28 June 1914, Europe was plunged into a frenzy of threat, counter-threat, diplomacy and preparation for war. Those who sought to avoid conflict found themselves out-manoeuvred by a combination of ill-defined treaties, territorial ambitions, years of arms building and good old-fashioned sabre rattling.

By early August 1914 the fire had been lit. In Germany, France and Great Britain the official line to be used was that it would all be over by Christmas. Following outbreak, cricket struggled on, unsure whether to pull stumps or see it through. The final game of the 1914 season epitomised this conundrum, as seen through the eyes of *Yorkshire Evening Post* journalist Alfred Pullin:

> While cricket was taking place, in the centre of the Hove enclosure Army recruits were being drilled in full view in the top part of the ground. The two things don't dovetail at all.

At 4.40 pm the game was called a draw so that the Yorkshire players could catch an early train home. Major Booth, Roy Kilner, Alonzo Drake and Arthur Dolphin immediately volunteered for service on their return. Only Kilner and Dolphin ever played first-class cricket again.

For all the public proclamations, politicians and military leaders prepared themselves for the long haul. At number 44 Wilbury Road, Colonel Sidney Wishart, commander of the 6th London Brigade, Royal Field Artillery, set to thinking how best to aid the war effort beyond following orders. He had made his fortune in the City, had been hugely influential in the development of the Territorial Army since its formation in 1908 and was a committee member of Sussex County Cricket Club. In these three capacities he called a meeting to discuss how the club could aid king and country. In early September 1914, officials from the Royal Institute of British Architects made the trip to Hove to look over his suggestions. On 16 September they wrote to Wishart with their thoughts

His offer had been to use the ground as a convalescent hospital. The pavilion was something of a possibility although considerable alterations would be required. Wishart's suggestion of the Cowshed was less enthusiastically received due to the lack of water, drains, electricity, windows and one wall. The concrete stepping was also an obstacle.

Undeterred, Wishart got the builders to quote on the pavilion scheme which would provide 27 beds split between the central hall, committee room and dining room. A sum of £93 7s would be required to improve lighting, draught exclusion, curtaining and heating. One rider he couldn't exclude was that the building would only be available until April 1915 if cricket continued. Not surprisingly the scheme was not pursued.

Meanwhile another colonel, C Somers Clarke, had gained the use of the ground as headquarters for the 6th (Cycle) Battalion, Royal Sussex Regiment, which also used the Ice Rink as their drill hall and the ground for ceremonial drill. In 1915 a rifle range was erected in the north-west corner for the 2nd (Hove) Battalion, Sussex Volunteer Training Corps.

Another officer, Captain Alan Luther, who played nine times for Sussex, was the first county cricketer reported killed in action though he had, in fact, been wounded and taken prisoner. He lived until 1961.

The band of the third battalion of the Sussex regiment parading on the outfield, October 1916.

During the war years, cricket was an increasingly rare sight but many other activities were on the menu. A stoolball match between one-armed soldiers and ageing lawyers was one. This traditional Sussex game was being revived by committee member William Grantham. There was also a country fair in aid of the Hove War Depot, closely followed by a baseball match between two Canadian teams.

In 1917 the club presidency changed hands on the death of the Duke of Norfolk with Lord Leconfield elected as his replacement. This was, however, just the home front. Across Europe and the wider world men were dying in their hundreds of thousands and when peace finally came the unthinkable cost was counted. Sussex had lost nine first-class cricketers in addition to county secretary Francis Oddie.

None of the nine could be considered regulars. John Nason was the most prolific, with 22 games before moving to Gloucestershire. Only one, Ernest Relf, younger brother of county stalwarts Bert and Robert, was an enlisted soldier. Of the remaining eight, four were Oxbridge cricket blues who had schooled at Harrow, Marlborough, Charterhouse and Westminster.

Developments Around the County Ground

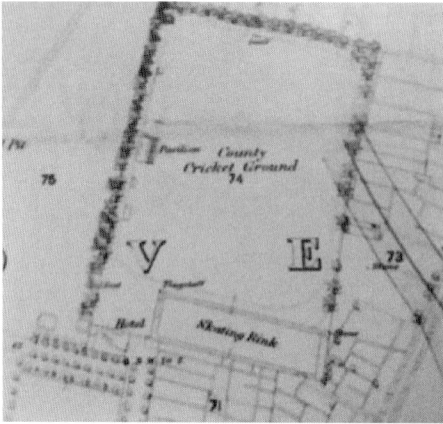

1873

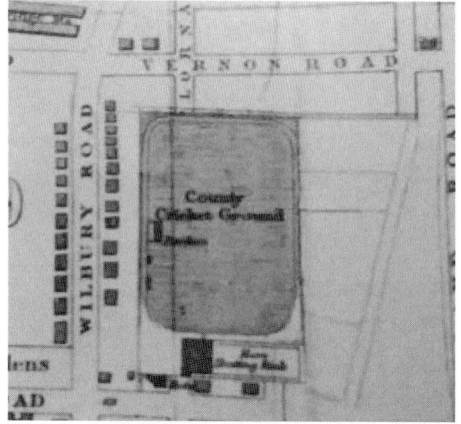

1880

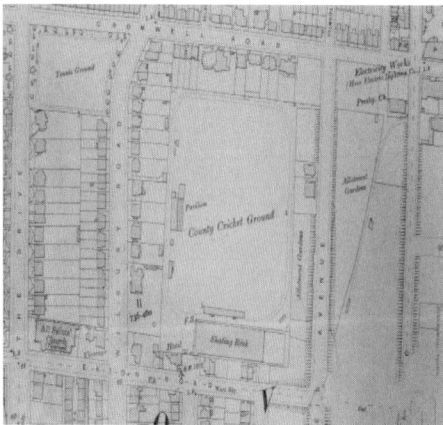

1911

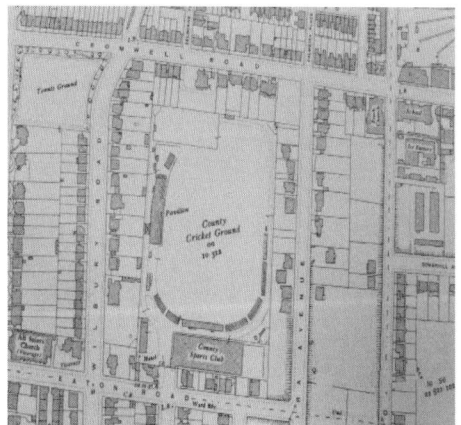

1931

-Three-

Between the Wars

Euphoria is not a word easily associated with the immediate aftermath of the cessation of hostilities in 1918, in spite of the initial outpouring of celebration. Exhaustion is a better fit. It was an exhaustion begat of four years of catastrophic loss of life amongst young men, with its consequent effect on their families. On top of this, Spanish influenza was racing across the world with an unprecedented mortality rate: 20% of those infected and an even higher percentage amongst young healthy adults.

For four long years, pleasure, house-building and planning for a better future had been put on hold while the European powers pummelled one another to the brink of annihilation. For all post-war governments there was the need to re-establish viable economies and find hope and optimism, putting the recent past to rest without forgetting the sacrifices made. Cricket had a part to play.

In 1919, a County Championship was hastily re-convened where matches were played over two long and tiring days. It was a thoroughly unpopular and short-lived experiment. Most counties struggled in the immediate post-war years. Some of the brightest pre-1914 prospects had been lost, facilities had been mothballed and finances had stagnated. When post-war account books were opened from Northampton to Leyton, the coffers were found to be horribly depleted. As ever, wealthy patrons were sought, membership drives launched and, as a last resort, assets stripped. Essex's Leyton headquarters was sold to the Army Sports Council with the county then leasing the ground as tenants.

Sussex's immediate response to avoiding a similar fate was not unusual. Despite careful financial management during the war years, only four professionals were employed for 1919, winter pay was abolished, and the club nursery was temporarily abandoned. With only 1313 members paying a total of £1404, the challenges facing new secretary Major WGM Sarel were profound. The ground had been well used but not well maintained during the war years. Arthur Gilligan described it as being 'in a rather primitive state as regards accommodation for both members and the general public'. Unwisely, Sussex took on 20 Championship fixtures and with the late demobilisation of some of the professionals, drafted in various amateur 'talents'. They fielded no less than 35 different players during the season.

Fortunately, the real talents of some of the old stagers such as Joe Vine,

Albert Relf and George Cox seemed undimmed in the immediate post-war years, and these men oversaw the rise of Maurice Tate, the Gilligans and Tich Cornford. This was a pattern replicated at most other counties as Wilfred Rhodes, Frank Woolley and George Gunn mentored their younger colleagues.

A New Start

Membership doubled in two years and in 1921 Lance Knowles began his 21-year tenure as club secretary. When a profit of £925 was signed off for the year the outlook may not have been exactly rosy, but neither was the club on the brink of extinction. However, this profit, boosted by the presence of the Australian touring team and a £526 windfall from Test profits, was reversed the following year with £982 the resultant deficit. One consequence was the loss of Vallance Jupp, his 13,000 runs and 1000 wickets at a niggardly average for Northants were sorely missed by Sussex over the next decade.

In 1921 the finest observer and recorder of Sussex cricket between the wars, Laetitia Stapleton, attended her first match at Hove with her Scottish nanny. Her vague recollections of that game, when the Australians lost most sessions but won in the end, would become precise, and her diaries faithfully recorded her relationship with Sussex county cricket. A few years older was Ronald Mason who, half a century later when writing *Warwick Armstrong's Australians*, vividly recalled his day at Hove. The tourists had arrived after suffering their first defeat of the tour at the hands of Archie MacLaren's own England XI. Still, they had beaten England 3-0 and unleashed on an unsuspecting public the first sighting of a genuine pace pair bowling in tandem with the new ball. Mason was bewitched by Jack Gregory and Ted McDonald as they 'exploded upon the attention'. Other players were almost as memorable and the ground itself left an indelible impression:

> We made the excursion again to the same crowded, cramped, noisy beflagged, beribboned and everlastingly memorable ground...I can still see, from my timorous nine-year-old height, the bewildering, smoke wreathed, elbowing chattering crowds, hear the buzz and hum, visualize the scuffling knots of people eager to snatch scorecards as the belated salesman fought off the besiegers.

In Brighton, as all over Britain, the tourists had received a rapturous welcome, a 'pullulating throng' assembling at the station to greet them on their arrival from Eastbourne. Is this perhaps evidence that Britain had entered the first stages of recovery? Sport was helping to heal some wounds, offering a return to the rhythms of normality and of life as it had been before the war when county cricket and touring teams were synonymous with the sounds and scents of summer, and part of the national calendar.

There was, however, a mountain of national debt with which to contend. The post-war national economy struggled and things were no different down on the coast. Income tax had increased drastically and national unemployment stood at 11% in 1921, though by 1923 it had fallen to 7%. These figures were largely replicated in Brighton. The town was also beset by a lack of housing despite it being second nationally, behind only West Ham in East London, in terms of population density.

Seaside resorts and places of entertainment were particularly hard hit and not helped by the introduction of an Entertainment Tax. Sheets of stamps had to be purchased by the club and then affixed to entrance tickets issued at the gate. The rate was 2d in the shilling or 16.6%. Little wonder that, as ever, survival was top of the list of priorities. To this end, Sussex trimmed costs where possible (three amateurs in the side) and maximised revenue (arranging the Middlesex fixture for August Bank Holiday in the hope of attracting London visitors).

In secretary Lance Knowles, the county was blessed with an administrator of the highest calibre, if not a playing side to match him. In 1921 Sussex did manage their highest-ever score at Hove, 670-9 declared against a modest Northants attack featuring a stand of 385 between double centuries Ted Bowley and Maurice Tate, but other than that the season ended with the team ninth, a position occupied again the following year. In 1923 they improved three places.

In 1924 hopes were higher when Sussex briefly topped the table only for their form to fall apart. Injuries plagued them and, worse by far, wicket-keeper George Street was killed in a motorcycle accident in Portslade. They finished the season back in tenth place. *Cricket* magazine's review of the year was sure where the fault lay:

> It must be bluntly stated that the younger county players suffered from being badly coached. Many elementary and obvious faults were not eradicated. It was not good to see county cricketers dismissed for a trivial score coming out with a grin as if it did not matter. The team as a whole batted in one-day-club-style, not approaching county standard.

Laetitia Stapleton was spared the worst of the travails of town and club. Safely ensconced, a stone's throw from the ground, at Kenilworth House School she became fan, observer and friend to generations of players. Her first clear memory of a game was in 1925 when the national press descended on Hove with the expectation of seeing Jack Hobbs match Grace's record of 126 centuries. Maurice Tate ensured he failed on that occasion but the following month he both equalled and overhauled the record at Taunton. The details of the matches up to that point may have eluded her, but Stapleton's memory of the ground was still crystal clear over 50 years later:

> In 1924 the County Ground at Hove presented a very different picture to the one you will see today. The pavilion was about a third of its present size…the ladies were severely segregated in what was called the 'Enclosure'…The only shelter provided for the female sex was a rather rickety stand, known affectionately as the 'hen coop'…The 'cowshed' at the southern end had a high wooden front, painted white, against which the ball would hurtle with a satisfying thud to register another four. To the northern end were some nice red brick Victorian houses and there was a tennis club on that part of the ground where the nets now lie. There were only two rather dignified and handsome houses in Palmeira Avenue: I have watched all the others being built, each one becoming less attractive than its predecessor.

There was much else to pique her interest, from the old horse clad in huge leather bootees pulling the heavy roller, to the Sports Club, as the old Ice Rink was now known. This was now equipped for badminton, squash and indoor nets with a shop selling sports equipment and postcards of players.

Near the hotel, amply-refreshed men would be lying in the sun in their caps and braces in sartorial contrast to the MCC and club ties in the pavilion and the long dresses and gloves in the ladies' enclosure. Provision of refreshment had been supplemented by the construction of The Chalet in 1908 and this 'temporary tea pavilion' lasted 100 years and would fulfil all manner of functions from indoor school to bat factory.

The telegraph boy would often rush out onto the field at the end of an over to deliver an orange envelope containing no-one knew what urgent news. 'Just occasionally the rest of the team would approach him and shake hands and then we knew that the tidings were good', wrote Laetitia Stapleton. With no loudspeaker, public announcements were chalked on a blackboard and carried round the ground by boys from the groundstaff, while always there was the clarion call of the newspaper vendors announcing 'latest edition' and 'stop-press' cricket scores from across the country.

The Age of Tate

Hovering in mid-table through the 1920s, Sussex relied heavily on the efforts of Maurice Tate with support from his captain Arthur Gilligan and Ted Bowley. In 1928, the batting bloomed under the peerless Duleepsinhji, with seven players reaching their 1000 runs for the season in his wake. The names of first Parks and then Langridge joined Cox and Vine on the scorecards and Sussex were becoming the hardest county to beat in the country. It was unfortunate that Gilligan's ability as a fast bowler had been severely curtailed in 1924 when he was hit over the heart in a Gentleman v Players match, but his influence on the team was profound. He oversaw the early development of some of Sussex's finest servants and instilled a spirit in the team that long-standing professional Tommy Cook recalled:

> We of Sussex, all Sussex born and bred, seem to have that county spirit that can never be so strong in teams of mixed counties and nationalities. This county spirit seems to give us a will to win stronger than any incentive of the £2 bonus.

Gilligan was also regarded as one of the finest outfielders in the country and he ensured that his team followed his example. But despite good team spirit and good fielding, with Tate being the only match-winning bowler in the side, an upper-middle position in the table was the best that could be hoped for.

Nonetheless, Gilligan had nursed Sussex through the 1920s alongside his faithful and tireless lieutenant Tate. There was no question of matching the might of the northern counties, but neither were they floundering near the bottom with Worcestershire and Somerset.

If Sussex were to join the twentieth century, and perhaps host a side that might, in time, challenge for the title, the ground needed attention. But overall the post-Edwardian era was one of cautious optimism down at Hove. Perhaps it was this spirit that led to a change in the club colours in 1929. The red, white and blue, replaced by the more regal dark blue, light blue and gold and the inverted pyramid of six martlets adorned sweaters rather than just blazer badges as previously.

Though right in the heart of the great depression, under the tireless work of Lance Knowles, membership had increased steadily and finances had stabilised. In 1921 the mortgage on the ground stood at £5450 but by 1927 the club had cleared the full amount and felt confident enough to plough £7000 into the pavilion extension – by far the biggest improvement the ground had seen in its 55-year history. FT Cawthorn was once again engaged to draw up plans to double the size of the pavilion on the inside, as well as provide covered seating capacity outside.

The original building had not been built as a rectangle with the length facing the pitch approximately twice that at the back. The plan was to increase both dimensions so as to extend the depth to create a perfect rectangle. This would of course increase seating capacity in front of the pavilion, but the club wanted more. A covered stand with room for some 250 spectators was placed on the roof of the new extension. The Brunswick pavilion that had stood to the north end was sacrificed and the pavilion could now amply house, from south to north, the committee room, common-room, amateurs' changing-area, players' common-room, professionals changing-room and a pavilion room at half-depth with service rooms and ladies' toilets behind it.

The Hencoop is now on the east side.

Though the building was now double in size and housed both professional and amateur players, much of the old ethos was unchanged. The professionals finally had hot water laid on with a chimney belching forth smoke at around 5 pm to indicate the boilers had been fired. The amateurs' dressing-room was virtually twice the size of the professionals', even though in most games the latter outnumbered the former by two to one. The amateurs' room had something of the air of a sombre London club with huge leather-upholstered armchairs and sofas, a vast table in the centre of the room and cricketing prints adorning the walls. There was still the same palaver of separate entrances onto the field, although Sussex proved to be more egalitarian than most counties and did away with this entry distinction in the early thirties. Still not sufficiently egalitarian to allow ladies into the pavilion, however.

The grand opening took place in the spring of 1928, overseen by Lord Leconfield, Lord Lieutenant of Sussex and president of MCC, who still held a share of the hotel through the loan he held jointly with David Reuben Sassoon. The following year Sussex were able to report a record crowd for the ground in the game against Yorkshire.

A knock-on effect of the new building was the moving of the 'Hencoop' across the outfield from its original site near the pavilion to the south of the main scoreboard This stand, at 85 feet long and 15 feet high, was dismantled, hauled across the ground and rebuilt, initially as a 'ladies enclosure', on the spot where it stood for another 40 years, rickety and draughty to the end despite only just surviving a storm in January 1930.

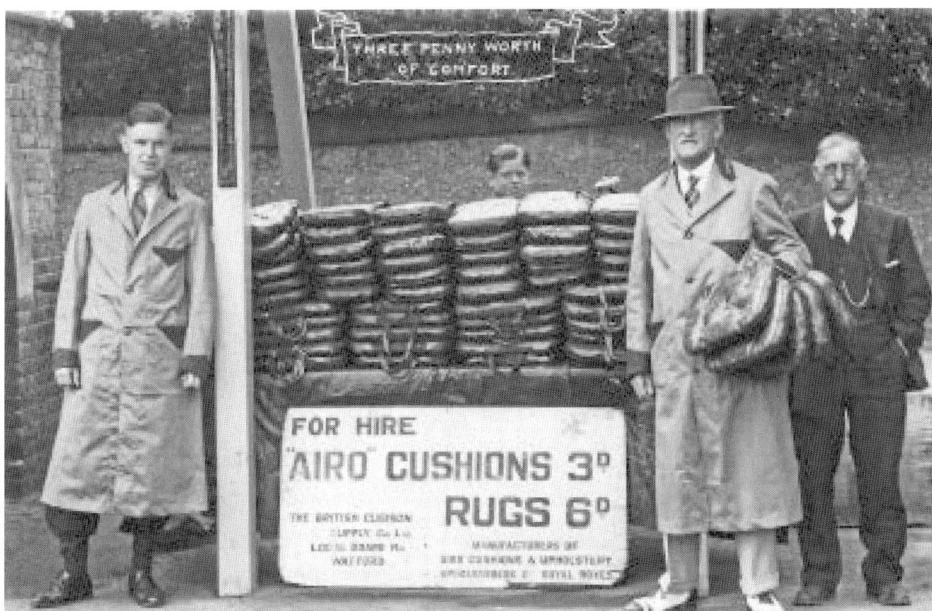

'Three Penny Worth of Comfort': Cushions with Lance Knowles.

For Laetitia Stapleton, after a brief sojourn in London, the county ground had become a home from home. Players that she idolised became acquaintances and then friends and figures around the ground became embedded in her imagination and then memory. There was the 'elderly gateman' who opened and shut the entrance for batsmen with unfailing courtesy while patrolling the line that women dared not cross. There was 'Cushions', offering his 'three pennyworth of comfort' and head groundsman Tom Burchell, whose father had worked on the ground since 1874, patrolling and tending the hallowed turf with his team. She was not alone in being beguiled as a youngster by the sights, sounds and smells of cricket by the sea. Cricket writer Gerald Brodribb vividly recalled trips from his home in Hastings:

Armed with my sandwiches a cheap half-day ticket I tried to endure patiently the seventy minutes journey [from St Leonard's] with all its tiresome stops till at last the train came curving round into Brighton station. There was always an anxiety lest it might be late and I might miss something. Then a rush from the exit to board the bus outside – 5a was it? Would it never come? And might not play have started at 11.00 instead of 11.30? On big days there was an army of spectators clutching their fodder and binoculars, all eagerly anticipating the day's play. We rocked our way up the steep hill from the station, 'standing room only', and laughing as we lurched past the Seven Dials. Not long now; and I leapt off boldly at the Palmeira Avenue stop.

I really preferred the quieter days when the ground was rather empty. First we grabbed a place near the screen from where we could feel the ball was being bowled almost at us…At last the bell would be rung in the pavilion, as sweet a sound as any boy could desire. There were no loudspeakers to tell you who had won the toss…Instead, a ground boy would carry a board round; 'Sussex won the toss and will bat' were the words that brought rapturous applause. If the weather was fine – and it usually seemed to be – this meant a more or less guaranteed 400 runs in the day's play, though not all of them would be made by Sussex if they were in one of their brittle moods.

I remember one day wearing my new membership tie – then red, white and blue – and I thought this might bring luck to the side, and it did. There were always people going round the ground: the men with up-to-date score cards, price 2d, with their roving eyes looking for buyers, the old man with the straw hat and one spectacle for his right eye only, selling 'three-pennyworth of comfort' in the shape of rubber cushions, boys offering 'tea tickets 1/6' if you felt like sitting at a table amongst tents, which we didn't because you couldn't see properly from there. There were also evening papers to be bought after 2 o'clock, which might include the lunch-scores of our rivals, racing results, local murders, declarations of obscure wars…

Those days seemed always to be fair and fresh and full of colour, the grass green even in August, white clouds off the sea and the clouds rocketing in the breeze. The county ground at Hove seemed a very paradise to me, and the only thing I could not understand was how those unfortunates playing lawn tennis where the nets now are could indulge in such a pursuit when Maurice Tate was on the warpath a few yards away. I often hoped that some Sussex batsman would land a ball amongst them.

Writer and poet Gerald Martineau saw the county ground in Hove as an escape from the nightmare of the 1926 holiday-season's great unwashed:

Thick-bodied, thick-lipped, and shining with heat,
Light brownish people are filling the street –
Filling the street from the sticky, grey trains,
Holiday-making while summer remains.
Lancashire lady, grey bonnet, old lace,
Smiling all over her frosty old face,
Hustled and trodden on, gay as can be,
Goes with the dago-rush down to the sea,
Down to the beach where they strengthen the air,
Thousands of grease-spots from Heaven-knows-where.

This is the town which, they tell me, is gay:
"Frolics in Brighton," the photographs say.

Nausea grips me; I rush from the drove;
Get me a taxi! I'll hie me to Hove;
Spin through the streets till I hear the glad sound,
Echoes of cheering all over the ground.
What an oasis beyond the old gate!
There will be Gilligan, Bowley, and Tate;
Far from the surge of the heated unclean;
Sussex and England – the game on the green.

At the much disputed north-east entrance, matters had finally been resolved. In April 1928 a further strip of 10 feet of land was purchased from a Mr Nash which allowed free passage into the ground from Palmeira Avenue. Initially a request to vary the 1906 covenant in order to allow ingress to motor cars had been refused, but when the inconvenience of parking outside the ground became an issue for residents, permission was granted for parking at the north end.

Near Misses

On the cricket front, the expansion of the ground indicated optimism for the future and the early years of the 1930s repaid this optimism on the field, each detail now being faithfully recorded on the impressive new Harmsworth scoreboard. With no more Gilligans to call on, Duleep added captaincy to his imperious batting. As the 1930s dawned he found himself blessed with a powerful team. The loss of George Cox in 1928 was a grievous one, but he had first played in 1898 and his retirement was well deserved even if, at the age of 52, he was capable of taking 17-106 (still the best match figures in Sussex history). George senior took over tuition of the next generation of players at the county Nursery at a salary of £200 a year, much the same as he had been earning as a player. Amongst the Hove records Cox still holds are most first-class matches (224) and most wickets in a season (86 in 1905). His replacements were more than adequate, not the least among them, his son, George Junior. Ted Bowley, the brothers Langridge and Parks and Tommy Cook were a supremely solid middle order, largely untroubled by national selectors. With them Sussex entered the silver years – runners up three times in a row from 1932-34. As ever, the bowling was the problem. Though he remained one of the finest in the country, Tate was past his prime and he had little specialist backing. The all-round skill of James Langridge, Bowley, Harry Parks, Bert Wensley and assorted part-timers was certainly no match for the likes of Verity and Bowes in Yorkshire.

In 1932, defeat at Hove by Yorkshire ended home hopes of a first title. Duleep struggled with a pulmonary disease that would end his career and Tate was also increasingly distracted by worries over health, a new baby and his chances of being selected for the England touring team to Australia.

The achievement of John Langridge and Ted Bowley is celebrated on the Harmsworth scoreboard.

'No triumph would have been more heartily welcomed throughout the length and breadth of the land than that of the southern county', was *Wisden's* response to Sussex's failure to stay the course

In 1933, Yorkshire were beaten twice but a further dip in Tate's form, followed by injury, was enough to scupper their chances. The following year, under new captain South African Alan Melville, it seemed that the pennant would at last be secured. With 10 games to go the Championship was seemingly in the bag only for just one of the remaining 10 to end in victory. A workmanlike Lancashire side edged over the line. Sir Home Gordon was not impressed:

> Until these fine fellows realise they cannot win fifteen points by pawkily playing for safety and being content with a mere five, they will never get the Championship.

The team coach, Bert Relf, was inclined to agree: 'Sussex were beaten by the mentality of their batsmen. If their brains had been equal to their skill all would have been well.' True, Sussex retreated into their shell after playing attractive and match-winning cricket until mid-July, but did they really lose their nerve? The temporary collapse in form of leading wicket taker Jim Langridge couldn't be over-estimated. Whatever the answer, the stigma that they didn't have the necessary killer instinct would remain for another 69 years.

In April 1933, in far-away Jamnagar, Ranji drew his last breath. The following year the scoreboard on the pavilion side was rebuilt in his memory. But it is through words that his memory is most eloquently enshrined. For sculptor Eric Gill, over the Downs at Ditchling 'when I have a little quiet wallow in the thought of something delightful and perfect, I think of Ranji on the county ground at Hove'. For Ranji's biographer, poet Alan Ross, he 'transmitted down the generations a shiver of the spine at Hove or Lord's, the air signed with that latest of late cuts, that silkiest of glances'.

This new scoreboard was

The Parks brothers Jim and Harry flank James Langridge behind the pavilion.

erected just in time to record still the biggest ever partnership at Hove – 490 for the first wicket between Ted Bowley and John Langridge against Middlesex in 10 minutes short of a full day.

Riding high in the table did not, however, equate to cash in hand. In 1929 the basic membership fee had risen sharply from 12 shillings to one guinea without bringing any great increase in income. Though membership stayed stable until 1939, it took an alarming dip in 1932, and the success of the side was not reflected in gate receipts. Even though two of these 'silver summers' were pure gold in terms of the weather, no attendance was as high as 1926 when Sussex had finished only 10th. A measure perhaps of cricket followers in Sussex, for whom success was not the be all and end all of the experience of a day at Eaton Road.

An even greater problem was the wages. By now Sussex were largely a professional side with the bill to match – £3685 in 1926 had risen to over £5500 in the seasons after 1932. With little or no increase in revenue, balancing the books had become impossible. In both 1926 and 1930 an end-of-season profit of over £2000 was recorded, but in the three runner-up seasons combined it was just £241. This paltry return proved to be just a precursor to losses of £3000 over the next three seasons. Amateurs were proving to be a good investment, with their expenses rarely rising above £300 for the year. But finding amateurs that didn't prejudice the form of the team was no easy matter.

Not that the professionals didn't earn their money: Tich Cornford received his benefit in 1934 and recorded an unbroken stint of over 400 games for the county and 484 in total, all the while standing up behind the stumps to Tate. The Langridge brothers played 1189 games and scored 63,000 runs, the Parks brothers, Jim and Harry, 914 games with 41,000 runs, Cook 459 games, Bowley 458 games, Tate 525. Even unsung Bert Wensley made 373 appearances. Aside from Tate, these players combined managed just 14 appearances for their country. Nine players whose careers were either largely or wholly played out between the wars played for Sussex 4402 times. The captains may have changed but the professionals were settled.

One consequence was a run of benefits: Tate 1930, Bowley 1931, Cornford 1934, Wensley 1936, Cook 1937 and Jim Parks 1939. The other three had to wait a while. With these loyal servants, Sussex could boast a home-grown side to rival anyone except Yorkshire. All bar one was born in Sussex; Ted Bowley was the odd-man out, hailing from the far-flung township of Leatherhead, although the family soon moved to Liss where, reputedly, the Sussex/Hampshire border ran through the centre of the parental home.

These ominous financial figures had not been envisaged when money was spent on ground developments. A further blow came with the death of David Reuben Sassoon in 1929. Together with Lord Leconfield he held the outstanding loan of £2000 on the hotel and this loan was now called in by his executors.

On the upside, Tamplins brewery had become a dependable partner. It had taken over the license to run The Chalet in 1923, and in 1928 paid £500 to extend its lease on the hotel until 1942. A series of whist drives raised most of the £400 required annually by the Nursery as well as enhancing the club's association with villages and outlying towns. The Brighton Brunswick and Martlet clubs were still using the county ground while the Sports Club and hotel were also valuable earners and even car parking had begun to appear on the balance sheets. In 1930, 1000 Girl Guides rallied at the ground and small rental incomes from the Sussex County Lawn Tennis Club and both Belmont and Claremont schools all went some way to bridging the gap between gate receipts and expenses. Perhaps the most forward-looking move of all was the appointment of Mr AE Quick as publicity agent, even if his annual fee of £25 (£2600 today) indicated a certain lack of belief in such things.

But the club was still stretched; a bank loan the only answer. Barclays came to the rescue with £5000, but with the deeds to the ground be deposited with them as surety.

Notwithstanding perennial financial precarity, they had been three glorious years at Hove on the field, in each of which the Championship pennant seemed to be within reach. They are years fondly recalled by Dudley Carew in *To the Wicket*:

Rather do I think of overs from Tate I have seen at Hove at the beginning of a day's play. The pavilion there is square to the wicket and to see bowling properly one must be end-on; so, as the players pour down the steps, a judicious stroll past the tennis courts to the sight-screen and watch the first few overs from there. Are there any overs like the first overs of the day? Those who come to cricket-grounds in the afternoons miss the beauty and quietness which brood over a cricket-ground when it is only half-past eleven by the clock and the crowd is small and scattered. What an incomparable freshness there is in the air and the game itself seems less an affair of practical runs and wickets than some *ballet*, some design, devised solely for delight and idleness. Never do the cricketers seem so near, never is such intimacy with them established from the ropes. After luncheon the bloom has gone, pieces of newspaper, the wrappings of sandwiches personify the desecration and the match, absorbed now in strategy and calculation, has receded from its first state of happy innocence. It is always June, somehow always

June, and a blackbird is running across the tennis courts and the numbers click in the score-board as the batsmen turn for their second run.

A Slide Towards War

After coming close three times in succession, perhaps it was inevitable that Sussex would fall back. The lack of bowling was again the reason. Tate was still plying his trade but was now a good county bowler as opposed to a match-winning champion, and the support from James Langridge, Jim Parks and Jim Cornford (no relation to Tich) was honest but not the stuff of Championship pennants.

The following year was worse. Alan Melville returned to South Africa to be replaced as captain by AJ Holmes, the team fell to 14th in the table and it rained and rained. With the pips squeaking in the treasurer's office, cost-cutting was once again top of the agenda. The secretary and his assistant took voluntary pay cuts and the players lost 5% of their earnings. Membership had stayed steady, but the 3518 gentlemen and ladies were regularly asked to dip into their wallets and purses beyond their annual subscriptions.

The saga of Maurice Tate continued; he was still just about the best bowler in the side but his newspaper columns and popularity in the cheap seats certainly rankled with some in the corridors of power. It was a miserable year, the club showed a substantial loss and there was no sign of anything getting better anytime soon.

For Tate, 1937 finished with a pay-off of £250 (he had collected £1900 from his benefit in 1930) and some spiteful words from Home Gordon:

> The premature ageing of the county's greatest cricketer was obvious. The popular play-boy has now become a mere trader on his past reputation of having been the best English bowler since the War, and is still held the idol of the faithful non critical.

'It was the way they did it', was Tate's verdict. Years later, Sussex's elegant captain Hugh Bartlett would delight Alan Ross by describing Home Gordon as "a shit". Tate wouldn't be the last to feel aggrieved at his treatment after decades of service and there is no doubt that this had not been forgotten by some when the committee was challenged in 1950.

Against all the odds, however, Sussex enjoyed a revival in 1937, a glorious summer of batting and record breaking. Jim Parks had first played for the county in 1924 and here he was not only scoring 3000 runs but also taking 100 wickets, a feat unmatched. Many believed that after the death of his wife in the winter of 1936, he found solace on the cricket field. He was never the same player thereafter: "1937 did for old Jim", said Hugh Bartlett, and little wonder – 63 innings, 3003 runs, 1047 overs, 101 wickets. He wasn't flashy, but taking Larwood and Voce for 100 before lunch at Hove in July was hardly stodgy. Six other batsmen recorded their 1000 runs for the season including the Langridge brothers, who became the first siblings to both make 2000 runs in a season. All this meant that Sussex scored 15,358 Championship runs, a figure not approached by any other county in any season. Although the perennial problem with the bowling meant any challenge for the title was still unlikely, it was a remarkable rallying around the flag in a time of adversity. It still didn't translate into profit in the accounts.

As it transpired, Sussex had been punching above their weight in 1937 and proceeded to fall to eighth and then 10th before war once again intervened. The appearance of two new varsity amateurs, Hugh Bartlett and Billy Griffith, was more than welcome but neither were bowlers and that is what Sussex needed. Bartlett's debut season was as dramatic as any in Sussex history, the left hander topping the county averages and treating Hove to the fastest century of the season, 57 minutes against the Australian tourists. He was promoted to captain in 1939 and toured South Africa with MCC in a run-drenched series, but sat out all five Tests before war ruined what could have been a brilliant career. Bartlett was a throwback to an age when the power of Jessop, the elegance of Woolley, and the panache of Edwardian amateur masters such as Kenneth Hutchings and Reggie Spooner set the tone. Griffith's career and influence proved, however, to be longer. The stalwart brothers Langridge, Parks and George Cox were as reliable as ever and a new pair of brothers, Charlie and Jack Oakes of Horsham, had appeared.

If Hove had a reputation for *laissez-faire* that could border on the louche, there were occasions when she could show her teeth both in and outside the ground. The game against Nottinghamshire in 1936 was one such when Sussex needed nine runs to win in the fourth innings but with only five minutes showing on the clock. Five extras and two runs came from Bill Voce's opening over and at 6.28 the Notts players trouped off claiming the rain. Umpires and visiting players were 'boo-ed to the echo', the 'uproar was tremendous'. Days later the Notts captain apologised. A similar set of shenanigans occurred in 1939 when Middlesex, due to the complexities of the points system, found it advantageous to not bowl Sussex out and proceeded to miss all manner of chances to rounds of booing. Outside the ground Hove residents were out in force at the railway station to heckle a German Police football team on the same day as Len Hutton was heading towards a Test record.

An aerial view of the ground in the late thirties looking north east. Little changed over the next 30 years.

The final game at Hove in 1939 proved to be one of its most famous. Just as at the outbreak of the First War, Yorkshire were the visitors and though they could not know it, the crowd under a blazing sun was seeing Hedley Verity for the final time in first-class cricket. The heir to Wilfred Rhodes, he was heading the English bowling averages, and had once taken 10-10 and bowled England to victory over Australia at Lord's with 15-104 in a day. He had also been thrashed all round the ground by Sussex skipper, Hugh Bartlett, the previous year. The game had been set aside as Jim Parks' benefit and Yorkshire were staying on the South Coast having wrapped up the Championship. Their captain, Brian Sellers, told his players "We are public entertainers and until we have instructions to the contrary we will carry on as normal."

The atmosphere was almost surreal. Balmy weather, Hove cricket week and war an inevitability. George Cox recalled the first day, on which he scored 198:

> The tension was awful, there was a feeling that we shouldn't be playing cricket. Yet there was also a festive air. We knew that this was to be our last time of freedom for many years and so we enjoyed ourselves while we could.

66

One man who couldn't was Herbert Sutcliffe; an officer reservist, he was called back to his regiment from Bournemouth before the game began. On 30 August, Sussex won the toss and casting cares aside hit 387, Yorkshire replying with 112-1 by the close. The *Times* cricket correspondent Dudley Carew was at the ground:

> It was crowded but nothing like so crowded had there been no threat in Poland. Groups of people were gathered around cars parked in the ground listening to the wireless as it spoke of the hopeless, last-minute efforts to save a peace that was beyond aid.

An overnight storm flooded the ground and when play was possible Len Hutton gave a masterclass in batting on a wet wicket, leading Yorkshire to 330-3 at the close. The following morning news was received that Germany had invaded Poland and the Yorkshire team were offered a quick getaway. They refused it in deference to the game's beneficiary. Yorkshire's remaining batsmen quickly succumbed and then Verity set to work under a drying sun: he needed just six overs to take seven wickets for nine runs. By mid-afternoon the Yorkshire team was on its green Southdown hire coach, arriving back in Yorkshire again 16 hours later. Despite the best efforts of the visitors, Jim Parks' benefit season brought in a paltry £734 and Hove was plunged into darkness once again.

Maurice Tate

ON MAY 17 1958, almost two years after his death, gates named in the honour of Maurice Tate, Sussex's greatest cricketer, were unveiled at the main entrance of the County Ground.

Nearly 50 years later, at a dinner to celebrate the county's first Championship success, the supporters still voted Tate the club's greatest-ever player. His career spanned 25 years, he took 2784 wickets at 18.16 (of which 774 were taken at Hove), and hit 21,717 runs, many scored with crowd-pleasing, if sometimes rustic, blows. Brighton born, with an easy, down-to-earth, charm, he was Sussex through and through, and universally popular. Little surprise, his name carries such enduring resonance.

County cricket has produced many loyal single-county servants, but rarely, if ever, can one have been touched by genuine greatness on the field as Maurice William Tate. Perhaps across the Pennines the names of George Hirst and Brian Statham might be offered up, but it is Tate who performed the most prodigious feat of sustained bowling in Ashes history.

England lost the 1924-25 series in Australia by 4-1. On the rock hard pitches, Tate hurled himself into no fewer than 316 eight-ball overs; an average of over 84 equivalent six-ball overs per Test. It wasn't just his endurance. In a high-scoring series he took 38 wickets at 23.18. Australia's main strike bowler, Jack Gregory, managed just 22 at 37 apiece. Never in Ashes history has one bowler performed so outstandingly in a side suffering such a crushing series defeat.

For Sussex, Tate carried the bowling for year after year. Having discovered the joys of seam-bowling, from 1922 until 1935 only injury prevented him from taking 100 wickets in a season while getting through around 1300 overs. Only once in this period did his wickets cost more than 20. Without ever taking his batting over-seriously he still scored above 1000 runs in a season eight times. In 1924 he topped both batting and bowling averages for Sussex, scoring 200 runs more than anyone else and taking more than twice as many wickets. He was simply a phenomenon of consistency, tenacity and talent.

But there is something much more to Maurice Tate than spectacular figures. His cricketing story began as a boy when his father, stalwart Sussex pro Fred, determined that his young son would eventually make amends for the crucial catch he himself had dropped in his one and only Test in 1902.

It would be fully 20 years before the father saw the debt he felt he owed begin to be repaid. A world war and an initial dalliance with off-spin delayed

Maurice's early progress. He'd been on the county books for nearly a decade, primarily as a batsman, when towards the end of the 1922 season he discovered, almost by accident, the fast-medium cutter. It was then, at the relatively advanced age of 28, that his career began in earnest.

Tate was a tall, heavily-built man. The nickname 'Chub', and the frequently applied epithet 'ungainly', had rendered both his batting and spin-bowling less than things of beauty. But those strong shoulders, wide hips, powerful legs and huge feet were made for the relentless workload that would be his staple over the next 15 years, while a sunny disposition and an appetite for the game of cricket made light of a burden few, if any, bowlers of his pace could equal.

Within a year he was opening the bowling for England alongside his county captain Arthur Gilligan. Together they removed South Africa for 30 in less than an hour. The following winter he was in Australia as the one threatening weapon in a flimsy armoury. Relentless accuracy of length and direction stifled all batsmen (he did once bowl a wide, a floater caught by the wind, but never a no ball) and his ability to move the ball both in the air and off the seam made defence an activity ever fraught with danger. But his key weapon was the seeming ability to gain pace off the pitch. This is, of course, a scientific impossibility but generations of batsmen would swear that Tate, and Alec Bedser after him, were not subject to the laws of physics.

His 1930 benefit was generously supported across the county, even though the actual game at Hove was a disaster, lasting just two days. 'Chub' managed just three wickets and five runs, bowled for a duck by Joe Hulme, who was better known for exploits at Highbury in the winter game.

Tate was John Arlott's first cricketing hero:

> He had…the finest bowling action of our time. The approach, delivery and follow-through, gathered, concentrated and directed every fraction of their combined energy into the pace of the ball.

Once even contracted to bowl in a London department store, 'Chub' was feted wherever he went, With a grin on his face, a pipe in his mouth and a word for anybody and everybody, he took it all in his stride. Like Statham, 30 years later, he was no analyst; he claimed to just hit the seam and see what happened. And a lot did: right up until 1937 when age finally caught up with him and the club's chairman, Brigadier-General D'Arcy Charles Brownlow, informed him abruptly that his services were no longer required. He was sent on his way, eventually becoming landlord of pubs in Rotherfield and Wadhurst.

Thankfully the club, and the cricket world in general, have shown greater appreciation than the Brigadier-General. The Tate Gates are a fitting bricks and mortar commemoration of Sussex's greatest son. But it is the memory of his sterling deeds and the smile of the doer, still handed down from generation to generation, that form his lasting legacy.

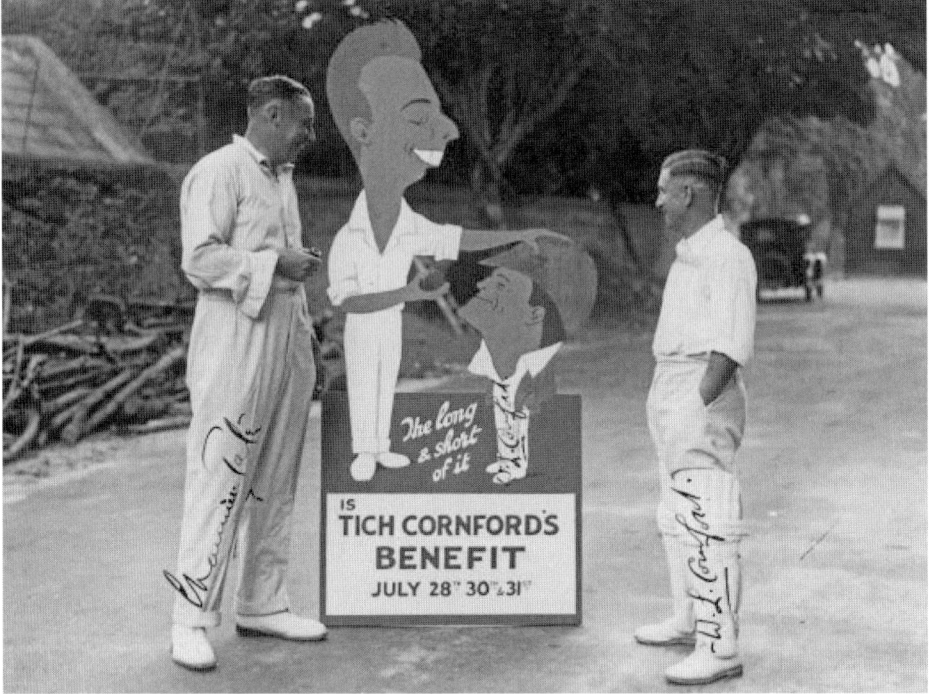

Tate adds his considerable help to Tich Cornford's benefit in 1934.

A Cricketer in Retirement
For George Cox
-Alan Ross-

The marine and the regency, sea frets,
And somewhere the Downs backing a station
Like a Victorian conservatory. I come upon
A scorecard yellow as old flannels and suddenly
I see him, smilingly prowling the covers
In soft shoes, shirt rolled to the forearm,
Light as a yacht swaying at its moorings,
But socially dangerous. An element
Of silk, of ease, with none of the old dutiful
Sense of the regiment, the parade-ground
Posture that gave even the best of them the air of retainers.
Instead, a kind of compassion linking top hats
With turnips, the traditional turning to devilry.
One apart, yet part all the same,
Of that familiar pattern of families,
Parkses and Langridges, Tates and Oakes and Gilligans
Griffiths and Busses, Sussex is rich in,
The soft air phrased by their fickleness.

Never one for half-measures, as generous
With ducks as with half-centuries, he seemed
To calculate extravagance, waywardly spendthrift
With the cold calculators, Yorkshire, the Australians,
Hove and the Saffrons ablaze with his fireworks
Dad wincing in his grave. With others,
Less challenging, he was often vulnerable,
Giving his wicket to those who were glad of it,
Indulgently negligent against parachuting spinners.

Now there are no scorecards, just pulled hamstrings
In village cricket and instead of fancy-free
Strokes in festival arenas the soothing
Of successors. The forearms make gardens,

And the journeys have lengthened, a sunset
Of orchards and vineyards, where reclining in a bath
Of imperial proportions he observes a wife
As delicate with pastry as he was at the wicket.

Cricket Weeks Again

AFTER 1918, CRICKET weeks were once again a huge draw across the county. The Brighton and Hove contingent would duly travel east to Hastings and Eastbourne or west to Worthing and the favour would be returned, weather permitting, at the end of August. Perhaps it was just as well that nothing fancy was planned for 1919 – just a two-day Championship game against Yorkshire, one half of which was washed out.

The following year was a different matter. Committees were formed, marquees and all manner of other attractions erected as cricket tried to put a respectful distance between itself and the recent carnage. Sussex had had a poor year but both Leicestershire and champions Yorkshire were roundly trounced to double their number of Championship victories. The baton had been passed and in this, at least, life had picked up where it had left off in 1914.

Dudley Carew was a regular and enthusiastic visitor and one who, learning at the knee of Cardus, saw much more than just a cricket match:

> Sussex cricket and Sussex players have a way of giving pleasure and memories of the Brighton week at the end of August, with its matches against Yorkshire and whatever touring side happened to be in England, insist on intruding….Not that the matches were frivolous or came as an anti-climax. They did not normally, perhaps, compare in intensity of feeling with the games against Yorkshire – alas, that those too often had the last edge taken of them by the knowledge that the title of Champion County was already on its way North – but the whole week was serious enough so far as the cricket went. Yet it was, the Festivals apart, the last fling of the season, and the summer and the elements conspired to make the thought of football, already edging its way into the top press columns of the evening papers, intolerable. The sun would become a kind of burning-glass, the outfield turn to the colour of corn and, visible at the far end of the avenue that runs down from the gates of the ground to the front, the sea would merge with the sky in a beneficence of blue. The heat would shimmer up from the hard ground and the contrast between the dark mahogany of the players' faces and the white of their flannels would give them the crude contrast of figures in a poster. It did not need arrival at the ground and the sight of Sussex men batting or bowling to release the springs of enjoyment – it was enough to be at Victoria, to be taking a place on the 'Brighton Belle', with its glass-covered tables, its Schweppes menu-cards, its raffish collection of passengers…Whiskies-and-sodas were ordered at

an impossibly early hour while, on the arrival platforms, hordes of office workers were streaming in to spend the June day with files and artificial light. Holiday was always aboard the 'Brighton Belle', holiday with too much make-up and a hat tilted at a tipsy angle, but holiday unabashed and determined to make the most of its time. The cricket might be serious enough on Sussex grounds, and few of those who travelled to revel found their way up to the Hove ground, but there is about the game whenever Sussex play it the faint suggestion of sand-shoes, of a breeze off the sea, and of people inordinately enjoying themselves.

For Laetitia Stapleton even if, as for any cricket enthusiast, it was tinged with late-summer sadness, the week was a highlight of the year :

Brighton and Hove Cricket Week before the Second World War was a grand occasion. Enormous marquees went up, flags flew and a band played. Teas were provided by the lady members of the Club, and their domestic staff washed up behind the scenes. There were six different sections and since there were always two matches in Cricket Week, each section was host to the teams during this time. Competition was rife as to who could produce the best cakes and sandwiches...Often the tea interval would be prolonged as on the day [in 1930] when Amy Johnson, back from one of her triumphal flights [solo to Australia], arrived on the ground to meet Don Bradman.

Collection on the outfield for George Cox snr's benefit match in 1920 cricket week against Yorkshire. George Street and Curly Roberts doing their bit.

Bradman wasn't actually playing. He played just twice at Hove and managed 'only' one century.

Eastbourne, Hastings and, later, Worthing also had their 'weeks', all offering their own charms. But it was at the county's headquarters that the season came to its climax, even if that rarely meant anything significant in terms of Championship positions.

Women's Cricket at Hove

WHILE EATON ROAD had always been more than happy to accommodate 'ladies' in a spectating capacity, there was considerably less enthusiasm for them to be active as players. Not that there wasn't some history, a women's match had taken place in July 1747 at the Artillery Ground, Finsbury. The formation of the Women's Cricket Association in 1926 was to provide a significant fillip to the game, giving it a national standing rather than being reliant on isolated outposts of enthusiasm.

The Sussex Association was formed in 1935 under the presidency of Mrs Peatfield, with the affiliation of three schools and three clubs. Four county fixtures were arranged for the following season. The big event in women's cricket in 1935 at Hove had been the game between South Women and The Rest of England. Despite a century from Amy Bull, the Rest's captain, the South Women won comfortably thanks largely to the efforts of Molly Hide of Reading. A member present reflected on his experience, "It was a well spent afternoon". The cost of staging the game was covered by Sussex CCC, to the tune of £14 2s 4d. The following year the fixture was repeated and the WCA annual report highlighted a growth in interest:

> More and still more converts to women's cricket were made at this match among sceptical members who, not coming to see it last year, heard such tales of the women's prowess that they came to see for themselves and went away rejoicing.

The local press wheeled out its predictable witticisms: 'Eve at the Hove County Ground Wicket', 'Mere Man Holds His Breath', and 'Woman Cricketer's Hit For Six'. The Sussex WCA failed in a bid to make stockings no longer compulsory in all fixtures. The successful argument against such a revolutionary move was

> that there would be many difficulties in the future over grounds, and that the WCA was not yet firmly enough established to enable us to ignore public opinion.

In 1936 a county side emerged after trials at Roedean School. Matches were then played against Hampshire, Surrey and Kent. The highlight of 1937, and a major advance for women's cricket in general, was the visit of the Australian tourists. In 1934/35 an English team had underscored the slow pace of the game's development in Australia, but just two years later roles were reversed. The Test series was drawn 1-1, England's victory at Blackpool being the only loss suffered by the tourists. A second nearly came at Hove, when South Women came within two wickets of victory in the inaugural first-class game played at the ground. Perhaps the most significant feature of the tour was the crowds. For the first time spectators took the women's game seriously. Over the two days of the Hove game, some 5000 paying customers were admitted with receipts of £162 10s. By this time Sussex also had an England player in the form of Peggy Sulman

There was, however, no rush of schoolgirls waiting to don whites and the war years rather crushed the life out of the burgeoning women's game.

World War II

AN EMPTY SILENCE settled across Hove, as it does across all county grounds in September, but in 1939 the atmosphere was very different. The whole town was bustling with preparation for war. With the news emanating from Poland and France, it was clear to all that these preparations needed to be both fast and thorough.

The evacuation of children from London under operation 'Pied Piper' began on 1 September and within months Brighton and Hove had accepted 30,000 refugees. Many of these were moved on the following year with the South Coast under threat from invasion from across the Channel.

The county cricket club made its facilities available to the forces; the outfield and sports centre for drill, a portion of the pavilion for the home guard and their sustenance from the Silver Lady canteen, as The Chalet had become.

During the summer of 1940, the club was also minded to use the ground for cricket as much as possible. Members were asked to pay a reduced rate of 10 shillings for the duration of the war and most obliged. Many games were arranged but most were then cancelled or re-located, a move that gave the citizens of Lewes a chance to see Wally Hammond make a century.

Towards the end of the season, on 14 September 1940, two cricket teams took the field at headquarters for a charity match in aid of the Spitfire Fund. A Sussex XI, captained by Arthur Gilligan, fielded such familiar figures as Maurice Tate, Tich Cornford and John Langridge (on leave from fire-service duties in London). The opposition was Brighton Clubs, led by Spen Cama of Preston Nomads. Gilligan had captained a Royal Air Force side the previous day at Hove against a Sussex side including Tate and the Langridges.

The game progressed sedately under cloudy skies with a hint of rain in the air, but with spectators and players alike happy to be out in the open, thoughts of war were, temporarily at least, consigned to the long grass. The rest of Brighton was going about its Saturday business and it seemed that even London might gain a reprieve from the Blitz as, despite attempts to jam British radar, there was a hiatus in the daily wave of bombers heading across the English Channel.

Although the low cloud cover had scuppered any mass attack, Luftwaffe command had sanctioned a number of small individual tip-and-run raids along the South Coast and the south of London. One of these 'small raids', featuring just one Dornier bomber, was to inflict the highest daily death toll that Brighton would suffer during the entire war.

Tracking the events of the day is something of a historical riddle, with conflicting accounts easily accessible in contemporary newspapers, internet reconstructions, and oral and written memories. Faithful chronicler of Sussex cricket, Laetitia Stapleton, was a spectator at the cricket and recalled the first siren sounding just after midday but not creating enough alarm to halt the game. At 3.30 sirens sounded again, followed closely by explosions across town.

Even this wasn't enough to halt the 'flannelled fools'. It wasn't until a German bomber made two passes across the ground that the players threw themselves to the ground and the spectators rushed to the depths of the pavilion boiler room.

On emerging, it was clear by the crater in the south-east corner that a bomb had been dropped; it was equally clear that the crater had been caused by the weight of the bomb and not its explosion – it was a dud. As was the bomb that had gone through the roof of the County Sports Club (the old Ice Rink). Maurice Tate was hugely aggrieved – "Fancy THEM doing that to US", he muttered to Arthur Gilligan. Even these doughty cricketers had to admit that continuing play with an unexploded 100 pound bomb at cow corner was probably unwise, and finally came the 'abandonment of the game owing to the insistence of the authorities'.

Across Brighton, in Kemptown, there was no comedy of any sort. A stick of bombs had wreaked havoc around Edward Street and Upper Rock Gardens, destroying houses, businesses and lives.

Some accounts of the raid have it that a lone bomber had become detached from its squadron and, pursued by a Spitfire, was dumping its load in order to enhance manoeuvrability. This hardly tallies with the fact that no large raids were mounted that day. Whatever the whys and wherefores, the fact remains that 55 people were killed and many hundreds injured. Cricket at Eaton Road recommenced two days later.

The following year was considerably more productive. Sussex hosted the RAF three times and Hove became a place to see some of the leading cricketers of the day. Ken Cranston of Lancashire so impressed the locals that Sir Home Gordon, now acting secretary (unpaid), set out to find him a dental practice in Brighton so that he'd be able to play as an amateur in peace time. Cranston would have been a fine addition; he later captained Lancashire and played for England. Another cricketer who expressed an interest might have been the greatest catch of all. Keith Miller was stationed at the Metropole Hotel and became a familiar figure at South Coast cricket grounds. Performances such as 134 in two hours for United Services against Sussex and his cricketing *joie de vivre* made him a perfect asset for any side. Unfortunately, Australia had greater hold on his soul. Slightly less spectacular was a Trevor Bailey century for the Royal Navy, and there were also appearances from Alec Bedser, Denis Compton and Charlie Barnett.

By 1942 some form of routine had been achieved. Sussex managed five games, while an inter-services league held matches on Wednesdays and Saturdays. This was quite a feat of organisation as Lance Knowles explained:

> All the lads are serving in some capacity or another, we have not one left – Tom Burchell and Beach look after the ground and old Billy [Newham] aged 80 and myself look after the office. There is quite a lot to do as the Home Guard use a portion of the Pavilion and some of the ground for training.

Sadly, neither Knowles nor Newham were to see the return of peace. After overseeing no less than 60 games at Hove during the summer of 1943 Knowles died in September and was followed next summer by Newham, who had served the club for 57 years.

Testing the mini aircraft 'Hoppity' on the outfield during WWII

The following year was quieter inside the ground but certainly not outside. With the allied assault on France approaching, the entire South Coast was a hive of activity either preparing for D Day or seeming to be preparing for D Day in an elaborate plan of deception. With restrictions on movement and a ban on watering there was no cricket until September.

In 1945, with the war now all but won, the club began to look to the future. WN Riley, president of the Sussex Cricket Association wrote:

> This association will provide a wide net of fine mesh through which no young

cricketer will be allowed to escape. We want real cricket democracy in the County so that every young Cricketer will know that if he has the requisite ability he will have the opportunity of representing his County.

Only 11 matches took place, none of them first class, but Billy Griffith was appointed secretary/captain and the club could proudly report that 'a deficit left in 1939 was turned into a profit by the end of 1945'.

-Four-

1946-1971

The message running in the local papers of Brighton, Hove and surrounding areas was 'Increased Membership is Essential'. With a new Labour government under Clement Attlee having swept aside the 'war-time leader' Winston Churchill, and with the County Championship back on the agenda, there was some optimism in the air in the spring of 1946.

But any optimism also had to be tempered. Cities such as Southampton and Coventry had suffered catastrophic bomb damage. Rationing of clothes, food and petrol was not likely to be eased anytime soon. Grieving families were having to come to terms with the loss of fathers, sons, husbands and breadwinners. Most adults were still haunted by the aftermath of another world war which had ended just 27 years earlier.

Despite all this, the mood was not that of 1919. There was a genuine belief that under a socialist government, recovery would be both quicker and fairer. The creation of the welfare state was a true reward for the privations of the last six years; a defining gift delivered by men such as Bevan, Morrison and Bevin.

Emerging from the Wreckage

In deepest Hove, members remembered well how Sussex had emerged from World War I and how long it had taken for the county side to re-establish itself. All were fully aware that history might well repeat itself; hence the calls for young players of substance to step forward.

Their worst fears proved well founded. Sussex's reward for their endeavours in 1946 was a wooden spoon, the worst season since 1896. Only Jim Parks of the pre-1939 vintage had retired, but the others were all older and no young Turks had emerged to add much-needed vigour. Poor Billy Griffith found out, as Billy Newham had in 1889, that the jobs of captain and secretary did not mix and he rapidly jettisoned the former in favour of Hugh Bartlett.

Arthur Gilligan had spoken of the county ground as 'rather primitive' in 1919 and there was certainly room for improvement in 1946, especially as crowds were expected to flood to cricket in a post-war return to normality.

The ground had been well-used, even over-used, during the war but, with altogether more important matters in play, little attention had been paid to its upkeep. 'Tired' would be the adjective now used. The groundstaff had done wonders under the circumstances but all corners now required sprucing up, and in some cases total overhaul, a verdict that could also apply to most of the town. Cricket could hardly be a high priority for most people, money to devote to such pastimes was tight. Patching things up was the best that could be done at Eaton Road and even the players put their shoulders to the wheel. Planned ground expansion would have to wait. Meanwhile with amenities in short supply in the town, the ground was put to any suitable use: a county rugby match was held at the southern end of the ground against Gloucestershire. But the first priority was to establish a team that could win some cricket matches.

The season of 1947 was a little better, before 1948 saw Sussex sink again. Six batsmen made their 1000 runs; all of them had been playing before 1939. The leading three bowlers managed just 203 wickets between them (Tate's haul in a good year) and all were of the pre-war generation. Crowds and membership remained steady despite the lack of success on the field but there was little feeling of the bonanza and bonhomie exuded by Compton and Edrich in 1947 and Bradman's Invincibles in 1948. When 'The Don' did come calling, however, the Hove crowds turned out in their thousands, as can be seen on the BFI website.

However, good-natured hard work by players, officials and volunteers was simply not cutting the mustard. A cash injection was sorely needed in all areas of the club and when a buyer arrived with an offer for one of its oldest assets, the financial committee was unanimous in its decision.

The looming presence of the old Ice Rink had been ever present since a roof was added in Edwardian times. In the intervening years it had been put to many uses. In 1946 the Hove manufacturer CVA Jigs, Moulds and Tools were looking for suitable premises and alighted on the site. A deal was done, the Rink was transformed into CVA's machine assembly plant, and the club earned a handsome profit which transformed its finances. By 1948 the cheque had cleared and for once there was money in the bank. The first move was to sign Patsy Hendren as replacement for coach Bertie Chaplin.

The 1949 edition of *Know Your Cricket County* outlined the task facing the genial and popular new recruit:

> Hendren's is a case of team-building almost from scratch. Several established players have retired since the war; others are now reaching the veteran stage and must soon follow. But no more comprehensive efforts could possibly be made to obtain suitable replacements than those being put into operation by the Sussex authorities. "Patsy" frankly admits that the going will be hard, but is confident

that he can, in time, achieve the desired ends. Good luck to him!

Though, given their history, it might have been wise for the county to invest in a bowling coach, Hendren was an eye-catching addition to the staff. In that same publication are youthful pictures of the 'green shoots' of a Sussex revival – Hubert Doggart, Don Smith, Alan Oakman, Ted James, David Sheppard and Rupert Webb. Not yet worthy of a mention, but not far behind, were Jim Parks jnr and Kenny Suttle. Grounds for optimism for sure, but it can't have passed Hendren by that all bar one were batsmen.

The Cricketer Spring Annual of 1948 reported on how some of the Ice Rink windfall was being spent. The tennis courts that had been a feature of the northern end of the ground for half a century were closed, to be replaced by practice pitches on which the new coach could hone his protégées.

The old professionals' pavilion, which had been largely redundant since the move to the main pavilion in 1927, was now converted into two offices, both equipped with a snug coal fire. The wooden verandah and staircase to the front were found to be defective and removed while the ground-level storage area was concreted and made watertight.

Further improvements followed to the pavilion itself. The 1928 extension was further extended, the players' changing-room enlarged and given proper viewing facilities and a glass-sided VIP area constructed above the committee room (it turned out to be uninhabitable on sunny days).

The decision was taken to run all catering, including the hotel, directly through the club rather than leasing it out – a move that resulted in considerable losses. An internal telephone system was installed connecting gatemen, scoreboard and press box with the pavilion.

From the Duke of Norfolk's estate at Arundel, turf was brought to create a tiered banking along the northern end of the ground. As *The Cricketer's* correspondent stated: 'It is well that the public should know a little of the care and thought that is put into the running of a modern county cricket club.'

A semblance of financial stability and ground improvements did not, however, lead to improvement on the pitch. The highlight of the late forties was John Langridge's Indian summer of 2850 runs – which would have been over 3000 but for a bad back – including 12 centuries and the accolade of being named one of *Wisden's* five cricketers at the age of 39. Harry Parks retired after 22 years' service, his passage eased by a benefit of nearly £2000.

Prospects behind the scenes may have been positive, but most members and spectators trusted the evidence of their own eyes and 1950 was one of the most difficult in the club's history on the field.

Down, Up, Down and Rebuild

Like most county sides, Sussex had had their fair share of boardroom strife, but unlike most others, there had been a general absence of such things throughout the first half of the twentieth century. Who knows what might have happened between the wars without the steady hand of Lance Knowles at the helm?

However, the second half of the century was a mere 76 days old when a very local display of bloodletting and washing of dirty laundry broke out at the annual general meeting.

The 'Great Walk Out' of 1950 has been well documented elsewhere but its seed and bloom are worth recalling. It is safe to say that if Sussex hadn't been floundering at, or near, the foot of the table for four seasons the vote of no-confidence and abrupt departure of the Duke of Norfolk from the AGM in the banqueting hall of the Royal Pavilion, would never have happened. Bartlett had resigned as captain and Griffith decided his future lay in journalism rather than as secretary at Hove. The committee saw fit to appoint two new captains and behind it all members and supporters felt that unpopular and damaging decisions were being made without due process or clarity.

The national press descended on Hove. The fact that a duke was involved was too good to miss. The skirmish lasted just a month and on 17 April at Hove Town Hall the Duke of Norfolk resumed his presidency. George Grimston was appointed secretary, a position he would hold for 14 years. Jim Langridge became Sussex's first ever professional captain in more than a stand-in capacity. Just maybe the briars of socialism had pricked the old order into accepting greater egalitarianism.

The following year was George Cox's benefit, an event that was to have positive repercussions for both player and club. Many felt that asking John Langridge and Harry Parks to share a benefit season in 1948 hadn't shown the club in its best light, so Cox's benefit was delegated a committee from the boardroom to assist him. So successful was this group that it was decided to make the Sussex County Welfare Association a permanent organisation dedicated to fundraising and supporting beneficiaries. Their efforts with football pools, raffles, social evenings and assorted other functions was to bolster the coffers enormously over the coming decades.

These initiatives did little to improve on-field form over the next few seasons, though the likes of 'Young Jim' Parks, David Sheppard and Robin Marlar brought a welcome whiff of youth. Within a short space of time these new men formed the backbone of the side. Cornford had gone and the Langridges and Cox were well into the evening of their careers. In the case of Jim Langridge, the end was hastened when he was laid out by a lifter from Cuan McCarthy of Cambridge University (and later South Africa). He would fill the vacant coaching position in 1953, which promised to be an exciting year, albeit beset yet again by financial concerns.

Around £20,000 was required annually to keep the books balanced and subscriptions were bringing in around £15,000. Another membership drive was ordered with a restructuring of prices to follow. Life membership was fixed at £50 and full membership, at an annual £4, included the perk of facing the professional bowlers in the practice nets.

Business House Membership was introduced to encourage local businesses to get involved in the club, and 54 companies received the three-guinea ticket; two transferables for all Sussex grounds with entry to the members' enclosure except at Hove. The scheme ran until 1972.

The real problem was that cricket was not attracting the masses. After the Compton and Edrich summer of 1947 and the Invincibles of 1948, crowds declined in the face of increasing competition from other forms of entertainment – a state of affairs that was echoed across all counties and that would never improve. Considerable plans for Sussex headquarters were put on hold until fortunes on the field and through the turnstiles showed an upturn. Unexpectedly they soon did.

In 1953, under the bold and imaginative captaincy of David Sheppard, Sussex found only Surrey impossible to overhaul. The mixture of wily veterans combined with young grammar-school boys Parks, Suttle and Oakman were superbly led by Sheppard both in manner and method. A crowd of 15,000 on August Bank holiday (overnight not-out batsmen Compton and Edrich being a significant attraction) was an indication of how quickly Sheppard had invigorated the spectators as well as the side.

It all came down in late August to the match at Hove where Surrey needed only to avoid defeat. In a damp squib of a game, they did so comfortably. Nonetheless, exhilarated by the season's bold showing, crowds formed in front of the pavilion to express their appreciation. Best of all, it was the new crop of young players who had blossomed under a young captain whose own form with the bat was inspirational. Sussex were not only successful but played with an élan that was the envy of others. EW Swanton singled them out as a 'shining exception' to the rather moribund approach adopted by many sides at the time.

Marlar, Parks, Oakman and Suttle continued to progress and were now joined by Ian Thomson, who would become the first post-war Sussex bowler to take 100 wickets in a season. This resurgence played out in front of no fewer than 1800 new members. The 1930s successes has brought little response from the public, but apparently the 1950s vintage were more interested in results.

Despite this success there was a growing feeling that Sussex were top-heavy with committees. Every aspect of the club had its own organising group and the main committee itself numbered no less than 36, all of whom were unpaid. With a windfall payment of £3000 from the Australian tour of 1953 and Rab Butler's welcome rescinding of the Entertainment Tax, the coffers were refreshed and a series of ground improvements undertaken.

Ladies lavatories came under scrutiny. An overhaul of the conveniences in the south-east corner was undertaken in 1954 and a new one was sandwiched between The Chalet and the boundary wall in the same year. With the club now in full control of the hotel, two rounds of improvements followed. Remodelling of the bar, dining room and amateur players' toilets in the pavilion completed the minor alterations.

It lasted 149 years. The Sussex Cricketer at the Tate Gates.

Far more significant was work on the long-serving Cowshed at the south end. The essentially flimsy nature of the entire structure now offered some advantage as it was deemed possible to lift the entire thing backwards and onto concrete supports, thus creating a refreshment hall underneath. This in turn freed up space for 'garden seats' on the concrete steps in front of the stand while deck chairs encroached on to the grass round the boundary. The cherry on the cake was provision of a small 'commentator's box'.

An even more ambitious plan was the 1955 building of a three-bedroom groundsman's cottage next to the hotel, until recently number 1, Eaton Road. Within the ground, the gap between the new secretary's office and the scorebox on the western side was filled by a two-storey building, housing office space. Two years later the box itself was substantially redeveloped at a cost of £2750 to encompass a press and scorers' box incorporating teleprinting, printer's room, umpires' room and press terrace.

The end of the 1955 season saw another break with the past with the retirement of John Langridge. He had made his debut in 1928 and played 574 first-class games for the county (161 at headquarters yielding 10,081 runs and 228 catches, both club records). At the age of 45 in his last game, against Somerset, he took five catches to establish a Championship record of 66 in a season.

Gloom as to the fate of the game in general was encapsulated in a 1956 report by Political and Economic Planning (PEP). *The Cricket Industry* declared ominously that 'in crudely economic terms, county cricket is fighting a losing battle against shortage of capital, income and the highly-skilled labour the game requires.' Numbers of paying spectators had plumetted since the golden, first post-war summers and there seemed no way to arrest this decline.

In 1957 it was decided to commemorate Sussex's greatest cricketer. Maurice Tate had died in May 1956, and gates in his memory were opened in May the following year. The memorial panels were unveiled by Arthur Gilligan and Hove resident Jack Hobbs with the ceremony overseen by the Duke of Norfolk and attended by Kathleen Tate and her three children This

The Tate Gates, opened in 1957.

time Sussex didn't stint – a sum of £2500 was set aside and the wrought iron made by Ernest Nailand of Hurstpierpoint.

The outgoings didn't stop there – another £2200 was invested on redeveloping the tea bar and building boys' changing-rooms to the north of the pavilion. It had been a real spending spree.

Events on the field during the mid-fifties barely justified such extravagance.

Sheppard's captaincy tenure lasted just one glorious year before he followed his vocation by commencing study for the priesthood, and in 1954 he asked to return to the ranks. He was replaced by Hubert Doggart who, in turn, was soon replaced by Robin Marlar, then librarian to the Duke of Norfolk at Arundel, thus guaranteeing his amateur status.

Although the side slipped to ninth in 1956, there was a feeling that better could have been expected. The team was largely unencumbered by England call-ups (Smith three, Sheppard two, Oakman one). Thomson was increasingly carrying the attack alone while at the Oval Surrey could draw on Bedser, Loader, Laker and Lock. At least, with Parks to the fore, Sussex were attractive to watch. No mean feat in an era where negative cricket was the norm. Most counties seemed hell-bent on strangling the game; Glamorgan taking 823 balls to score 143 first-innings runs but one example. An antidote to such stultifying fare came in 1957 when Don Smith launched a vicious attack on the Gloucestershire attack at Hove, his blaze of sixes landed one spectator in hospital with a broken jaw and saw another invading the field armed with an umbrella begging for mercy.

Sussex were invariably entertaining, but became increasingly incapable of winning. Each season seemed so full of hope and each season ended in disappointment. With the exception of 'Sheppard's Year' in 1953, the decade which had promised much, delivered little. Perhaps it was down to attitude. In 1948 an 'ex international' (more than likely Arthur Gilligan) wrote:

> Sussex have never won the County Championship and somehow I don't think they ever will. Points and percentages have never formed part of their make-up. They play to win, of course, but to them the game has always seemed more important than the result.

By the end of the 1950s, mid-table had become lower-table. New names and new hopes such as Les Lenham and Don Bates appeared, Parks enchanted, Suttle and Oakman scored their thousands and Thomson ploughed indefatigably on, but there was no magic. Without the efforts of Poona White in encouraging new membership, Sussex were reported as facing the prospect 'of having to close down through lack of public support'.

Members and spectators had seen enough false dawns throughout the post-war years to have become weary of the repetitive failure to deliver on promise. No better example was the final game of the 1958 season. Champions elect Surrey were facing a trouncing at Hove, the home side needing just 54 to win with all wickets standing. They lost by 17 runs. The dream of a first Championship seemed further away than ever.

Robin Marlar, writing in 1959, criticised the expansion of the Championship, calling for it to be reduced in size and for the introduction of a 'knock-out cup competition'. Presumably he had one-day cricket in mind. Appropriately enough, the man that Marlar had lured to Hove, a certain ER Dexter, was awarded his county cap.

Ted Dexter had silenced the many naysayers in 1959 by scoring 2000 runs in domestic cricket before travelling to the West Indies and outbatting all bar Garry Sobers. He was handed the captaincy of Sussex on his return.

Dexter and Gillette

From the moment the new captain eased his pale blue Jaguar SS100 (the replacement for his red Borgward Isabella), into his reserved parking place at Eaton Road, Sussex cricket entered a new era. With Lonnie Donegan's *My Old Man's a Dustman* topping the charts, Dexter brought the swinging sixties to that 'pleasingly dozy scene'. Outgoing captain Marlar described the tone at the time:

> The atmosphere of Sussex cricket in those days wasn't attuned to winning. The club was into entertainment and nurturing cricketers' careers, but it seemed bizarre to us to start a championship season feeling we had to win it. At that time, we were in the majority, and it was this attitude, which would now seem complacent and unambitious, that Ted was landed with.

It is easy to apply a retrospective view where, in the words of Alan Lee,

> …the impression that it was always Lord's in the June sunshine and that Lord Edward was forever, by royal decree, batting at number three and hitting Wes Hall on the up through extra cover.

If Dexter ever displayed this magisterial and devil-may-care attitude in county cricket, then it was in the opening weeks of the 1960 season. Arriving at a club 'prone to somnolence, pretty much asleep on its feet', his first two games in charge, at Edgbaston and Taunton, were a clear indication that a new broom had arrived – sweeping, driving and cutting. Dexter also applied his mind to the problems faced by captains at 'this idiosyncratic ground', where the vagaries of moisture, sea breeze and atmosphere made decisions after the toss fraught with danger.

The season's opener at Hove was against reigning champions Yorkshire.

The crowds rolled in but Yorkshire overhauled Sussex's first-innings total without losing a wicket. In poor weather, declarations were made to force a result and Sussex snuck home by 32 runs. Three more victories followed, with runs flowing off Dexter's bat, catches being held as never before and players such as Bates and Suttle responding to the new regime. Membership rose by 1200. It wasn't just the results, it was the manner in which they were achieved.

The effort could not be sustained, largely because Dexter was required five times by England. But still Sussex were 'in many ways, the team of the year'. When Marlar came to write of the season in *Wisden* he couldn't resist comparisons with Keith Miller and the way Dexter 'captured the imagination of those inside, outside and far from the boundary ropes of our big cricket grounds'.

Even Dexter's allure, however, wasn't enough to stem an overall decline in attendances. The same questions were being asked in cricket grounds and committee rooms up and down the country. How to halt the tide of people flowing away from attending matches in favour of television and days out in the car? How to balance the books when crowds had halved in just over a decade? How to increase the appeal of cricket to a new generation desiring a more immediate fix, be it a three-minute pop record, deep-fried chicken or clothes that your parents would never, ever wear?

Not that all the problems were external. The amateur/professional

Business at the Tate gates in the 1960s. Scorecards for sale, cushions for hire.

delineation was seeming increasingly archaic, even if it remained significant in other sports such as tennis, rugby and athletics. Chucking was a blight on the game as was dreary cricket with no thought of entertainment, until Richie Benaud and Frank Worrell briefly galvanised Test matches.

There was also the problem of South Africa and how far politics, or more precisely morality, should be allowed into the game. It was all very well to speak about 'winds of change', but it was action that was required and, bar the likes of Sheppard and Arlott, people of action were distinctly lacking. Dexter's debut season as captain had been a roaring success, as had Sheppard's, but Dexter was staying put for that tricky second season.

Neither of the next two years went as planned. Sussex slipped back to mid-table despite the best efforts of Suttle and Thomson who were now Sussex stalwarts in the best Bowley-Vine-Langridge tradition. Sheppard made a brief return, auditioning for an England place. Future captain John Barclay, a schoolboy down with his parents from Horsham was enraptured:

> It was then the traditional bank holiday match against Middlesex, and we sat on the splintery wooden benches in the south-west corner of the ground. Hove was full, or so it seemed, and this impressionable little seven-year-old [he was actually eight] watched Sheppard make a hundred amidst sunshine and picnic and much happiness. I was captivated by the magical strokeplay, by the majesty and elegance of both class and style. I was hooked and from then on all I wanted to do was play cricket and try to imitate those golden moments of my childhood.

Rather beautifully, Barclay has forgotten that he was there on the third day and a draw was inevitable from the first ball. It clearly didn't matter a jot.

Is this how it should be? Why are we at the ground watching cricket? We all have our own reasons. Take a straw poll: how many would rather see a glorious double-century from Brian Lara coupled with a crushing defeat for Sussex as opposed to a duck from him and a win for us? In footballing terms, would any home supporters at Old Trafford relish a mesmeric display from their 'noisy neighbours' and a 4-0 defeat? Having personally never been a 'supporter' of any team, it's hard to tell. But we all have our own reasons to be there, whether as members of the Shark Army or just to idle in the sun drinking warm beer from Sid's Shack and hoping to see the best players on the field (from whichever team) showing just why they are the best. It's sport without tribalism; it suits some and not others and Eaton Road has offered a sumptuous choice for 150 years.

County Cricket

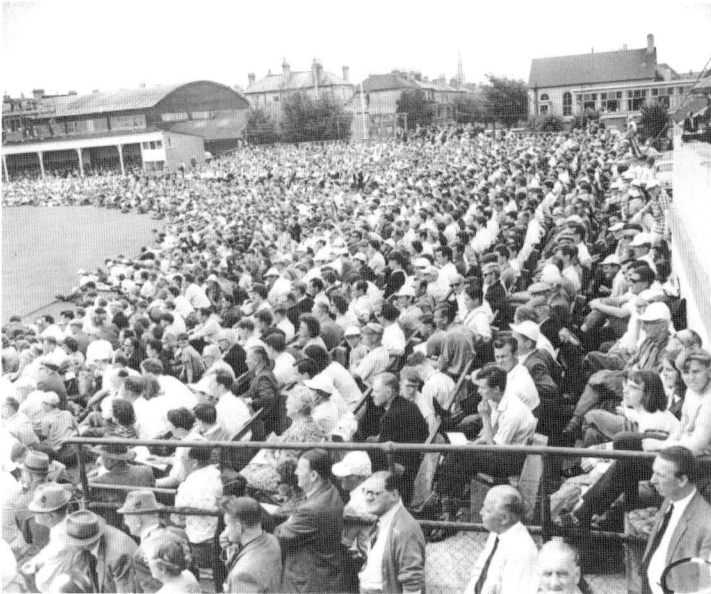

Gillette Cup and TV

The recruitment programme was now beginning to pay some dividends as the Buss brothers and John Snow inched their way towards the first team. Still, Dexter bemoaned the lack of a 'reserve force of any quality' emerging from 'groundstaff training and club activity outside the ground'. With good reason. Sussex, especially without Parks and Dexter on Test duty, were no world beaters.

The following year, 1963, was different. Gillette pulled off one of the great sponsorship coups of the era for just £6,500; their 'KO Cup' attracting crowds and interest far beyond their wildest dreams.

Many aspects of the one-day format had not been properly thought through and Dexter turned this to his advantage. While Colin Cowdrey at Kent would keep two slips and a gully throughout the 65 overs, Dexter wasn't afraid to ring the boundary with fielders. And, while others were happy to be 40 without loss after 20 overs, he wasn't afraid to attack from the start. He also had a good and enthusiastic fielding team, disciplined bowlers and two natural one-day batsmen in himself and Jim Parks.

Sussex won the first two trophies of the nascent one-day era, collecting just over £4000 for their efforts. Not bad, and small beer compared with the cash injection brought by the crowds who had shown an enthusiastic appetite for the new competition. The only home match in 1963, against Yorkshire, was a complete sell-out and the 1964 semi-final saw 3000 waiting outside the ground at 8.30 with 5000 failing to find a way in, as shown on the front cover. One who did was 10-year-old John Barclay, 'squeezed…next to the old Cowshed at the sea end'.

Despite this fresh infusion, attendances for Championship games continued to fall as running costs rose. The club was back in the financial doldrums. One bright spot on balmy summer Sundays was the sight of the International Cavaliers. Hanif Mohammad, Garry Sobers, Lance Gibbs and Bobby Simpson were amongst the cricketing greats who graced Eaton Road, bringing with them holiday crowds, ice-cream shillings and sense of light-hearted, one-day fun.

The sights at Hove during this period are for all to see on the BFI website. Marvellous colour footage of the West Indies, Australian and South African tourists playing at Hove in 1963, 1964 and 1965. These short films show better than any still image how the ground looked and what kind of crowds these exotic cricketers could attract. The highlight is certainly the best footage of Wes Hall's bowling ever taken.

Struggling to Survive

For the rest of the sixties, it all went downhill. Other counties wised-up to one-day tactics. Sussex's Championship positions went from moderate to catastrophic and various players became embroiled in conflicts with the club. Even the ground fell into disrepair. The pitch was, according to Arthur Gilligan, 'in a disgraceful state', and new groundsman Len Creese was tasked with digging it up and relaying it with turf from the outfield. As a result, four games finished in two days, including the potentially remunerative one against the 1966 West Indies tourists, who were beaten by nine wickets.

It's a lockout! Kenny Suttle and Ted Dexter at the wicket against Surrey in the 1964 Gillette Cup semi-final.

Creese's remedial work was recognised the following year when pitch inspectors gave Hove a clean bill of health. His work extended well beyond the playing surface. He was proud of the whole ground. Flowers, newly-planted trees and fluttering flags adorned the arena as if in protest at the urbanisation that was encroaching. Brighton and Hove were now increasingly commuting satellites of London. It was no longer unthinkable to make the return journey five times a week. The effect on the growth of the town, housing and cultural life were to prove immense. One development that was to have a negative impact at Eaton Road was the appearance of Sussex University in 1962. The pressure to find undergraduate accommodation saw the demise of hundreds of boarding houses that had attracted holidaymakers to Brighton, many of whom had enjoyed days at the cricket as part of their sojourn on the South Coast.

Sussex had only previously had one truly match-winning bowler in their history and Tate was not a fast bowler. Now, once Mike Procter and his South African team-mates were banned, they had the fastest Test bowler in the world. John Snow had taken 11-47 in the shortened West Indies' game yet somehow Sussex managed to estrange their prize asset. Snow was not a man to be dictated to; a proud bowler, he believed that he should bowl as he saw fit even if that meant half-pace cutters off a short run when the situation demanded it. Down at Hove, this was deemed a lack of effort, not a charge levelled at Fred Trueman or Brian Statham when they did the same. Snow had every intention of extending his career beyond the age of 30 and saving his very fastest for the national side – more than likely he was aware of what various captains had done to the ever-willing Wes Hall.

While arguments between officials and Snow flared there was the issue of the retirements of Suttle and later Parks, the county's two greatest post-war servants. Suttle had played an astonishing 423 consecutive games for Sussex (beating Joe Vine's 421, though Vine did play two Tests) but his retirement was handled with all the lack of skill of Maurice Tate's 30 years earlier.

Parks had a short spell as captain after the equally brief but elegantly breezy reign of Nawab of Pataudi. Parks' aim had been to bring vim and brio to the side. Writing at the beginning of the 1967 season, he vowed to make cricket a sport and not a 'drudge' and to play the kind of positive cricket which had always been associated with the club. He certainly succeeded in bringing about a more exciting brand of cricket, but not a more successful one. By 1968 the lack of materials at his disposal and the weight of captaincy, leading the batting and keeping wicket, was proving too much. He resigned in favour of Mike Griffith and Sussex finished bottom of the table.

Griffith was categorical that 'it is "behind the back" rumblings that have brought this club down and these must be properly aired in future'. Lack of money was an even bigger threat. The losses for the year were £8000. Despite a healthy membership of nearly 7000, debts had risen to £21,000. Any balancing of the books was only achieved thanks to a steady catering income. To add to the misery, when new regulations for overseas players were introduced in 1968, Sussex missed out on signing Barry Richards.

Tony Buss and John Snow laying waste to Surrey in August 1967. Sussex still failed to win!

Not that Sussex lacked ambition when it came to the ground. In 1969 a grand plan was unveiled which involved demolishing The Chalet, building a new hotel and flats in the south-east corner and raising a 'restaurant-bridge' above the Tate Gates. On a more modest level, *Aerosigns* were contracted to oversee in-ground advertising.

As ever, players had come and gone with others waiting in the wings. Some, such as Ian Thomson, who completed his 100 wickets in a season 11 years in a row, had reached their full potential. Hove was heaven for him as John Barclay saw it:

Sussex cricket has throughout its history been dominated by the weather. Sea frets, high tides and moisture have contributed to the well-grassed pitches at ... Hove, on which Maurice Tate and later Ian Thomson, with swing and seam, proved so deadly.

Alan Oakman's 20,000 runs, 700 wickets and 594 catches made him a significant servant through difficult times. Parks, Suttle, Lenham and Bates, who retired in 1971, had sustained Sussex over many years and been a major part of the Gillette Cup-winning side. Others, such as Richard Langridge, Graham Cooper, Euros Lewis and Ron Bell, had, for one reason or another, flattered to deceive.

As the 100th anniversary of cricket at Eaton Road approached, the county was once again in a state of flux. The old-stagers had been replaced by a more international flavour in the form of Geoff Greenidge, Uday Joshi and Tony Greig. Roger Prideaux (whose wife Ruth was hugely influential in Sussex women's cricket) arrived with bundles of experience from Northants while Peter Graves, John Spencer and schoolboy John Barclay provided some home-bred input.

The Buss brothers and John Snow were now the senior players, but all eyes were on Greig. He had served a long apprenticeship having been 'noticed' by various Sussex players while coaching at Queen's College in South Africa. By 1970 his blond hair, height and all-action approach had made him a must-watch commodity and captain in waiting.

With so many changes in personnel it's not surprising that these were not years of plenty for the county. Despite early success in the one-day game, the side had not taken well to the new John Player League, launched in a 1969; a year for the club only marginally better than the nadir of 1968.

Off the field, things were thrown into further disarray by financial shortfalls and allegations of mismanagement. The club was struggling to come to terms with the new age of sponsorship and commercialisation. As the swinging sixties transitioned into the austere seventies, a booklet was published to celebrate 100 years at Eaton Road. Its pages were richer in reflection on the past than hopes for the future.

Hubert Doggart described an atmosphere that could have been Edwardian:

> Tents and deck chairs have a festival flavour, as if demanding that matches should, by rights, be played at holiday time, and in a holiday spirit. The spectators, themselves on holiday, seem a part of, rather than apart from, the drama enacted before them...Perhaps it is the ground's informal friendliness that one savours most.

Jack Arlidge, the *Evening Argus* chief sportswriter for over 20 years, had spent more time than most on the ground:

> You can never be certain who you will meet at the County Ground. Turn a corner at the top of the pavilion, or in the 'ladies' bar, or stroll along by the trees at

the top of the ground, or go into the 'Long stop' for a reviver, and you meet someone famous in the world of sport, theatre, films or art. In the days shortly before the last war, Sir Aubrey Smith of round-the-corner fame, dropped in for lunch; Lord Olivier brought his son in for Easter nets last year; Norman Wisdom accompanied his son for coaching.

Alan Ross, a committee member from 1985 to 1989, was, as ever, reflective and poetic:

First and foremost, it is a seaside ground, a mixture of the regency and the raffish, from which, almost alone in England (or anywhere else for that matter) you can actually see the sea. Not much of it, it's true, but you are always conscious of it, in a quality of light, in the feeling of the air. The sea has shaped Sussex cricket and Sussex cricketers, it has given both an alternating exhilaration and fallibility.

At Hove, sun and sea-mists, heat and cold, follow one another with bewildering rapidity, and Sussex fortunes on the field bear witness to this elemental instability. The Downs, too, are another physical factor, separating Hove from the flatness of southern England, a protective arm flung across the whole county.

As a *ground*, quite apart from its associations, Hove cannot exactly be called beautiful. It has always been suburban, with a touch of the exotic: an odour of Empire, of curry powder and whisky, retired colonels and actresses, the ailing old, the robust young. The ground slopes to the sea, so that the villas lining it have a precarious air, their verandahs tilted like pitching steamers.

In any case, the architectural frame of Hove was always a mess, lovable in its variety, but of little consistency and no merit. But the physical aspect of the ground is only part of its real character, and the lifting of the spirits, the *joie de vivre* that Hove seems to uniquely produce – at least for those in love with Sussex cricket – comes from the quality of the cricketers. As surely as vintage wines are the unmistakeable embodiments of local soil, climate, skills, care, cunning and luck, so is Sussex cricket, in the atmosphere of Hove, born of unique circumstances.

Despite the over-riding tone of nostalgia, the 'architectural frame' of which Ross wrote changed dramatically for the first time since 1927 in the lead up to the anniversary.

And John Arlott added his thoughts, when reporting on the first day of the Australians visit in June 1968 when Paul Sheahan scored a century and John

Snow took four wickets:

> The sun shone and, within the ring of Edwardian buildings their influence unaffected by the flats outside which are too large to belong in this private world, children stretched out, half-watching and waiting to start their own games on overlapping improvised pitches during the interval; their elders leant back in their deck chairs and sometimes dozed; here and there a large figure lay, sleeping off the morning's beer and acquiring unwanted sunburn; and the cricketers gave it all diverting, and often absorbing, point and unity.

Down at the south end of the ground, the Cowshed and the Ice Rink/roller rink/sports club/drill hall/machine-tool factory had bitten the dust and the Ashdown flats and the Gilligan Stand risen from their ashes. The cash injection from this development enabled the club to reduce its overdraft. Still the finances would see-saw.

1969, the Cowshed still stands but the roof has been taken off the Ice Rink/factory in preparation for demolition.

In 1970 the club took out insurance on the turf as the 'stop the tour' movement gathered momentum and when the South African visit was duly halted a government grant of £2339 helped fill the coffers. In 1971 the combined profit of £13,000 from the hotel and Chalet failed to prevent a loss of nearly £12,000. Efforts to attract the local population into the ground continued – the Easter Monday Donkey Derby became an annual fixture and events such as the visit of Ed 'Stewpot' Stewart's Showbiz XI attracted crowds larger than seen at most county matches.

By 1972, bar two world wars, Eaton Road, Hove had been hosting county cricket for 100 years. It had been through crises aplenty and as the anniversary approached another was in full swing. The team wasn't good enough, the money wasn't plentiful enough and the club was struggling to adapt to times that were a changing.

Eaton Road under attack from anti-apartheid activists.

Big Hits at Hove
-Gerald Brodribb-

THE PRESENT COUNTY Cricket Ground at Hove was first used for big cricket in 1872. Though the whole area of the ground seems spacious, it is possible to hit a ball over the surrounding wall in all four directions. The greatest distance is from the south or sea end wicket to the wall at the north end of the ground and amounts to 138 yards. It is said that Robert Brann and CLA Smith achieved this hit, and Robert Relf certainly hit Haigh over the wall in 1907; FT Mann in 1920 twice in one over drove balls from MW Tate first bounce against the wall; one of these was a hit which AER Gilligan says was one of the very biggest he ever saw. In the opposite direction, the distance is 106 yards from the north wicket to the front edge of the south stand [Cowshed], and 120 yards to the wall running behind the stand [now demolished]. JH Sinclair hit Ranji over this wall in 1907; in 1925 Colonel AC Watson hit a ball from PGH Fender not only over the wall, but right against the vast factory building [Ice Rink] just beyond it, and during his historic innings of 189 in 1911 E Alletson cleared the stand and pitched the ball on the building and possibly right over its curved tin roof. The most recent big hit here was by Wesley Hall, the West Indian, in 1957, when he drove a ball from Marlar over the stand, over the boundary wall and it pitched just below the glass windows of the factory. Marlar says he can still recollect the sound of this beautiful free, lithe hit. A less straight hit more in the direction of mid-off could send the ball past the end of the stand in the direction of the main gates and possibly bounce even through them. The late Sir Home Gordon said the biggest hit he ever saw at Hove was one such hit almost down to the gates by R Slade Lucas of Middlesex off a lob from Humphreys.

PGH Fender says that the biggest hit he can remember was a drive by CB Fry down to the gates, and Alletson certainly hit one ball which ran right through them, and it is said was picked up by a boy who was found playing with it in the street. A left-hander could on-drive the ball in the same direction, and HT Bartlett in his famous 157 *v* the Australians in 1938 landed a ball from Ward on to the pear-shaped island of grass to the south of the secretary's office – a drive of some 125 yards.

Hits in an east-west direction over the boundary wall require less distance. From a centrally placed wicket the distance is 88 yards to the east wall behind the Ranji score box [*sic*, Harmsworth score box] and small east stand [Hencoop], and 94 yards to the line of the west wall running behind the pavilion buildings.

There have been several huge and unmeasurable hits into the gardens which back on to the east wall, and hits right over the pavilion and into the gardens beyond are not uncommon. MC Bird in his innings of 151 *v* Sussex in 1911 made three big hits right over the pavilion and into the gardens. The left-hander DV Smith when he scored his magnificent match-winning 166 *v* Gloucestershire in 1957 was assisted by the pitch being well off centre – in fact only 53 yards away from the pavilion rails, and therefore only 78 yards from the wall. No fewer than six of Smith's nine 6s were swept square right over the top of the middle of the pavilion and out of the ground.

A hit over the roof of the stand which was built on top of the north end on the pavilion in 1927, requires a great deal more loft to clear it, and is a rare hit.

The Gilligan Stand

THE OLD ICE Rink, dating back to 1872, had seen many changes. Firstly, the new American fad for roller skating supplanted its winter-only cousin. This proved to be a short-lived venture into Americanising Hove.

By 1896 it had become Hove Tennis Ground. After 1918, this became the County Sports Club and now featured a roof to facilitate wider usage. The war years hosted drill practice rather than sport. After the war, the club's asset was sold to Hove Machine Tool manufacturer CVA, who re-purposed it into their machine-assembly plant. CVA had several factories around the Brighton area and at its peak employed 2000 people.

In 1947 the company started manufacturing milling machines under licence from Kearney and Trecker Inc. The relationship was such a success that in 1957 the American giant swallowed the Hove minnow.

Within a decade it became apparent that having sites littered across Brighton and Hove was uneconomic and the parent company decided to consolidate into one centralised plant. Hollingbury Industrial Estate not The County Ground, Hove, was the preferred option. This was much to the disappointment of the Eaton Road workforce, who had enjoyed the summer lunch-time perk of sandwiches on the roof watching cricket. By 1967, it was clear that the factory was to be vacated. Sussex CCC appointed a sub-committee to ensure it was involved in potential developments.

The initial plan was to sell the factory *in situ* to another company, with a price tag of £70,000 envisaged, but the Borough Council had no wish to see 'non-conforming industry' continuing in a residential area, and took the opportunity to revoke the site's industrial production license. As a result, agents valued the plot at only around £40,000. Demolition and residential redevelopment was the only viable use.

This lower price brought in developers and in 1968 the site was bought for residential use. It soon became apparent that if the Club were to offer up a relatively small part of the ground, the number of flats could be doubled.

In exchange for this sale, the club obtained three benefits. Firstly, the developers would build a new stand to replace the Cowshed: this would contain squash courts and the indoor school which had, to that point, been in The Chalet. Fitted offices for radio and TV commentary were also included, together with a new and spacious press box. Secondly, a cash bonus, initially settled at £26,000, would be paid along with all legal fees. Thirdly, all residents would become members of the club, and their subscriptions form part of the ground rent. This would ensure an annual income of £700. Unfortunately, this latter benefit would provide diminishing returns, as the club neglected to ensure the figure for membership was inflation-proofed.

The developers had happily reached an accord for the north side of their project, but on the south side were the houses at 3, 5, 7 and 9 Eaton Road which would be required if the new block of flats were to front the road. Numbers 7 and 9 refused to sell and Hubbard Ford and Partners were obliged to re-design the new block around them.

Publicity shots for a 'superior development of 125 flats including 8 penthouses.'

The club took advice from various sources, most notably from Middlesex and Warwickshire, into how best to create the new indoor school where Les Lenham could conduct his cricket clinics, and gently inform generations of Fatty Batters that perhaps cricket was not for them, before sending them home nursing shattered dreams amid swarms of bees.

Building work began in the autumn of 1970, the hope being that the stand would be completed for the new season – it wasn't. The official opening was finally arranged for 27 November 1971 with Arthur Gilligan cutting the ribbon in front of 120 invited guests. For whatever reason, a large number of invitees RSVP'd in the negative. The development wasn't universally popular. Various irate letters were received concerning the fate of the Cowshed, the lack of covered accommodation in the new Gilligan Stand and new deckchair arrangements, or lack thereof, on the grass.

With the flats nearing completion, a £50 prize was offered for the best name for them. 'Ashdown' was the winner, beating such unlikely efforts as 'Umpire

State Buildings', 'Wuthering Heights', 'Hoval' and 'Batsball House'. When the estate agents initially marketed the properties, the prices ranged from £6,650 for a one-bed flat without ground aspect to £20,000 for a three-bed 'penthouse suite' with a grandstand view behind the bowler's arm. By the time of completion, the range was £11,700 to £17,850.

The windfall at least enabled the club to clear some debts and embark on new projects.

-Five-

1972-2002

The Hove centenary year began in optimistic vein with big plans afoot and an aspect of the ground about to drastically change. The factory was gone, the Gilligan stand was up and behind it the Ashdown flats were taking shape. The club even had some money in the bank. It had the best fast bowler in the world, with Dennis Lillee hot on his heels, and it also had the coming man in Tony Greig, who had spent the previous winter in Australia playing for a Rest of the World team under Garry Sobers.

The Rise and Fall of Tony Greig

At the start of the 1972 season the captain, Mike Griffith, fresh from touring South Africa with The Sussex Martlets, wrote: 'The best way to celebrate this Centenary would be to win that elusive title.'

Snow and Greig immediately prospered against Australia, Snow with eight wickets and Greig with five, as well as top scoring in both innings of the opening Test at Old Trafford. At Hove matters progressed less well. Qualification for the new-fangled Benson and Hedges Cup ended in farce in Bradford with Yorkshire chasing down 86 to win in 51 overs. Defeat in the opening round of the Gillette Cup followed at Hove. The John Player League was barely better: four wins, three washouts and nine defeats. The Championship went the same way, the first victory coming in July when Greig took 11-46 (and top scored) against Kent. Second bottom was the final placing.

Mid-season, Mike Griffith was interviewed by Christopher Martin-Jenkins; the tone was downbeat to say the least. He talked of some players not being 'co-operative by nature', bemoaned taking a backseat to Deryck Murray at Cambridge and Jim Parks at Hove and admitted he was 'disillusioned with the professional game in England'. The son of the TCCB secretary was at least honest: 1972 was a horrible summer for Sussex. The only bright sparks were a victory over Australia, an £11,000 testimonial shared between Kenny Suttle and Jim Parks and a surprising reported profit of £8291, despite a loss on the centenary appeal. That first title remained a mere pinhole in the distance, a plaque commemorating 100 years at Eaton Road served only as a pointed reminder of this sustained failure.

In 1973 Greig took on the captaincy. With no member of the Parks' family in the side for the first time in nearly 50 years, a youthful squad with two overseas players in Greenidge and Joshi; who were hardly a match for Procter, Richards, Lloyd, Bedi *et al*; Greig had a challenge on his hands. But he loved nothing more. Before the season even started, however, all county clubs suffered a setback with the introduction on 1 April of Value Added Tax. On the plus side, the players would receive £6 for a six and £36 for six wickets from the Sussex Mutual Building Society.

Despite these incentives the season was, bar a Gillette Cup run to Lord's, little better than its predecessor. Greig threw himself at the job and the job threw itself back at him. Mid-season he talked little about Sussex beyond praising Snow and Roger Prideaux, but plenty about reorganising the game, all the way from neutral Test umpires to reducing the amount of Championship matches to 16 and scrapping batting bonus points. Another captaincy issue was decided at Hove, that of the national side. In May 1973 MCC's sub-continent tourists were pitted against The Rest in a Test trial that would effectively decide who led England against New Zealand the following week. Tony Lewis got a duck on the first morning and Ray Illingworth's team won. John Arlott felt pangs of guilt that he had treated Lewis to some sparkling Vouvray at nine that morning in order to 'approach the day with equanimity'.

Sunday market.

There was one change that Greig hadn't considered. But Frances Manning had. She proposed the unthinkable at the AGM, that women be allowed to stand for the committee. Voted down twice she returned in 1975 and won, and women were finally permitted into the 'Men's Pavilion'.

In commercial terms some enlightened thinking was abroad, although not sufficient to allow the idea of 'pop festivals' on the hallowed turf. Communications with London promoters had gone back and forth but the lack of enthusiasm on the part of Sussex wasn't hard to divine. Easter carnivals, Sunday markets, beer festivals, giant eggs adorning the four corners, more showbiz cricket and a contract with *Arena Sports Advertising* were all designed to raise revenue. This was easily spent on such necessities as the long-awaited sightscreen at the sea end, a major overhaul of the main Harmsworth scoreboard and the erection of a new one on the pavilion side. The construction of squash courts in the north-west corner in the winter of 1973 was altogether more significant. An outlay of £63,000 came with an estimated annual revenue of £16,000. This proved wildly optimistic. By the time damp problems had been resolved, the profit shown over repayment on loans was scarcely more than £2000. The newly-founded club shop, originally operating from a caravan, was proving to be more profitable.

The next season showed little improvement and Sussex settled into a run of mediocrity before reaching the nadir of 1975 – bottom of the Championship, lower mid-table in the John Player and out in the opening round of both cup competitions.

The repeated talk of youth prospects was becoming wearying. For once runs rather than wickets had become the problem, but mostly the potential of Peter Graves and John Spencer, amongst others, was not being fully realised.

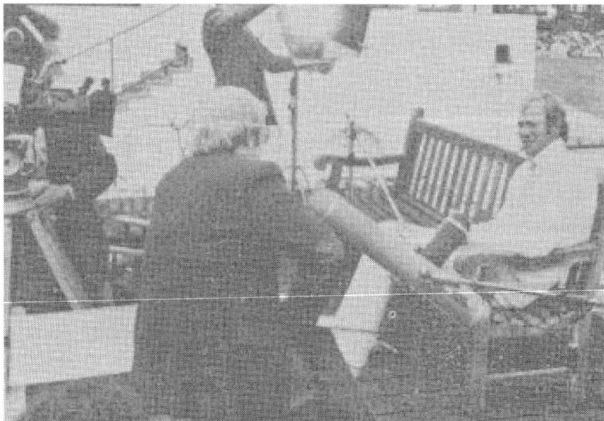

Tony Greig interviewed by David Vine, assorted consequences ensued.

What Sussex would not have given for Clive Rice, Andy Roberts or Majid Khan? The exchequer this time reflected this poor form – membership dropped to just over 3000 in 1975. County form had only rarely shown any direct correlation to membership figures, and possibly this falling-off was due to a lack of individual flair. Significant annual losses were becoming the norm, and led the committee to report it was 'generally disturbed at the trend of expenditure'. It might have been equally disturbed about the lack of income.

The mood in the country was correspondingly grim. The three-day week of 1974 battered the economy while unions and employers fought over control of industry as successive governments struggled to govern.

There was certainly no three-day week at Hove, but in other areas it sometimes seemed that the club was a microcosm of the wider country, riven by dispute and with no clear idea of how to find the exit sign. For once the season started well and Sussex found themselves briefly at the top of the table but as the drought-stricken outfields across the country turned light brown, it was a position they were never likely to sustain. For viewers of BBC1's *Sportsnight*, Hove became known as the backdrop to Greig's incendiary, pre-recorded 'Grovel' interview, conducted on the press balcony with Sussex in action behind him against, of all teams, West Indies.

The season was a mixed one. New signings Roger Knight and Arnold Long brought much-needed experience, Graves and Spencer showed their true worth and respectability was established. However, beyond John Barclay there was little evidence that the much-vaunted Sussex youth policy was bearing any fruit.

The most exciting prospect was undoubtedly Javed Miandad; four games, 500 runs and soon to be a Test-debut centurion in Lahore. One quiet triumph was that of Peter Eaton, the new groundsman, whose efforts in the drought-ridden summer were rewarded with £150 as the Watney Mann Challenge Trophy winner.

The year of 1977 was better for Sussex, though attention on discernible improvement was abruptly re-directed on the day Tony Greig faced the press when the Packer Circus came to town. Briefly, Eaton Road became the centre of the cricketing world. Hove had been warned of Greig's ability to attract publicity the previous year with his ill-advised comments on West Indies' cricket, but this was a new level. Within weeks, Greig had moved from being the saviour of English cricket to pariah and traitor, booed at every ground. Losing the England captaincy was the upshot. It wasn't totally unpredictable. John Arlott had astutely written that although Greig's appointment would be 'instantly refreshing...His merits are the parents of his flaws.'

Another problem brewing was foreign players. Geoff Greenidge and Udai Joshi had served the county well in the seventies but they were not the charismatic and match-winning pair that sides such as Gloucestershire, Hampshire or Lancashire could boast. Worse still, players of the calibre of Barry Richards, Ken McEwen, Peter Kirsten and Paddy Clift had slipped through the net.

That all changed in 1977 when Sussex found they had had two young batting prodigies on their hands in the form of Miandad and Kepler Wessels. As if these two weren't riches enough, a third soon arrived in the form of Imran Khan.

The April nets, 1978

The Odd Couple, Barclay and Imran

Having announced his decision to leave Worcestershire, Imran was granted permission by the Cricket Council Appeals Committee to play for Sussex without the statutory one-year registration period. It wasn't a universally popular ruling. Glamorgan secretary Wilf Wooller resigned from the TCCB in protest. Wooller would receive round-about compensation in due course when the Sussex committee decided to favour Wessels over Miandad, who then moved to Glamorgan.

Imran Khan, drawn to the bright lights of Brighton, though at this stage still raw and untutored, was a highly-promising young player. Who could have known that he would become perhaps the most influential cricketer in the world, not to mention prime minister of Pakistan? With Snow and Greig effectively finished as Sussex players, his immediate, and near-impossible, challenge was to replace both. Under new captain, Arnold Long, and Geoff Arnold from Surrey, Sussex finally had the kind of county side that won trophies. Experienced leaders, solid county professionals, the magic of the overseas Test players and youthful exuberance in the form of Paul Parker. It was the latter who top-scored at Lord's when Sussex beat mighty Somerset in the Gillette final, a first trophy for 15 years.

In the final year of the decade Sussex had become a strong county side, eventually finishing fourth behind runaway winners Essex and only losing at the semi-final stage of the Gillette Cup. There was talk of Alan Knott joining. Gehan Mendis, Paul Phillipson and Tony Pigott had strengthened the team and went at least some way to off-setting the loss of Javed Miandad. Overall though, it wasn't a bad place to be at the start of a new decade.

Much had changed at Hove in the 15-year gap between trophies. Not so much in the appearance of the ground, beyond the looming presence of Ashdown down at the southern end, but behind the scenes. The various committees were coming to terms with the new age of sponsorship and the fact that a county cricket club cost around £150,000 a year to run. Prize money, membership, gate receipts and so forth were all well and good but were never enough. Sponsorship filled some gaps; even the new pitch covers were adorned with the logo 'Save for a rainy day with the Alliance Building Society'.

The new decade began solidly on the pitch but with losses of £104,000 over the previous two seasons, concern over finances as ever loomed in the background. Club secretary Ray Stevens announced ominously that: 'The committee is reviewing the whole staffing structure of the club', and with that Tony Buss was sacked as manager and his workload dumped onto the coach Stuart Storey. Graves and Spencer departed as well; the former finally calling time on a career blighted by hand injuries and the latter choosing a career in education over match-by-match fees for Sussex. The foreign players more than paid their way with Wessels outstanding in accumulating 1500 runs at an average of 65. Parker's stock continued to rise, and young Colin Wells showed great promise.

This was just a precursor to what was nearly a great year in 1981. David Sheppard had almost dragged Sussex to a first title in 1953, and now it was the turn of new captain John Barclay. He was not equipped to lead by example as Sheppard had done, but he did manage to extract every bit of talent from his side while engendering fierce loyalty and a fine team ethic – much as Mike Brearley was doing for the national side in that same year. Not that Brearley and Barclay always saw eye to eye. In John Arlott's last Championship game as a journalist in 1980, he believed a spat between Imran and Brearley had encouraged Barclay to allow Wessels to bat Championship chasing Middlesex out of the game. Arlott watched sadly the 'sluggish death throes of a callously murdered cricket match'.

Where Brearley had Botham, Barclay had Imran. He also had Garth le Roux and the still-prolific Wessels along with new arrival Ian Gould. Parker was now an England player as well as being regarded as the best fielder in the world by Brearley, Alan Wells had joined his brother, Ian Greig and Mendis both had fine seasons and the County Championship went down to the last game, with Nottinghamshire holding a four-point advantage. Any self-respecting Sussex supporter will be well aware that this advantage was all courtesy of umpire Peter Stevens. In the game between the two contenders, Sussex were denied victory when Mike Bore was given not out when plumb lbw to Imran. With that contentious decision went 16 crucial points.

In the final round of games, Sussex did everything they could by battering Yorkshire from pillar to post, but at Trent Bridge Nottinghamshire virtually beat Glamorgan in a day. It had been a great effort from the perennial bridesmaids and one that made their captain proud:

> We had aspired to excellence and had played a lot of wonderful cricket along the way. It is only with the passing of time that the disappointment of not winning has grown.

The Angry Eighties

On the field all was well, off the field it wasn't. Jack Arlidge's end-of-season report laid bare countless problems that had only been slightly softened by a £62,000 profit. Chairman Tony Crole-Rees was fighting for his job. His honesty in admitting errors of judgement and poor management of the *Sussex Cricketer* pub hardly helped his cause as a legal stand-off ensued. But his message was clear:

> If we are to continue with first-class cricket at Hove in the 1980s, then we must explore every avenue of finance. There must be no sacred cows in our struggle to keep alive this old and famous club.

The ground itself was definitely well down the pecking order in terms of investment. By and large, sponsorship was sought for any improvement while club funds were concentrated on the playing side.

The near miss of 1981 was partially redeemed by a runaway victory in the John Player League the following year – 14 wins in 16 games, and that without Imran, who was Man of the Series for Pakistan against England.

It might have taken a long time, but surely someone took notice of the effectiveness of a Pakistan leg-spinner at Hove? Abdul Qadir's match figures in the tour game against Sussex were 13-122. With the financial squeeze, some of the playing staff were delighted to receive one of eight sponsored Morris Itals provided by Caffyn Motors.

With Imran returning, le Roux in place and support from Tony Pigott and Ian Greig on the fastest pitch in the country, it seemed that Sussex were ready for a bonanza season in 1982. In the event, injury intervened and Sussex slumped, never more so than when John Barclay inserted Essex at Hove in a regional Benson and Hedges match. Graham Gooch scored 198 and Keith Fletcher 101.

More soul-searching accompanied this collapse. In the committee rooms secretary Stanley Allen became the latest official to wonder about the organisation of the club and its impact on the team and facilities. He questioned the power of members, given that they were responsible for only 25% of the revenue. He advocated a limited company approach with members (or anyone else) as shareholders and the secretary given free rein to run the club on the lines proscribed by an elected board of directors. It was a suitably hard-nosed Thatcherite approach to business management. And business is what Allen had in mind. This was the 1980s, complete with de-regulation and financial freedom, and the argument went that if one didn't run with the times then one ran into oblivion. On a lighter note, Alan Lee applauded a new initiative:

> Sussex have at last arranged adequate signposts in the maze of streets around their Hove ground. [No more will I be lost] somewhere between Devil's Dyke and the seafront.

The next two seasons saw Sussex prospering in the John Player League but firmly mid-table in the Championship where injuries to Imran and Pigott were only partially offset by the form of Colin Wells and Alan Green. Ian Greig was sacked by the finance committee with Mendis and Chris Waller soon following. The appointment of Gould to the captaincy, with his 'brash, jack-the-lad exterior', aided by the equally brash all-rounder Dermot Reeve, was quickly rewarded with victory over Lancashire in the final of the Nat West Bank Trophy. It would be a long time before anything on the field brought cheer to the hearts of supporters again.

Early in 1987 the word 'mutiny' was attached to the Hove dressing-room. Despite success on the field, it only 'papered over the cracks of the structure of the county', according to John Barclay. In February, the manager/coach, Stewart Storey was sacked, largely at the behest of the players, while in the boardroom Richard Renold, a financial controller by trade, was trying to bring some 'much needed sanity to the county's account books'. He was baffled by some aspects of his job:

> Success does not seem to have any effect on membership at all. We don't understand the psychology of Sussex – winning competitions doesn't seem to

bring in people at all.

This was a curiosity Sussex had experienced way back in the silver years of the 1930s. Andrew Longmore in *The Cricketer* tackled the same issue:

> A county's cricket club reflects the nature of the county. The rolling downs of Sussex have traditionally nurtured the spirit of the Gentleman amateur, someone who cares not for winning or losing, someone who plays for fun not money. Perhaps too that spirit has, until recently, affected the way the club is run. It certainly seems to affect the members. It is an astonishing fact that after the season of 1981 when the county played tremendous cricket and only just failed to win the Championship that membership fell off for the following season.

Imran's benefit season proved to be of the non-playing variety; injuries were so severe that Ian Gould commented that 'for a few awful weeks it did look as if we might be struggling to get any sort of side on the field'. Tony Pigott, an advocate of better pay, and also a co-lessee of the county ground squash courts, was involved in a bout of fisticuffs in Brighton.

Hot air ballooning in front of the Gilligan stand, bingo inside.

One wooden spoon was always on the cards and it was nearly two, both Championship and John Player League. Gould promptly resigned amid talk of a 'dissenting faction' which was presumably responsible for leaving copies of Van Morrison's new album *No Method, No Teacher, No Guru* in the dressing-room. Paul Parker was ushered in as the new captain, with John Jameson installed as coach. Both le Roux and Reeve moved on.

Despite the arrival of yet another new coach in Norman Gifford, the next two years were little better bar the batting of Alan Wells. Great performances on the field tended to come from opposition players – Michael Holding, aged 34, collected 8-21 in the first round of the 1988 Nat West Trophy.

The granting of permission to build on the Hastings' Central Recreation Ground in 1989 was a salutary reminder of the precarious nature of protecting an urban sporting arena when property developers are eying its potential. With the Hove ground worth an estimated £5m and the land being the club's only major asset, it was becoming clear that pressure might eventually lead to cashing in the cheque and finding pastures new. Just a stone's throw away, Brighton and Hove Albion were being posed similar questions.

The Ambitious Nineties

There was a certain cruel symmetry coming into view. It was exactly the same market forces that had landed Sussex at Eaton Road back in 1872, albeit not voluntarily. But for the time being, the club ignored the property speculators and, with a 1989 profit of nearly £200,000, and all debts cleared, turned their attention to ground redevelopment. "In 10 years' time the ground will not be recognisable", predicted the bullish vice-chairman Alan Wadey. "The pavilion needs a bomb put under it." Hardly words to endear him to a vast number of regular spectators. Ivo Tennant noted

> Sussex will have to contend though, with opposition from Hove Borough Council to the ground being turned in a commercial enterprise. So Sussex must now build a team worthy of a £5m venture.

The immediate response on the field was to finish bottom of the Championship. This barely affected profits. Did this represent blind loyalty or a lack of concern over winning and losing among the spectators? This had been a constant source of confusion since 1872. What drew spectators to the ground? Was it success or just competitive cricket? Was it great or glamorous players or just the prospect of good weather and pleasant day's entertainment? The answer probably lies in a combination of these factors, none being significantly more important than the others.

The determination to drive a rebuilding programme, costing between five and seven million pounds over 10 years, was undimmed. Wadey hadn't lied. Envisaged were the demolition of all existing buildings on the ground; the construction of a new pavilion/indoor school complex; new hospitality, function and conference facilities and new seating to increase capacity to 6500. Step one was to obtain 'outline planning permission' for a new hotel on land occupied by the pub, Chalet and groundsman's house.

This concentration on finding new income through sponsorship, corporate activity, non-cricketing pursuits and anything else that came to mind was the inevitable result of events, both within and beyond the surrounding wall at Eaton Road, throughout the previous 50 years.

Counties such as Somerset and, to a lesser degree, Sussex had always been reliant on amateur players to keep wage bills down. This saving was then aided by paying professionals a meagre sum for the duration of their careers before pensioning them off with a benefit which might enable them to set up in a pub or post office somewhere. The higher-profile players might find work coaching in public schools while the lesser players were likely to enter the job market penniless, untrained and 35 years old.

As the amateurs drifted away and professionals demanded better remuneration, a process accelerated by Kerry Packer, so the pressure grew on county coffers to increase player rewards. Wage bills spiralled and became by far the biggest expense.

For Sussex in particular the choice was stark – turn Hove into a viable business centre or be forced to crack the golden egg and move out. With the need to generate the requisite running expenses, allowing the ground to stand idle from October to April was palpably absurd, just as it had been 70 years earlier. Unfortunately the winter months were those least suitable for using the outdoor facilities so hotels, bars, wedding receptions and the like had to be squeezed into the somewhat inadequate perimeter area. That, at least, was the theory. Putting theory into practice was always likely to be challenging.

The early 1990s brought little success on the field. Sometimes it seemed as if Sussex were treading water and waiting for the big fish to arrive. Alan Wells continued to score heavily and took over the captaincy; 'colourful personality' Ed Giddins and Ian Salisbury transformed the bowling attack; Bill Athey and Eddie Hemmings arrived as an antidote to the avowed local-youth policy, and the club continued to show a profit season after season, aided by outside agencies. Merrydown Cider arrived as chief sponsor and was happy to throw in a three-year, £200,000 deal.

The two veteran signings proved to be astute but couldn't prevent Sussex suffering one of their most painful days. Despite setting a short-lived record total, they were defeated at Lord's in the 1993 Nat West Trophy final at the hands of Sussex old boy Dermot Reeve's Warwickshire.

As 1994 dawned, 'anticipation hangs in the sea frets at Hove' chirruped one pre-season report rather unconvincingly. Players chopped and changed but the big plans for ground development were finally revealed four years after Alan Wadey had first spoken of mass demolition.

In December, the Sussex committee gave the go-ahead for a four-storey pavilion and a multi-purpose sports hall at the north end of the ground. On the east side, hospitality boxes and a restaurant were to be built at a cost of £250,000 with a further £4.6m earmarked for the north end.

The size of the debt incurred would be partially offset (to the tune of £1m) by selling the lease on the pub. The 'go-ahead' came from financiers and the club committee. But it was far from being signed off by either local residents or Hove borough council. The 1994 accounts showed a slight profit but a breakdown of income underlined how the club still remained only just in the black. Revenue from spectators at £300,000 was heavily outweighed by commercial revenue at £478,000 which was, in turn, dwarfed by the TCCB payment of £560,000.

Within two years the grand plans for Hove had been 'deferred', much to the delight of many. Profits remained tiny and results poor. Every spring came the talk of 'potential' and every autumn the familiar lament of that potential failing to be realised. Franklyn Stephenson worked hard and Alan Wells remained one of the best county batsmen, but the promise of Giddins seemed to have fizzled out even before he was sacked for cocaine use. Gifford resigned, the Hastings' ground disappeared under concrete and then, at the end of 1996, came a mass exodus. Alan Wells was clumsily dismissed as captain and left for Kent, Ian Salisbury and Martin Speight were looking for better opportunities and promising youngster Danny Law was allowed to join Essex. The arrival of Mark Robinson and Billy Taylor was, at first sight, scant compensation.

One thing that certainly hadn't changed at Hove was its reputation as a high-scoring ground. In 1991 Sussex were making light work of chasing 437 for victory against Kent, needing just nine runs with four wickets standing. They lost all four in making eight and the game was tied. Two years later Sussex and Essex shared 1808 runs over four days (one double-century, six centuries and nine half-centuries) for just 20 wickets.

If 1996 finished badly then 1997 boded no better. Brighton and Hove Albion left the Goldstone Ground and feelings were running high at Hove. The team had been poor in 1996 and were now shorn of four of their best players. Little surprise the insurrectionist *Sussex 2000* movement found ready support around the county.

Sussex 2000

The ball started rolling when former player Tony Pigott, now at Surrey, succeeded in gaining the requisite 50 voting members' signatures to force an Emergency General Meeting at Hove Town Hall on 8 April. This wasn't soon enough for those who flocked to the Annual General Meeting on 19 March. No less than 800 people crowded into the Grand Hotel, four times the normal attendance, only to hear themselves being branded as 'rabble rousers'. Secretary Nigel Bett had become a laughing-stock after his appearance in *British Naturism* but far more damaging was the perception of the committee as 'aloof, autocratic and arrogant', while presiding over a club in freefall.

Alan Caffyn had already stood down as chairman after an ill-judged interview with the *Brighton Argus* and by the time the evening ended the rest of the committee had followed. Into the vacuum stepped Robin Marlar as chairman with Pigott as chief executive and director of cricket. A new structure was quickly established with clearly-defined areas of responsibility. Former players Spencer and Snow were brought on to the committee. The pledge of *Sussex 2000* was:

> To develop Hove into a ground capable of staging international cricket and to implement policies that would improve communication, finances and development as well as bringing playing success.

'All one can do is wish them luck', commented Alan Lee, without sounding especially convinced.

Long-standing club librarian Ossie Osborne left, feeling unable to accept making room for the coaching staff by moving from his offices to a portacabin.

The new crew was not short of ideas. At the first AXA Life League match, under 18s were admitted free and music was used between overs. Sussex lost by nine wickets. Late in the season floodlit cricket came to Hove and 4000 turned out. Sussex Tigers lost by five wickets. The team was weak and could not afford to lose strike bowlers Jason Lewry and James Kirtley to injury. The upshot was bottom placing in the two leagues but a surprising run in the Nat West Trophy, before a heavy defeat in the semi-final.

For once, gate receipts reflected performance to the tune of an £83,000 loss. Undeterred, Pigott went shopping and returned heavily laden. Ex-Australian Test player Dave Gilbert moved in from Surrey as director of cricket thus allowing Pigott to concentrate solely on his administrative roles. Even more eye-catching was the signing of a disillusioned Chris Adams from Derbyshire. He didn't come cheap – a £250,000 three-year deal made the new club captain the highest-paid player in county cricket. This was a high-risk strategy; rather than cutting his cloth, Pigott had elected to buy a bigger suit. It might not have been exactly Maradona to Napoli but there were similarities.

More was to follow with the recruitment of Michael Bevan, certainly the most exciting foreign signing since Garth le Roux. Around the ground, the efforts of Pigott began to become visible with *King's Cuisine* taking over the catering contract for £100,000. The *Dexter Room* opened in the pavilion, the players' dining room was spruced up, the *Jim Parks Bar* appeared, players now dined in the *Greig Room* and plans were laid for the *John Snow Terrace* bar above the club offices. Around the ground a baguette bar, hot-food outlet by the main scoreboard and three mobile units were available on match days. Another initiative, the *Willows* restaurant/bar in the squash club, was singularly unsuccessful.

On-the-field performances improved, largely due to the form and fitness of bowlers Lewry, Kirtley, Mark Robinson and Robin Martin-Jenkins. Peter Moores retired from playing and was immediately installed as manager/coach, allowing Gilbert to follow Pigott's lead in paying more attention to administrative matters. The reward for all this effort was a debilitating yearly loss of £193,000.

The big news of 1999 was Hove becoming the first cricket ground in the country to install permanent floodlights. Under the sponsorship of *Stonegate Farmers*, five 100-foot towers each containing 12 halogen lamps rose above the Hove skyline. The Sussex batting was strengthened by the signing of Richard Montgomerie and Tony Cottey, and with the four quick bowlers taking 200 Championship wickets Sussex were slightly unfortunate to miss the cut when the split into two divisions came into force for the first time. But Pigott and Moores did succeed in imbuing the club with a new, competitive culture that appealed to local youngsters such as Michael Yardy and Matt Prior. Moores' move into coaching was as to the manner born, Adams recalled his effect on the entire squad:

> You were constantly challenged to get better, no matter how old you were. He had this brilliant way – not in an aggressive way – of challenging you. Peter's greatest

skill was being able to make you feel super confident, but also make you aware that you could still get better.

Central to this new side was the revitalisation of the new-ball pairing of Kirtley and Lewry.

In May two noteworthy matches took place: India and South Africa attracted a crowd of 6216 for a World Cup group game, with hundreds more locked out of a ground clearly not yet fit to host international cricket. In the Championship, Sussex chased down 455 to win against Gloucestershire, the second highest score of its type in history.

But in the same month a familiar theme was ominously revisited with the news that 'Sussex are seriously considering leaving their ancient home'. It was hardly a surprise given the spiralling debt, not least that caused by expensive signings.

The considerations were not complex: the club could borrow against the security of the £5m ground but if that borrowing became too costly then there would be no money to re-locate, even if the ground were sold. The travails of the local football team, exiled to Gillingham, were a stark illustration of where this could lead.

By the end of the year Pigott cried enough and left, to be replaced by Gilbert, and despite a moderate season with the bat Adams was selected to tour with England in South Africa. He played all five Tests but scored few runs. With county sides increasingly being seen as feeder clubs for the national side and the influence of central contracts keeping Test players away from their counties, the failure of Adams to cement a national place would prove good news for Sussex.

Not that Adams prospered as the new century dawned; a poor season was compounded by a daft spat with ex-Sussex player Danny Law in which he narrowly avoided a ban. With his rising profile, the legality of Kirtley's action was called into question and the team slid from top to bottom of division two in the last six weeks of the season. A small profit was little compensation, as, without the benefit of hindsight, was the signing of Murray Goodwin as temporary cover for Bevan.

During the course of the summer *The Cricketer* sent out their reporter Anthony Meredith to all 18 county grounds to compare and contrast on 10 categories. Hove faired well enough on 'basics' (amenities), 'welcome', 'shop' and 'club annual'. The marks were low for 'scorecards' and 'heroes' and Hove was plum last for 'access' (only motorists were considered), 'buzz', 'pizzazz' and 'setting'. According to this somewhat subjective analysis, Hove was bottom of the pile.

For the next two seasons the team moved gently upwards without ever looking like champions in waiting. That said, winning the Championship division two was a big step forwards: Kirtley's action passed muster, Goodwin settled in quickly and Robinson moved into coaching.

On Friday 14 September Hove was completely silent for three minutes, five days after the terrorist attacks in New York. Only seven months later, this sombre pause was echoed by Sussex and Surrey players following the deaths of Umer Rashid and Ben Hollioake in Grenada and Perth.

The resignation of Dave Gilbert and chairman Don Trangmar, four years after replacing Robin Marlar, were offset by the good form of the batsmen, in particular Adams, Goodwin and Martin-Jenkins. One-day form though, remained miserable. The 2001 success in the Championship division two may not have caused any waves across the country, but in the Sussex dressing-room, and around the county it marked a, albeit nascent, winning mentality.

The big(gish) news at the beginning of 2003 was that Sussex had signed a new bowler, described by Brian Scovell as a 'rotund, part-time television analyst'. The good news was that Mushtaq Ahmed would not be part of Pakistan's plans and that he had every intention of putting behind him the troubles of his latter years at Somerset.

Women's Cricket Continued

BEFORE THE OUTBREAK of war in 1939, there had been indications that Hove was likely to become a regular venue for women's cricket. However, the six-year hiatus saw the Sussex County Association disappear due to a lack of personnel and funding. Enthusiasts grouped together to re-launch the organisation in 1947, and the following year Surrey and Sussex women played Kent and Middlesex over two days at Hove, the first significant match for almost a decade.

In 1949 county trials were held at both Hove and Eastbourne. The latter match attracted far more interest, and for the best part of 20 years the women's game largely disappeared from the county ground. When the Australian tourists played The South in Sussex in 1951, it was The Saffrons that hosted. Twelve years later, the Australians played twice in Sussex, this time at Worthing and Hastings. Throughout the period, schools and clubs showed little interest in expanding the game across the sexes, and it was left to a dedicated few to keep the embers glowing.

In 1966 it seemed as if a turning point had been reached. Sussex Women were now strong enough to almost beat a strong New Zealand side, and Eaton Road was seen as a suitable venue. Sadly this was a blip, only to be rectified when the women's game received an enormous shot in the arm in the form of the inaugural World Cup in 1973. At the back end of the previous season two 60-over trial matches were held at Hove, England losing to The Rest on consecutive days.

England's first game in the tournament proper took place on 23 June 1973. As part of the build-up, there was perhaps the strangest match ever to be played at Eaton Road between a Sussex XI and England Women. Suffice to say, the game was reduced to six-a-side and only five overs per innings – Rachel Heyhoe-Flint was caught and bowled by Norman's son, Nicky Wisdom. When the real cricket started, Enid Bakewell and Lynne Thomas set a new record opening partnership of 246, leading their side to an easy victory against an International XI.

Again there was a long gap before international cricket returned to Hove, this time for a Test match against Australia in 1987 when four days on a flat wicket were insufficient to produce a result. The game was, however, at long last beginning to find a wider audience and greater participation across the county. After decades of struggle, the Sussex Women's Cricket Association's positive annual reports now reflected reality rather than wishful thinking. Numbers attending winter coaching sessions under the Gilligan stand in the 1970s had been depressing, but by the early 1990s a new atmosphere was sweeping the club.

The 1998 merger of the WCA and ECB was not universally popular, but along with the inception of the Women's County Championship the previous year, there began a steady rise in the popularity and profile of the women's game. This process was particularly rapid in Sussex. The appointment of Terry Burton as coach of the senior side in 1995 and the emergence of Clare Connor as one of the finest players in the country were initial drivers which in turn led to a closer co-operation with the county club. John Barclay led coaching sessions at Arundel while Peter Moores was amongst those leading at Eaton Road. There was also tremendous support for the Sussex WCA from the late ex-England international and 1993 England World Cup-winning manager Ruth Prideaux. Although most matches were played at 'out grounds', there was one regular fixture per season at Sussex's headquarters: an important step in providing a greater sense of inclusivity governing both forms of the game.

In 1999 Sussex were promoted from division two of the Championship. The new century was full of promise And the wearing of stockings was no longer a requirement.

Hove at the Centre of World Cricket

TONY GREIG WAS a publicist's dream, he loved the limelight and it loved him. He was also a captain's dream; he could do almost anything, he always tried his best, he brought the best out of others and people loved to see him play. No wonder then that from the day on Championship debut at Hove in May 1967; when he hammered 156 off a Lancashire attack containing Statham, Higgs and Lever; until 1978, Sussex couldn't believe their good fortune. There were dissenting voices of course: too loud, too brash, plays too hard, something of the pop star about him. But even these voices had to admit that he really could play. For a club in the financial mire nothing could be better than a man who could make turnstiles click.

Brash and bold. Greig and his sponsored Jag on the outfield.

History will, however, always tell that when Greig brought the world to Hove it was nothing to do with his activities on the field. For those who shuddered at his comments about the 1976 West Indian tourists he had already queered his pitch. Yet one year later more was to come, much more.

The 1977 Australian tourists were having a grim time. Their first two county fixtures had been all but washed out. Saturday 7 May wasn't going much better – 35-1 at the close of play. At least there was a barbeque at Tony Greig's house at Dyke Close, and he'd hired a marquee and laid on the Fosters.

Players, journalists, friends, administrators and rumours were all present.

Everybody knew, and had known since the Centenary Test in Melbourne a few months earlier, that something was afoot. Greig himself had prepared a statement with his agent Reg Hayter that would appear the following day. There was little point in pretending nothing was going on and Kerry Packer agreed: "Rub the lamp, Greigy." Big money and a game-changing schism were in the offing; it wasn't the Fosters talking, Greig was choosing his moment.

Once the statement was released the implications were clear – 'most of the world's top players' were due to start playing for big bucks in Australia in just six months time, irrespective of any ICC sanctioned Test schedule.

Next day the sun shone and Greig belted a half-century as Yorkshire were beaten in the John Player League in front of a good crowd and a media scrum. After play, it was back to business off the field:

> Pressmen have been very patient over this matter, especially those waiting at the Hove County ground, and it is only fair they should be the first to hear from me. I shall be meeting them tomorrow and later appearing on television.

On Monday came the newspapers' reaction – the *Daily Mirror's* 'Test Pirates' was the most succinct, with even more considered articles scarcely more positive. It was now clear that the other English players recruited were Derek Underwood, Alan Knott and John Snow. Australian journalist John Crilly, working for World Series Cricket, brought a television crew to Hove. They were allowed free entry but charged £30 on leaving the ground.

On 11 May the cricketing press descended on the banqueting room at the *Sussex Cricketer* to hear Tony Greig give full details, or at least as much as he knew. His words were hardly a surprise. The involvement of South African players had been published on 24 April, Packer had spoken bluntly in Sydney on 9 May and then there was Greigy's garden party. Ian Wooldridge wrote: 'Far from being a shock development, I suggest that the only surprise was that it was so long delayed.'

Greig had already done two interviews for the BBC and IRN on the day, but for the English press an open conference with the current England captain, now Packer's *de facto* playing lieutenant, was manna from heaven. In a heaving room thick with smoke, lights, lenses and anticipation, Greig was relaxed, smiling and friendly in a loud check jacket. As Richard Streeton wrote in the *Times*:

> Greig spoke fluently at a press conference at the Hove ground for 90 minutes. If

there were brief moments of arrogance and naivety present, too, he was never less than frank.

Greig had little or nothing to hide now that matters were out in the open. His mantra was that his actions were a forward step for the greater good. He would be seeking compromise with cricket boards all over the world. But there was a steely resolve behind his words. It was clear Packer could and would survive and thrive alone:

> When the authorities know all the facts they could well take a different view of it all. Lord's and the others must sit round a table with him [Packer]; I know no better way of sorting things out. The door is open.

The assembled throng listened intently but Greig had no doubt that the seeds he was throwing were falling on distinctly stony ground:

> I experienced the odd sensation of knowing that many of my listeners did not believe a word of what I was saying. When I insisted that cricket would benefit in the long term they stared and muttered as if I was a creature from another planet.

As events gathered pace towards a move which would change international cricket forever, three Australian journalists placed a notice in the *Times*:

In affectionate remembrance of International Cricket, which died at Hove, 9th May, 1977.
Deeply lamented by a large circle of friends and acquaintances. RIP.
NB: The body will be cremated and The Ashes taken to Australia and scattered around the studio of TCN9 Sydney.

The View from the Away Dressing-Room

THE WONDERFUL COLLECTION of letters in the ownership of Tim Burges, paints a picture of Hove during the sixties and seventies from the perspective of the visiting player. First-class cricketers of the era relished their trips to the South Coast, either to Hove or when imbibing the festival atmosphere of games at Hastings and Eastbourne.

Memories, appear fresh from players who, by and large, have not often been asked to tell their stories – the county stalwarts. Malcolm Scott of Northants particularly recalls the humour of Kenny Suttle and Alan Oakman. The camaraderie and friendships shine through in the words of Richard Jefferson and Roger Davis who also recalls 'a wild night out with Greigy' and 'smashing Mike Griffith at squash'.

Some games were not so perfect. Andrew Miller of Middlesex only made one visit and managed a golden duck, a drug test and was then defeated by Colin Wells in a 100m sprint across the ground. Jim Yardley did better, his 94 being inspired by dire threats from his captain, Don Kenyon, who had discovered him dancing with a lady at 9.30 pm the previous evening. For Surrey's Michael Willett, Micky Stewart was the intimidating captain. Willett ran him out and then, after injuring a knee, found his skipper emerging as his runner just as he approached his century. He got there. On a return visit in 1964 he was somewhat embarrassed, this time in front of a 15,000-strong Gillette Cup crowd, when his grandfather ambled out onto the field for a chat at the fall of a wicket.

Like other Surrey players, David Sydenham relished the warm atmosphere of Hove matches, even more so after following Alec Bedser's inexplicable advice to drink two pints and eat a portion of cheese at lunchtime. Thirty minutes later and opening the bowling he found himself giggling and 'drunk in charge of a cricket ball'.

Derek Pringle saved his drinking for later, touring the town's Harveys' hostelries and musing on 'those silly eggs round the boundary'. Barrie Meyer had the misfortune to be fielding on a certain summer's day in 1966 when cricket was very much off the agenda as play was repeatedly interrupted by messages brought out to keep the players apprised of events at Wembley. Clearly the authorities in charge of the loudspeaker system felt that the sparse crowd would have no interest in the goings on of England and West Germany in the winter game.

Above all it is John Snow, Imran Khan and Garth Le Roux that remain etched in most memories. Clive Radley had the misfortune to meet Snow on their respective second XI debuts and can't recall him bowling faster. Alan Castell faced up for Hampshire in the game after the 'Gavaskar incident' – 'express pace' was the verdict. Dennis Amiss, Geoff Ellis and John Holder were equally impressed and intimidated. Gwyn Richards has a fonder memory of Snow, as he allowed him a single to get off a king pair.

For those with a longer career, such as Roy Palmer, it only got worse when Imran and Le Roux were operating together. This was a verdict echoed by Graham Monkhouse, Jim Love and Tim Tremlett. Happy days for the spectators, less so for batsmen.

Spen Cama

No HISTORY OF Eaton Road could conceivably be written without reference to the players that have graced its turf over 150 years: Fry, Ranji, Tate, Parks, Snow and Mushtaq Ahmed to name just a very few. Likewise, no history is complete without due credit paid to those whose efforts were behind the scenes: Lord Sheffield, Lance Knowles and Spen Cama spring readily to mind.

Cama was born in London in 1908, to an Indian father, a successful carpet importer, and Welsh mother, a nurse. His father died shortly after the birth of his only child and his widow re-located to Brighton. He started playing cricket at school, aged six, and he was just 18 when he founded the club with which his association will ever be remembered. As the name suggests, Nomads had no home ground to start with, but Spen would see to that.

After attending Brighton Grammar School, he trained as a barrister. While studying for the bar, he would often drive off into the countryside for a bit of peace. A regular destination was in the lee of the Downs at Fulking. There was land for sale and Cama, who had branched into property, bought it at auction. Ground, pavilion and everything else at Fulking owe their being to his deep and generous pockets. And along with the buildings and lovingly curated turf, his legacy is also one of spirit, as Dave Bowden, chairman of Preston Nomads, has said:

> All of our members strive to honour Spen's other legacy to the Club, which is to play our cricket the "Nomads way" – the way that Spen pioneered. That is to play to win, but always in a fair and sportsmanlike way – with genuine respect for the opposition, officials and each other.

Another plot of land to benefit from Cama's munificence was the County Ground at Hove. When he wasn't playing and after he'd hung up his bat, Spen was a regular at Eaton Road right up to his death, aged 92; sadly, before Sussex secured their first pennant.

Cama had no family but neither of the two cricket clubs to whom he endowed much of his estate, could have expected to be such fortunate beneficiaries. It took many years to untangle his property interests and apportion the inheritance. Preston Nomads received £7m, Sussex received £12m.

Once tax matters had been settled, Sussex were in the enviable and unusual position of being able to ignore the lurking developers and invest in their home ground. Virtually all the subsequent developments over the last 10 years, from the new south stand and seating to the changing-rooms and indoor practice facilities and much more besides, have been courtesy of Cama's legacy. A man who loved his cricket has allowed countless others to enjoy theirs, whether in the shelter of the Downs at Fulking or down by the sea at Hove.

Nobody did more to save Eaton Road than Spen Cama.

The Groundsmen

AT THE HEART of the Eaton Road ground is the grass of the playing field, and at the heart of the playing field is the square. For 150 years this green oasis has been tended by a dedicated team of men, always men.

Once the 1871 barley crop had been safely harvested, the first job was to level the 10-acre plot on which the turf from the Brunswick ground would be laid. The chalk slurry overlying the deeper chalk provided for ideal drainage in the long term: in the short term there was the question of providing a surface fit for play in less than 12 months.

The original groundsman, Peter Pearce, had received his training at Leonardslee estate of William Hubbard, and was offered the best assistance the town could find. Edward Spary, 'nurseryman, florist and seedsman' at Queen's Park was brought in to ensure that the turf would settle and knit in the shortest possible time. Together, Pearce and Spary succeeded, to the degree that within two years Pearce had been poached by Lord's where the playing surface was downright dangerous. His departure led to nearly seven unbroken decades of the Burchell family.

Tom Burchell senior took charge of the ground for 23 years before being succeeded by his son of the same name in 1897. Junior Burchell was in charge for half a century and even played twice for the county as an emergency wicket-keeper. For regular visitors he was part of the fabric of the ground. Stern and sober in his three-piece suit, trilby and studded collar, Burchell, along with his ever-present henchmen Beach and Prior, formed a formidable barrier to any child, or adult, with the temerity to move too close to the square.

What the Burchell's did, was produce good batting wickets. Not always, rain on uncovered surfaces made the art of pitch preparation more of a lottery than it is today. Generally a combination of short boundaries and dry wickets made Hove a ground more fondly imagined by batsmen than bowlers. This, of course, makes the career of Maurice Tate even more remarkable.

Should the heavy roller be required, the captains needed to give Burchell due warning. The mare, stabled behind the hotel, would be produced, harnessed and fitted with her giant leather boots and patiently led up and down the wicket. For economic reasons this picturesque procedure disappeared in 1925 and a band of volunteers were called for in her place.

To say that the Burchells took pride in their work would be to tell but half the story. Like all the best groundsmen, their patch of turf was their domain;

a living thing, they took responsibility for maintaining it and nurturing with diligence and devotion:

> Tom Burchell has the reputation of being astir as early as five o'clock in the morning, and he seldom leaves his task till close on nine o'clock at night, and no matter what time during the day you visit the Hove ground, you can always see Tom hard at work with his very loyal staff.

The 68-year Burchell dynasty came to an end with the retirement of Tom junior. His successor in 1942 was Charlie Holden, a groundsman of 20-years experience before coming to Hove. In 1955 Holden moved into the newly commissioned cottage at 1 Eaton Road, where he battled pigeons and children bent on stealing his cabbage seeds and scrumping his apples: 'I think I'm better at growing grass', he reported reflectively. In 1958 Sussex took the unusual step of awarding Holden a testimonial. On his retirement, nine years after the testimonial, he was replaced by Len Creese.

With the mare lame volunteers push the heavy roller.

Creese had been a reliable allrounder for Hampshire before the war, much admired by John Arlott who described him as 'sturdily built, strong, brave and combative'. One of his team-mates, Gerry Hill, had good reason to consider him 'mad as a hatter' after Creese had accidentally shot him in the leg while he was running in to bowl at a net session. Quite why Creese was carrying a loaded gun is unclear. After minor counties cricket for Dorset he was made groundsman at the Hastings Recreation Ground, combining this with a spell as a landlord at the *Dripping Well*. In 1967 he moved into the cottage at Hove and took up his post. Accompanied at all times by his Alsatian, Nikko, Creese immediately set about making the ground more attractive to visitors, alongside digging up and re-laying a square which over the previous few seasons had displayed a Jezebel temperament – both fast and unpredictable. The success of the venture was rubber-stamped the following season.

Working under Creese for a decade, and his natural replacement, was Peter Eaton, who assumed control in 1976, becoming, at 33 years old, the country's youngest head groundsman. In that famous parched summer, Eaton and his team won the Watney Mann Challenge Trophy (cash prize £150) for his efforts. His tenure was to last for another 25 years with his wife running the club shop for a number of them. He produced hard, bouncy wickets that were the envy of quick bowlers around the country, although less popular with the batsmen who faced Imran Khan and Garth le Roux. Eaton died at only 57, after collapsing with a heart attack at a conference in Durham. His legacy was well expressed by John Barclay:

> Peter was a great ally, a great friend, and will be greatly missed. The wickets in my day were tremendous. They had pace and bounce which is very difficult to produce and Peter was one of the best. He was a shrewd old thing who always knew what the wicket was doing and if it would turn. It's a very sad loss for Sussex cricket and his family.

Christopher Martin-Jenkins added that 'he was an essential part of Sussex cricket literally for as long as I remember going to Hove, and it simply will not be the same without him'.

Eaton's approach to the job was neatly summarised by his own pitch report, given shortly before South Africa met India in the 1999 World Cup. He had the spectators in mind:

> It's got to be a batsman's paradise. I don't think bowlers come into the reckoning really. For the Championship we'd leave a bit more grass on, but in one-day games people would rather see runs than wickets. No one wants to see, say, South Africa bowled out for 80. So, really, it's got to be as dry and hard as possible.

Next in line was Derek Traill. By comparison to his predecessors, Traill was inexperienced and had no previous connection to the county. What he did bring, however, was the ability and desire to employ new methods and technology. With one-day cricket bringing new pressures to bear on the 18-pitch square, innovations such as linear aerators and modified dwarf rye grasses were essential to speed up the recuperation process. Speaking in 2005, shortly before leaving Hove for

Houston Texas, Traill expressed his concern at the difficulties facing groundsmen, having prepared pitches for no less than 21 days' first-eleven cricket before the end of May of that year.

Andy Mackay was appointed immediately following Traill's resignation and his 15-year tenure included no less than eight ECB awards for the quality of his pitches. During his time, Mackay oversaw a 10-year pitch relaying programme, reconstructed the outfield (including installing irrigation and drainage) and led the renovation of the practice areas. In his final season of 2019 he also collected the Institution of Groundsmen Industry Award. The citation from the ceremony at the Birmingham NEC gives a good indication of the changes that have come to the groundsperson's areas of responsibility since the days of Tom Burchell and his horse-drawn heavy roller:

> The 11-strong grounds team at the brightonandhovejobs.com Hove County Ground is charged with the provision, planning, improvement and maintenance of all playing and practice facilities at the stadium, the Allfield Academy ground, the Brighton Aldridge Cricket Academy (BACA) and at Preston Nomads CC to accommodate a busy fixture list:
>
> 1) Fifty-one days of pro-cricket matches, three days of women's cricket matches.
>
> 2) Ten days of other cricket games, 50 practice days and 25 days of use of the outfield for community or corporate events.
>
> 3) Two 20,000-seater music concerts.
>
> 4) At the academy ground – over 100 match days over two grounds plus 30 training sessions and the off-field net area is used five days a week.
>
> 5) At BACA - 50 match days and the ground is in use five afternoons a week.
>
> 6) At Preston Nomads CC – over 120 adult matches across two grounds and around 40 colts games.
>
> The quality of the playing and practice surfaces are consistently outstanding, and the stadium site continues to have superb practice nets and outfield, both in terms of presentation and performance. Indeed, since reconstructing most of the cricket square over the past several years, the pitches now have genuine pace, and all of the squares and practice facilities at the other grounds are playing at their peak.

Mackay resigned to take up the role of Pitches and Grounds Advisor to the ECB, an accolade for what he had achieved at Hove. His parting words tell something of the groundsman's lot:

Being a groundsman is not simply a job that you leave at the end of each day, it is a lifestyle: something that you live and something which mentally occupies you constantly. I leave happy that I have given everything I was able to give to Sussex Cricket, holding nothing back, and I feel blessed to have been part of this club.

Being a head groundsman is an exceedingly lonely place at times, but most of the time I have had a great deal of fun and I am very proud of what my team and I have been able to accomplish with all of the playing surfaces.

The next appointment, in March 2020, went to local man Ben Gibson. He had already been part of the groundstaff at the ground for nine years, having been apprenticed at Horsham Cricket Club. After two years he joined the Hove team as an assistant groundsperson in 2011, before being promoted to senior groundsperson in 2015. Shortly after landing the top job, Gibson spoke about the pleasure he took in the challenges that lay ahead:

I couldn't be happier to have been appointed head groundsperson. I've got big boots to fill but am delighted to be getting started. It's a really exciting time to be part of the club and it's a privilege to be playing a part in that.

I've got a great young and enthusiastic team working with me here at Hove, as well as at Blackstone [Academy Ground, sponsored by Hurstpierpoint College], the Aldridge Cricket Academy and Preston Nomads where we also look after the facilities.

What he couldn't have predicted was that no paying spectators would watch any cricket at Eaton Road in his first season. But games were played and the grass still grew and the Sussex players needed to practice. Gibson had intimated that nothing could be taken for granted: certainly the plague of leatherjackets that hit the ground just before the opening of the 2021 season was an unwelcome twist of fate.

Nine head groundspeople in 150 years. Every square on every ground must have its ups and downs over a century and a half, but Hove has been fortunate in its natural advantages and the men who have harnessed and exploited what nature has provided in the preparation of sporting surfaces fit for first-class cricket. And there has been a lot of it. Over 1250 first-class matches have been played over 150 years, only Lord's, The Oval, Trent Bridge, Old Trafford and Edgbaston can boast a greater number. None of those grounds can rival Hove in one matter – only three games have ever been abandoned without play: another testimony to the drainage and those who have managed it.

The 300 Club

Trumper

BILLY MURDOCH SHOULD really have been the first triple-centurion at Hove. In May 1882, captaining the touring Australians, he led his side to the biggest victory in a first-class game ever recorded to that point in time – an innings and 346 runs. As the scores would suggest, Sussex were a weak side and the tourists very strong. Murdoch's contribution to this massacre was an unbeaten 286, the 'demon' Spofforth being the unfortunate number 11 who couldn't see his skipper over the line for what would have been in his second triple in four months.

Seventeen years later, Victor Trumper succeeded where Murdoch had narrowly failed. The young buck had been taken on tour at half money as an investment in the future; a financial arrangement that was reversed when he showed that he belonged firmly in the first XI and played in all five Tests. Trumper's reputation grew quickly throughout the tour and his century at Lord's in the second Test sealed his name as the finest young batsman in the world. To some degree the rest of the season was a slight disappointment, something he was to correct in spades three years later, but he did take advantage of good weather and a flat pitch at Hove in late July 1899.

Centuries on the first day by Fry and Killick meant that a draw was always favourite. Australia spent the second day catching the Sussex total. A large part of the final day saw Trumper gliding to his 300, at which point Joe Darling belatedly declared to try and force an unlikely victory. Sussex easily saved the game.

It was, by all accounts, 380 minutes of batting 'of the most perfect character', with runs being scored all round the wicket. The *Times* talked of his 'brilliant cricket' and *Cricket* attested that Trumper's batting was 'of a kind which could not be improved upon from any point of view'.

The postscript to the innings was typical Trumper – he put the bat he had used in his skipper's second cricket bag and a few weeks later the bag's owner found the bat inscribed 'To Joe Darling with Victor Trumper's compliments'. On Trumper the immediate effect of the innings was, however, not positive. Exhausted, he scored barely a run for a month. Even for the most gifted of batsmen, 300 is a lot of runs.

Duleepsinhji

It was 31 years before another batsman passed the magical mark at Hove. In 1930 England was accustoming itself to a certain Don Bradman, on the first of his four tours of 'the old country'. When Sussex took the field for their opening home fixture against Northants at Hove on 7 May, Bradman had played just twice, batted twice and scored 421 runs for once out.

This was a red-letter day in the history of the ground for more than one reason: the sons of long-time Sussex member, and brother of Lords Rothermere and Northcliffe, Sir Hildebrand Harmsworth, had donated money from his will to erect a new scoreboard on the east side of the ground to replace the contraption that had stood there since the early years. This scoreboard still stands. It can rarely have had such a busy day's cricket to record. A flat wicket and moderate bowling attack offered a perfect chance to test its mechanism, even if poor light and a slow outfield made conditions short of ideal. The ceremonial opening was made by one of the benefactor's sons, and he duly recorded a hit for three scored by Kumar Shri Duleepsinhji.

For the first few hours, wickets fell regularly enough even if Duleep seemed to be batting in a different game to his partners. His innings hummed along at around 50 runs an hour, the highpoint of the day being when he was joined by Maurice Tate and the pair added 255 in 105 minutes for the sixth wicket. Duleep moved from 200 to 300 in 70 minutes, thereby passing his uncle Ranji's Sussex record of 285. He was eventually stumped for 333, the highest score in a day in Championship cricket to that date. Legendary umpire Frank Chester said many years later that he had never seen batting like it – and he saw Bradman, Hobbs, Macartney and Headley.

Brilliant and flawless as this performance was, it was not the highest score of the season. Bradman bettered it by one, in a day, in the Leeds Test match.

Paynter

Eddie Paynter of Lancashire was in the form of his life in 1937 when his side arrived at Hove. The home county was in good heart, sitting second in the Championship table, albeit a fair way behind Yorkshire. Paynter didn't actually turn up with the rest of his team. Having been in action for England at Old Trafford, he had taken the midnight sleeper to London and arrived at Brighton's Pier Hotel at eight in the morning. 'This meant I had just time for breakfast and a shower before walking to the Sussex County Ground.'

Lancashire won the toss, chose to bat, and at lunchtime Washbrook and Paynter, who had found that 'the sea air gave us both a tremendous appetite for the Sussex bowling', had passed 200. Paynter was already in three figures and Washbrook joined him soon after the interval. After two quick wickets, the afternoon offered little respite as first Oldfield and then Hopwood joined the hitting while Paynter continued to strike the ball to all corners of the ground. Paynter passed his 300, eventually falling for 322 in 300 minutes, the highest score by a left hander in England:

> I had thoroughly enjoyed myself but I was feeling the effects of my overnight train-journey by the time I was lbw to a full toss from Jim Parks.

By the close of play Lancashire had annihilated the Sussex bowling to the tune of 640-8, still a record for a day's play at Hove. Paynter's role as entertainer was not finished for the day. That evening at Brighton's *S.S. Britain Ice Palace*, on West Street, he was summoned on to the arena to take the applause from the audience and in particular 'the many Lancastrian holiday-makers in the throng':

> I shuffled reluctantly on to the ice and, before I could reach the compere, completed a pirouette in attempting to keep my feet on the slippery surface. I brought the house down in more ways than one.

Goodwin

Sixty-six years later, in mid-September 2003, Sussex sat proudly at the top of the table. They needed just six points from their final fixture of the season at home to Leicestershire. Surely this time the Championship pennant would fly over Eaton Road?

On a beautiful day, with a sense of great things in the offing in the balmy late-summer air, Nicholas Sharp settled back in his seat 'and got ready to watch history unfold'. He also recorded the day in his record of the season, *Some Magic from Mushy and Much More*. A veteran spectator of 55 years, it had been a long wait.

At lunch, with Leicestershire at 111-2, the picture was less than rosy, though Mushtaq Ahmed had just collected his 100th wicket of the season. Surely the afternoon would be better? It was. The visitors tumbled to 179 all out and three of those precious six points had been banked. During the tea interval, groundsman

Derek Traill was content with his pitch and blamed the batting for the low score. Further grounds for optimism.

Traill's opinion was emphatically supported by the events of the next two hours. At 137-1 at the close, with Murray Goodwin an untroubled 71 not out, the trophy was within touching distance. A score of 300 would bring the necessary points.

At 8.30 the following morning queues were forming around the ground in a throwback to the golden days of 1960s Gillette Cup matches. On top of the pennant being within his grasp, Goodwin had plenty at stake with rumours that his contract might not be renewed.

Once Chris Adams came to the wicket the run-rate increased, and with it the crowd continued to grow as Sussex bore down on the magical figure of 300. By lunch it was all but in the bag at 284-2, with Goodwin now 143 not out. During the interval interviews were recorded and champagne corks popped. At 1.44 pm Goodwin pulled Phil DeFreitas to the mid-wicket boundary and the deed was done. The pitch was invaded by the rest of the team, the squad, the physio. The crowd rose as one and stayed firmly off the grass. At last.

Now freed from the shackles of team responsibility, Goodwin upped his pace. Having passed the team landmark, he decided to hit out and was dropped on the boundary before the 12th man was sent out with new gloves and the target of Duleep's 333. Goodwin re-organised himself and at 335 not out he was called back in by his captain. Jason Lewry knocked Leicestershire over on day three and that evening Phil Tufnell's cricket show was broadcast live from the *Sussex Cricketer*.

The man from Harare had joined the exclusive Hove 300 club, joining his predecessors from Sydney, Sarodar and Oswaldtwistle. Tommy Cook's 278 against Hampshire in 1930 is the best for a player born in the county, matched by Robin Marlar's nine for 46 against Lancashire in 1955.

-Six-

Champions, at Last

Nobody could have foreseen how all the pieces would fit into place in 2003 and make Hove the most intimidating cricket venue in England. How Goodwin would flower, ably backed by Cottey. How young wicket-keepers Prior and Ambrose would drive one another on to ever greater achievements. How Martin-Jenkins, Adams, Montgomerie and Mark Davis would produce match-winning performances and, above all, how Lewry and Kirtley would stay fit and underpin the mesmeric skills of the country's best bowler, Mushy. Adams was in no doubt as to the effect of his spinner:

> Pre-Mushtaq, I would constantly be trying to find wickets and a way of unlocking opponents. I'd constantly be feeling under immense pressure myself to score runs.

The story of the season and how Sussex finally broke their duck in the Frizzell County Championship has been lovingly told by Bruce Talbot and Paul Weaver in *The Longest Journey*. The season itself was some journey: from Lord's in April, when Sussex managed to lose a game they had largely dominated for three days, to the lap of honour at Hove in September when the Sussex juggernaut, steered by Goodwin and Lewry, ran Leicestershire off the road.

Eaton Road had never seen anything like it, Kirtley wondered if *any* cricket ground had seen anything like it:

> How were we allowed to go onto the pitch? We had a lap of honour. There was a 10-minute delay. I don't think that's ever happened before. How we got away with it I'll never know. It was an incredible memory.

Adams was later able to reflect on what his side had done and what it meant to the ground and its spectators:

> It was special. It captures the beauty of a club like Sussex. It's got that really old, long-standing relationship with its supporters. You think through time, the Ranjitsinhjis, the Dexters, the Parks, the whole history of the club…To be able to do something for the first time is truly incredible.

After the longest of waits the triumph of 2003 was always likely to result in something of a hangover. The headache and dry mouth weren't long in coming.

The opening match of the 2004 red-ball season at Hove resulted in a thorough thumping from Lancashire. Poor weather then led to a series of draws and the kind of momentum that had been so important in 2003 was never re-captured. The team was largely unchanged; Ian Ward replacing Tony Cottey the only significant alteration, but the vigour was lacking. Goodwin wasn't the same dominating presence, both opening bowlers were often absent and even Mushtaq was a lesser force. The upshot was a slip to fifth in the table and a no-show in limited-overs cricket.

Tim Ambrose and Matt Prior's battle for the gloves was resolved for the 2005 season when Ambrose left for Warwickshire. His departure, along with that of Ward, was more than compensated for by the resurgence of Goodwin and the emergence of Michael Yardy and Naved-ul-Hasan. Even the departure of Moores to the England Academy was managed smoothly when he was replaced in-house by Robinson. A climb to third in the Championship and victory in division two of the National League gave rise to a feeling that, granted a fair wind, 2006 could be a bumper year.

Back Row: Rosalie Birch, Alexia Walker, Kate Oakenfold, (sponsors' rep), Sarah Taylor, Sara Lord, Caroline Atkins, Laura Marsh. Front Row: Mandie Godliman, Charlotte Burton, Clare Connor (captain), Holly Colvin, Charlotte Russell, Emily Hopkins.

A parallel rise to the top was also taking place in the women's game in Sussex. Having been promoted in 1999, and then immediately relegated, the side was building towards being the best in the country. They had already made history at Hove in 2000, by hosting the first floodlit women's game (narrowly losing to Surrey). The dominance of the team over the next decade was almost complete: between 2003 and 2010 Sussex won the Championship five times and were runners-up on three occasions. Led by Clare Connor, the team could boast nine England internationals covering all skills from Sarah Taylor behind the wicket to Laura Marsh, and Holly Colvin with the ball, Arran Brindle with the bat and Rosalie Birch with both bat and ball. Colvin's first international game was the stuff of dreams. On 8 August 2005 she was giving the England side net practice at Hove. The following day (at the age of 15) she was playing for England, also at Hove, against Australia. The match was drawn, largely due a defiant century by Brindle.

Behind the scenes, the club was faced with one of the biggest decisions of its long history. As ever, the ground itself was in urgent need of upgrading. Stands needed replacing, amenities improving, the pavilion refurbishing and new training and practice facilities building. Yet again, serious questions were again being asked as to the viability of a prize piece of Hove real estate staying as a cricket ground. The death of long-serving patron Spen Cama in 2001 and his £12 million legacy provided an answer in the nick of time. With such a large and complex estate, accessing the legacy was never going to be quick but the two principal beneficiaries, Sussex CCC and Preston Nomads CC, were undisputed. Shortly after Cama's death, it seemed that HMRC had accepted that Business Property Relief was available to the estate, which essentially gave the club a free hand to invest. However, in October 2005 another section of HMRC was questioning the earlier decision and all further expenditure was frozen.

By 2006 the situation in Fulking was clear as Nomads had created a charitable trust to protect their money. At Hove, there was still the crucial question of whether corporation tax was due. In June 2006 the *Brighton Argus* was reporting a the stand-off:

> The Inland Revenue's Capital Taxes Office have begun an investigation into whether they can claw back a slice of the £12 million legacy in corporation tax. Sussex have been promised a decision in the next two or three weeks. Chairman David Green has admitted losing that amount would mean their plans to redevelop the County Ground would have to be drastically scaled down The legacy was bequeathed to the county when Cama, who had no dependents, died in 2001 at the age of 92 and left an estate worth £30 million. Green said: "There

have already been two separate investigations into the Spen Cama estate and we have been advised that the legacy is not subject to inheritance tax. But we could be liable to corporation tax which is why we have put any development plans on hold for the moment."

These uncertainties delayed plans that were already well developed. The Gilligan Stand had passed its sell-by date and was described, quite rightly, as 'dilapidated'. It was due to be replaced with 'a public pavilion and improved conference and corporate hospitality facilities to increase revenue streams on non-cricket days.' There were also the proposed magnificent new indoor practice facilities, benefitting not only the professional players, but also the wider community. Schoolchildren were offered the chance to see into the workings behind the scenes and what was required of top-level sportsmen and women.

In the bleak midwinter, the end of the Gilligan stand.

In addition, the committee was keen to increase spectator capacity on both sides of the new 'public pavilion'. Further doubts were cast on longer-term plans to develop the site of the *Sussex Cricketer* by uncertainties in the property and financial markets. The club chairman, David Green, expressed confidence that the club would not 'get whacked', but there was nervousness. At least the interest on the money enabled the club to return a profit of over £200,000, despite an operating loss in excess of £300,000.

In February 1999 David Stoner had presented a critique on the club's accounts for the previous year. His proposals highlighted shortcomings in the methods then in place, and led to his being appointed treasurer in 2000. A tightening of financial procedures followed, in order to ensure greater accountability as to how money was spent.

There was also the question of the freehold of the ground to consider. At this point it was under the jurisdiction of trustees acting on behalf of the club and its members. The club itself had no legal status. In 2003 Stoner submitted an extensive proposal with the intention of seeking incorporation as a bona fide co-operative society to be known as Sussex County Cricket Club Limited. This would ensure that the club, and not its members, were responsible for financial liability. The transference of the freehold of the ground would ensure the club's position as a legal entity as well as providing legal recognition of the ground as part of the main assets of the club, a route already taken by other counties such as Kent and Gloucestershire. Crucial to this procedure was the ability to prove that this entailed 'transfer' rather than 'sale' in order to avoid payment of Stamp Duty Land Tax. Once this had been achieved, the new registration took effect on 1 November 2006 and absolved the trustees and the committee and members from any personal liability with regard to the ground and the freehold,

While all these back-stage issues were being grappled with, the side were winning cricket matches. By the end of May 2006 it was clear that Sussex had re-found the formula that had served them so well in 2003 – finding runs right through the order and supporting Mushtaq as he picked his way through the opposition. Opening bowlers, Naved at first and then Yaser Arafat, proved adept at softening up the opposition in readiness for the 'rotund' magician's filleting of the middle and late order.

In the white-ball game, Sussex were proving equally effective, strolling through the south group to set up a final in late August with Lancashire at Lord's. And it was the Red Rose county that were proving a major irritant in the four-day game. After beating Sussex at Aigburth, they hung on for an unlikely draw at Hove to keep their hopes alive.

In the space of three glorious and unforgettable weeks, Sussex completely ruined Lancashire's season. First at Lord's, Kirtley's 5-27 allowed Sussex to defend a meagre 172 and lift the Cheltenham and Gloucester Trophy. Then at Trent Bridge, after Carl Hopkinson was run out for a duck, Sussex ran up 560-5 before Mushtaq took 13-104 ensuring the Championship pennant would once again fly proudly above the Eaton Road pavilion. Big runs and averages from Goodwin and Adams and 102 wickets at 19.91 from Mushtaq had been at the heart of the success, but once again support came from all quarters. It was a triumph for Robinson. He had inherited a good side, but he had tinkered with excellent effect and had recruited cleverly.

Much the same applied to the 2007 season. In the final round of matches, Mushtaq recorded figures of 67.5-10-225-13 at Hove and Sussex romped to victory over Worcestershire. But at the Oval some bad news was filtering through: Lancashire were making strong progress in chasing an unlikely 489 to beat Surrey and win the Championship. At 229 for two with VVS Laxman and Steve Law at the wicket it seemed quite possible that it could all go pear-shaped for Sussex. Then Ian Salisbury dismissed Laxman. While the Sussex players hung round on the Hove outfield and in the pavilion, together with supporters, wickets gradually fell in London. It wasn't until Dominic Cork was removed with Lancashire just 25 short of their target that the corks could pop.. Early in the season it had looked very different at Hove when the Marks, Ramprakash and Butcher, scored 407 together for the third wicket, treating Mushtaq like a net bowler before Goodwin returned the favour with 324 runs for once out in a game of 1363 runs for 16 wickets. Fry and Ranji must have been looking down with pride. Hove was still a flat track.

| *The captain and his sorcerer.* | *Jublilation in the pavilion.* |

Three Championships in five years after none in well over 100 was a phenomenal achievement. It justified all the risks and money expended on recruiting Adams, Goodwin and Mushtaq who were, in turn, ably supported by local players such as, Prior, Yardy, Martin-Jenkins, Lewry and Kirtley. Unencumbered by international calls, Sussex were able to field a settled side mixing resoluteness and brilliance. The sad inevitability was that the team would age – Montgomerie retired at the end of 2007, and Adams and Mushtaq left in 2008, though not before another trophy had been won in the Natwest Pro40 League.

It's rather sad to reflect that these triumphs took place in the autumn of an era when the Championship still had currency. The last days before central contracts and the IPL had had time to turn the old competition into a backyard.

A time when England players still, sometimes, played for their county. The days when you knew which county any England player played for. Who now knows or cares which county side owns the affiliation of Ben Stokes or Jos Buttler? Jofra Archer is unlikely to take 150 first-class wickets for Sussex even if he plays till 2030. At Old Trafford the Brian Statham end recognises 1,816 wickets for his county, the Jimmy Anderson end just 340.

Sussex's run of pennants happened just before players parachuted around in search of a game or played half a game that might give them some practice or a leg-up towards the national side. The sun didn't always shine but at least the best players were able to care about the county that had nurtured them and made them the players they were. If county cricket really matters, it can't exist just as a bloated training ground for the national side, and that's before franchises and Sussex CCC having to compete with the Southern Braves. Not to mention The Hundred.

Michael Yardy took the reins in 2009, and the emergence of local boys Chris Nash and Luke Wright, together with the signing of Ed Joyce,

The Harmsworth scoreboard receiving some brutal surgery

made Sussex the team to beat in all one-day formats. Another Pro40 title was collected together with the Twenty20 Cup. Only a disappointing showing at Lord's in the final of the Friends Provident Trophy prevented a clean sweep. The four-day game suffered and Sussex were relegated to division two, but would bounce back the following year. One negative aspect that

146

reached the local newspapers and beyond was the question of the fox – it was shot by a 'vermin-control marksman…amid fears it would dig holes in the ground.'

By now the question of the Cama legacy had been fully resolved. HMRCs questions concerning the status of the holding company for Cama's assets and its eligibility for Business Property Relief had been successfully challenged by the estate's executors and HMRC did not pursue the matter any further.

For followers of international cricket, the women's game at Hove offered a glut of spectating opportunities. Tourists from New Zealand, West Indies and Australia all played T20s, with India, New Zealand and Australia playing in ODIs.

Just before the beginning of the 2011 season, the Sussex chief executive, Dave Brooks, was hosting an open day at the ground to allow members and supporters to see what had been going on during the close season. Spen Cama's money was now being spent. The new south-west stand was complete bar the safety signs and would hold 1700 spectators. The old south-west terrace had always been at a strange angle, not exactly looking towards the pitch, which had resulted in generations of cricked necks being rubbed in the pub after stumps. The new south stand behind the bowler's arm on the site of the old Gilligan stand, was ready and 96 'exclusive seats' had been put on the roof to add to the myriad activities enclosed within its bright new façade.

Another development had been taking place over the period of the previous decade in the form of the Sussex Cricket Museum. The portacabin that had housed the library was gradually falling apart, hardly an attraction for housing valuable books and cricketana, but space had become available in the pavilion in the form of the old groundsman's unit underneath the committee room. Under the auspices of the curator, Rob Boddie, a team of volunteers catalogued the club's possessions and moved into the new space in 2011. Publishing ventures and the auction of Robin Marlar's collection were major actions that both helped fund the museum as well as develop its outreach. Reward came in 2020 with the Howard Milton Award for Cricket Scholarship.

With an outlay of £8 million the ground capacity for big nights under lights had now been raised to 7000. Those big nights were not just confined to cricket. Bonfire night became a hardy annual, drawing the biggest crowd to any firework display in the Brighton area. Then there were the concerts: Sir Elton John was a regular, joined by such as Sir Rod Stewart, Sir Tom Jones, Sir Cliff Richard, Lionel Richie and Madness. Such events may have been unpopular with some local residents and the groundstaff, but they kept the finances ticking over. Now, the challenge was to maintain a team that would attract crowds worthy of their upgraded home.

Rocketman at the County Ground.

Over the next half-dozen years, the performances on the field hardly matched the grand plans. The arrival of perennially under-rated Steve Magoffin was a huge bonus, and he led the bowling attack for the best part of five years. Joyce and Nash attempted to fill the gap left by the departure of Goodwin and for four years the county performed well in the Championship before relegation in 2015.

In the same period, one-day cricket brought a couple of semi-final appearances, but additions to the trophy cabinet appeared unlikely. Monty Panesar provided welcome change and wickets for two seasons and the hiring of Chris Jordan strengthened the side in all forms of the game, but still Sussex resided outside the promotion zone of the Championship, while a visit to the Vitality Blast final in 2018 under new captain Ben Brown was their best limited-overs performance. But 2018 also saw the full emergence of Ollie Robinson and Jofra Archer for the first time, which could only lead to a sense of optimism going into the 2019 season.

Under the leadership of Charlotte Burton, the domestic women's game continues to thrive in Sussex. The local side now plays on their own pitch at the Aldridge Academy at Falmer but Eaton Road is still a valuable and attractive venue, the Women's Super League semi-final and final of 2019 attracting good crowds.

It was in 2019 that plans for the next stages of the Eaton Road project were released. The *Sussex Cricketer* at the entrance gates, in the south-west corner of the ground, was to go after 147 years. The *Brighton Argus* gave the details in February:

The development would include a new bar and restaurant, as well as 40 apartments, commercial space and 'a much more visible and attractive entrance to the ground'. Likely to be phased over five to seven years, proposals include the redevelopment of the south-west corner of the site on Eaton Road, improving the main entrance to make it both more visible and more accessible.

Rob Andrew, CEO of Sussex Cricket, said: "Our goal is to make our club sustainable as an organisation and to effectively support our fantastic work across the whole of Sussex's cricketing community for the long-term. Our proposed Phase 1 redevelopment of the south west of the Ground will provide us with the funds necessary to invest in the further ground improvements we need to ensure our future here in the heart of Hove. We have been here nearly 150 years and hope to remain here for another 150!"

The proposed Phase 1 development will include replacing several buildings facing onto Eaton Road, including The Sussex Cricketer pub, with new leisure spaces and homes. A new conference and event space is also proposed at the south west end of the pitch, and up to date club offices will also likely move into the South Stand.

At the north end of the ground, new and improved seating for spectators is proposed, supported with bars, new toilets and refreshment facilities; and the existing hospitality rooms in the south-east corner will be replaced with new seating stands.

Mr Andrew said: "Our facilities can be improved and there are many aspects which would make them more efficient and financially effective, allowing us to offer a better range of events and activities at the ground and supporting our community work across the county."

The need for diversification still rang as loud as ever. The work of the last 10 years and next seven years is by far the biggest project undertaken in the 150-year history of the ground. Never before has the club had both the funds and organisation, maybe even the will, to transform Eaton Road and drag it into the twenty-first century. In some ways this was slightly reminiscent of the plans of Alan Wadey all those years ago. This time, the committee adopted a sensible balance of progress and history rather than a tone of gleeful destruction of the past.

By September of the same year, updates appeared in the local press with further details:

Plans to knock down a pub and create 37 new flats outside a cricket ground have been submitted. Sussex Cricket has revealed its radical redesign for the County Ground in Hove, complete with a replacement of the Sussex Cricketers pub. This week, the plans went on display for the first time to allow people to give feedback. The existing pub of the same name will be knocked down. More than £20 million will be invested in the ground and its surroundings, creating 153 jobs.

Rob Andrew, chief executive of Sussex Cricket, said he wanted the club to "secure its future". He said: "We have heard from our club members, neighbours, local businesses, amenity and conservation groups as well as the South East Design Panel and council officers and we have worked hard to integrate their feedback into our plans. Sussex Cricket supports 200 community cricket clubs and 340 league teams across Sussex, an academy training ground a centre for women's cricket, and community support bringing cricket to people of all abilities in the county."

As well as the new flat block and pub, changes will be made to the cricket ground. The old Tate Gates will be reinstalled at the ground's entrance alongside a new clock tower. The revamped Sussex Cricketer pub will be open-plan and have a terrace for visitors. The block of flats on Eaton Road will provide 37 new homes, including one four-bed apartment. Basement parking will be provided for residents.

Phase two of the development will see the club office [once the professionals' dressing-room] and south-west stand knocked down and replaced by a new main entrance, rooftop bar, and club shop. Then the club hopes to add two more seating stands at the north end of the ground, along with Astroturf terraces for visitors to put deck chairs. Finally food stands in the south-east corner will be replaced with a new 586-seat stand.

The club hopes to get permission for phase one of the project for the start of 2020, which could be finished by 2022. Then phase two of the project is expected to follow in 2023.

In 2020 two more phases of work were announced:

The third phase is for two stands to replace the informal seating area and better hospitality. The fourth phase is to demolish an existing hospitality area and build a new stand.

The work is not popular with all. Inside the ground there is regret for what has gone, and is going, mixed with recognition of the inevitability and necessity of adapting to a new age. Outside the ground there is the inevitable concern about potential negative effects on the local area balanced against job creation, increased housing and the underpinning of a business that brings visitors to the area.

As the new buildings take shape around the Tate Gates, any Eaton Road regular, or even occasional, can be forgiven for wondering where it will end. Most are aware of what happened over the border at the Goldstone and many know that without Spen Cama's legacy Sussex CCC would most likely have found themselves in the same boat.

The Sussex Cricketer replaced temporarily by a hole in the ground.

There is widespread understanding that without a business plan and steady revenue streams the ground has a limited future. There is no disguising its potential in real-estate terms. The custodians know this well, and have set in train developments to extend the lifespan of the ground. Eaton Road survived the urbanisation of Hove, it withstood the shadow of the Ashdown flats, it incorporated floodlights and new seating. The southern-end panorama is about to change again.

So what next? Banks of permanent seating at the north end? Further retail or building work on the east side? And the thorniest issue of all, the pavilion. Built in 1872 and extensively extended and realigned in the intervening century and a half, it is the jewel in the Eaton Road crown. This is not an imposing Victorian monolith in the manner of Lord's or Old Trafford but it is, increasingly, the only link to the origins of the ground. Various architects at Lord's have understood the value of their great piece. At Old Trafford this is less obviously the case, the integrity of the pavilion being severely compromised by developments over the last decade. If the current Hove pavilion were to be replaced by three floors of swish offices, what then? Would it still be a 'field of dreams' if enclosed on all sides by the trappings of the shopping mall or retail park?

Younger spectators would soon adapt and forget what had been there before. Anyone who has spent countless hours, days and years at the ground would mourn the loss of the icon. How deeply they would mourn it, is the question.

Afterword
Rob Andrew: Sussex Cricket – CEO

Fast forward the next 150 years and what will the County Ground at Hove look like? First of all let us hope cricket is still being played here – in whatever format is deemed appropriate!

One-hundred-and-fifty years since cricket was first played on this piece of ground and there has certainly been change. It is often said nowadays that the 'only constant is change' – how very true in all walks of life, but it seems especially true of cricket at the moment.

When I joined in January 2017 one of the first projects considered at the Board was 'what is the next phase of development at Hove?' This followed the ground improvements courtesy of the Spen Cama legacy, and a new opportunity was available due to the expiry of the lease on the *Sussex Cricketer* at the end of 2019. After a cursory review of whether staying in Hove was the right thing to do (it was decided it was!), we set about putting a masterplan together for this next period in the club's history during 2018. Following public consultations we finally submitted a planning application in September 2019.

The major challenge was to combine the old with the new and come up with a plan that set out to modernise yet retain all that has been special in the long history of the ground. We ultimately had the opportunity to create a new entrance at our front door on the site of the old pub, which will also include reinstating the famous Tate gates. We will retain the freehold of this land and create not only a much enhanced entrance but also a very valuable long-term commercial asset for the organisation. A modern new *Sussex Cricketer* pub will also be part of the development.

Planning permission was granted in March 2020 (just as the Covid pandemic hit) and we spent 2020 getting the site ready for construction in 2021 and 2022. Completion of phase 1 is due at the end of 2022.

The next part involves the demolition of the Wilbury offices and the creation of a five-star matchday and non-matchday conference and events facility adjacent to the south-west stand. Allied to phase 1 and the new concourse entrance, this will create an outstanding modern commercial heart to the club in the most accessible and appropriate part of the ground. On the back of this we can ensure the remaining parts of the ground retain the 'Hove feel' long into the future, including the deckchairs at the Cromwell Road end!

I am sure 150 years ago people would have been delighted to know that their efforts would still have seen cricket here in 2022, let us hope in 2172 they are saying the same.

Part II

PEOPLE

Jim Parks

"You could stand at the Cromwell Road End and look out to sea. I used to love that."

Ask anyone who watched the oldest county between 1949 and 1972, and the odds are that even through the sea fret of fading recall, it will be 'Young' Jim' who burns brightest in the memory. In the end, if you're exploring Sussex cricket, all roads lead to Jim Parks.

The road I take to on a flat October day is unmetalled. High in the hills above Worthing, it takes me to the bungalow Jim and his second wife have lived in for half a century. Jim's small spotlessly neat study reflects the unpretentiousness of the man: there are cricket photos and memorabilia on the walls, but few that feature James Michael. They commemorate rather, James Horace, his father. Pride of place goes to a framed match-by-match tally of the 1937 season, when Jim Senior became the first and almost certainly the last man to score 3,000 runs and take 100 wickets in an English summer.

Born in Haywards Heath in 1931, Jim looks light of his years. The eyes still hold a youthful shine, and only his frequent smile creases a face in repose unmarked by the years. "I've never really done any exercise, but all that bending down seemed to keep me fit. And I've never taken sugar. I've been very, very lucky." He remains, as the *Brighton Evening Argus* once dubbed him, 'Sunny Jim'.

Jim's first memory of the County Ground is when he was six years old: September 1st 1937, the opening day of Sussex v Surrey. Jim's mother had sadly died of tuberculosis just the previous autumn, and he was taken by his grandmother. He knew next to nothing about cricket and the whole day remains "a bit of a blur". But he does recall his dad repeatedly hitting Alf Gover over the slips to the boundary. Jim now thinks that his father's golden summer was a reaction to the terrible loss of his wife. "He had always been a cautious opening bat but that year, he seemed to decide to just go for it."

After that first outing, Jim and his grandmother went more regularly. They came to watch not just his father, but Uncle Harry too. Hours spent in the home dressing-room listening to Jim Senior and Harry, gave Young Jim a solid grounding in the game's nuts and bolts. Enough certainly, to appreciate the subtle skills of Hedley Verity when the Yorkshire left armer gently filleted Sussex's second innings in the last Championship game of 1939. When Hitler had invaded Poland on Wednesday 30 August, the rest of the Championship – and the country – had drawn stumps. The Yorkshire team elected to keep going in honour of Jim Senior's benefit. JH picked up £75 while Hedley Verity reaped the rich reward of 6-1-9-7 to win the game by an innings with time to spare on the Friday. By midday on Sunday, Britain was at war.

At the age of 11, Jim won a local authority scholarship and made the tortuous daily journey on blacked-out trains to Hove County Grammar School for Boys where his sporting life hit its stride. He played football for school and local club and was in the school cricket first team by age 14. As the War drew to a close, he was playing for Brighton Boys in the winter and for County Junior sides in summer. His father had played his last game for Sussex on the day war broke out before moving north for National Service and the Lancashire League, but the bloodline would continue down on the south coast. Still just 17, Jim Junior had already turned down an offer to join the ground staff at Lord's, when on April Fools' day 1949, he made his first-team debut for his home county.

For the next 22 seasons, JM Parks would emblazon a vibrant legacy on the turf at Eaton Road. If you caught him in the early years, it was his electric fielding and accurate leg spin which left its mark. Even a two-year spell of National Service failed to interrupt proceedings. The Wing Commander at Coastal Command Headquarters was "a cricket nut. I think that's why they sent me there", and Jim spent almost as much time in whites as he did in the blue serge of the Air Force. There were games for the RAF and Combined Services, and in between them he still managed to make 18 Championship appearances for the county.

After National Service, Jim continued to patrol the covers, until the morning in June 1958 at Brentwood, when Robin Marlar summarily told him he was keeping wicket. Jim had to borrow gloves from his Essex mate, Brian 'Tonker' Taylor. He couldn't get out of bed the following day and missed the next two matches. But at 27, the body still adapted quickly and Jim absolutely "loved keeping". And he did it with skill and distinction.

But it's the batting for which he's remembered with such warm appreciation. Season after season, for nearly a quarter of a century, Jim Parks was both swashbuckler and stalwart: 984 first-class innings, 30,000 runs, 42 centuries and 175 fifties to go along with 871 catches and 64 stumpings. He shone too in the then nascent one-day game and would have been a natural for T20. At a time when clearing the boundary was almost frowned upon, Jim did it often. With his open stance – "I learnt that from Kenny Barrington" – most of his sixes went flat and hard, 'inside out' over cover or extra-cover. He doesn't remember most of them now, but there is one, hit like a tracer bullet over point into the lower tier of the pavilion off Fred Trueman that remains vivid; Fred's glowering impersonation of a 'teapot', ensuring its permanent etching in the memory.

Jim, his mind still as quick as his feet were against the spinners, remembers his playing days at the County Ground as a life blessed. In the early days, the professionals were stuck away at the back of the pavilion in a windowless dressing room while the amateurs gazed out through plate glass or sat on their balcony to watch play. But apart from this early feudal geography, relations between the two dressing-rooms were cordial. They all drank together in the bar and Jim's first amateur skipper, Hugh Bartlett, was "a lovely man". And when Jim still graced Eaton Road, "You could stand at the Cromwell Road End and look out to sea. I used to love that." Jim and Jenny love the sea. From their bedroom window the Channel stretches out below them to the far horizon. "You wake up in the morning, look out the window, and there's it is. It's wonderful."

You didn't do it for the money. But Jim never had difficulty in supplementing his income with off-season work. In the early years he did a couple of winters in the laundry at St Francis' Hospital, just down the road from home. In 1951 he caught the bus to East Grinstead to work for the Conservative Party agent during an election. By 1954, and the first year of the new indoor school in the Chalet, he was doing the coaching. In 1959, via Learie Constantine, his father's great friend from the Lancashire Leagues, the coaching took him to Trinidad from where he was called up as an emergency replacement for the fifth Test at Port of Spain. Using bat and 'keeping gloves borrowed from the injured Keith Andrew, he hit a second innings 101 not out. And stumped Clyde Walcott for good measure.

Jim's England career of 42 matches spanned from his second full season as a pro in 1954, right up to the 1967/68 tour of the West Indies when he was nearer 40 and named one of *Wisden's* Five Cricketers of the Year. Two centuries, nine fifties and a Test average of 32 – good for a 'keeper at the time. Early on, selectorial nostalgia for the 'pure keeper' meant his place was not always assured, but between 1963 and 1968 he was England's number one. "Until Alan Knott came along. And that was clearly that", says Jim now with a philosophical smile.

157

The Sussex fans loved him. And, at least until the end, the club looked after him too. Jim was given his county cap and professional contract while still doing his National Service; there was a benefit in 1964; and in 1972, a joint testimonial with his great friend Kenny Suttle – "We joined on the same day and left on the same day" – which helped Jim buy the house he still lives in.

The testimonial, however, was the last token of largesse from the committee. Jim wanted another year but had fallen out with the chairman – "I still don't know why" – who offered him match money if fit. Jim was already working pretty well full time for Whitbread and decided to retire. Kenny was casually informed in passing that he was surplus to requirements. The manner in which the man who still holds the record for the most consecutive appearances for a county was consigned to the scrapheap still beggars belief: "I was with Kenny walking up the back and Eddie Harrison, the same bloke, said 'Oh Kenny, I need a word with you'. I went on, and then and there he told Kenny he was finished."

In the event, Jim's playing retirement was delayed when his old mate Brian Close persuaded him to come down to Taunton. He would play another two seasons and the odd match until 1976. His last game was at Worcester when a young Imran Khan whistled one past his nose and he finally realised it was time to call a halt. He was 46 years old. He'd had one helluva of an innings.

Despite the "disappointing" end at Eaton Road, Jim was not bitter. He always went along to player reunions at the ground and was delighted, in 1987, when the new regime at Sussex asked him to come back to head up the club's embryonic commercial department. "Going back was just marvellous." He did 10 years in the role until his 66th birthday; this time his retirement properly honoured with a dinner for 500 guests at the Grand Hotel.

Jim still goes down to the ground for at least a day of each home fixture when the Championship's on. Jenny loves cricket, and if they're not walking briskly along the promenade at Worthing and "checking what the sea is up to", that's where you'll find them. Jim has granddaughters but no grandson; his son Bobby, of Hampshire CCC and fleetingly England, is the last of the male line. No matter. As long as there's cricket played at the County Ground, the light from Bobby's forebears will shine on undimmed.

Nigel Russell

"It feels as if you're entering history. It's not a beautiful ground. A bit of a hotch-potch, really. But it's unique."

Nigel first went to Eaton Road in 1956, aged eight. Driven down from his home in Burgess Hill by his neighbours, two "lovely old dears", Mrs Manley and Mrs Morley, they sat in the pavilion next to the players' steps. He remembers little about that first game, but "fell in love with the place from the off".

At 10, he was given junior membership and would travel to the ground on his own, then steel himself to face the "fierce gatemen at the Cromwell Road End", who would invariably warn him to behave himself. This at an age when he had little or no idea what *not* behaving might entail. Having run the gauntlet armed only with his scorebook and his sandwiches, he would set up camp for the day in the Hencoop next to the main scoreboard. He logged every ball meticulously. Before long, rather than wait for the smaller scoreboard by the pavilion to catch up, the "regular coterie of old lags" made him first port of call for statistical updates. In time, he was granted honorary membership of their "gang". Fascinated, even at that young age, by the numbers and the stories they told, his passion was fuelled further when he was taken by one of his kindly neighbours to a flat on Grand Avenue and gifted a set of *Wisdens*. "Heaven."

Nigel's love of the game grew once he started playing himself. He began in the back garden with his father. His dad had played pre-war for Middlesex 2nd X1, and despite having lost an arm during the D-Day landings, could still bowl "an exacting line and length". While his father was quietly supportive, he never pushed him. His mother on the other hand, encouraged him wholeheartedly, in part he thinks, because she had a "crush on Les Lenham". Nigel's crush was Jim Parks. There were newspaper clippings and glossies cut from programmes featuring his hero plastered all over his bedroom wall. Though his mother didn't say anything, Nigel thinks she was probably a "bit relieved" when he was around 14 and Young Jim was replaced by a large poster of Avenger Honor Blackman, "in full leather".

Throughout the period of shifting hormones, Nigel played regularly for his school and local club, and in the close season there were winter nets at the Chalet under George Cox. George, another Burgess Hill neighbour, would sometimes drive him down to the ground in his "beautiful Volvo Coupe. The one with the fins." Nigel sat in the cramped backseat and was slobbered over by George's huge dog – "a St Bernard or something". The slobbering was worth it, the car was a different thing altogether to Mrs Manley's old Wolseley, and George was: "An inspiration. So positive and supportive."

An off spinner who actually turned it, Nigel's game progressed enough to catch the eye of the club. In his late teens he was playing for the Martlets and the Club and Ground. It was at one of the latter games, aged just 18, that he was standing in the slips with Les Lenham and, in between deliveries, Les enquired as to what Nigel planned to do with his future. Nigel hesitantly ventured that professional cricket was in his mind. Les asked if he had a back-up plan and Nigel told him he was thinking about the Army. At change of ends, Les gently put his arm around Nigel's shoulder and advised him to take up Plan B. "It was devastating at the time but just the reality check I needed."

Nigel served in the Army for 22 years, with postings in Belize, Brunei, West Germany, Gibraltar, and Northern Ireland as well as the UK. By the end, he was confined to the office. He missed working with the men and decided he might as well get paid decently for "pushing bits of paper round a desk" and became a school bursar.

In 2001, he saw an advert for the vacant CEO post at Sussex. He applied and was interviewed in the November. He heard nothing at all until the following March, when out of the blue, he was taken to lunch by the chairman, Don Trangmar and offered the job there and then. Don was interested in strategy and wanted someone to keep an eye on day-to-day operations and "to make things happen". The perfect role for Nigel. Unfortunately, by the time he took up the post, there had been a change at the top, and the new man clearly wanted to busy himself with exactly the nitty-gritty stuff Nigel had been appointed to take charge of. Nigel knew "from the outset that it wasn't going to work". After just six months, he resigned.

Despite its brevity, Nigel's short tenure was still massively impactful when it came to the playing side. He is modestly proud of his key role in recruiting perhaps the most significant player in the club's latter-day history. He remembers walking round the ground with coach Peter Moores during the Championship game with Surrey. Mushtaq Ahmed, on loan to the London club from the Staffordshire league, struck them both with his on-field energy. Nigel suggested that they have a word. Peter was wary at first. Mushy had a "bit of a reputation" from his Somerset days, but eventually a meeting was set up.

At *Al Fresco's* on the seafront, it was just the three of them for lunch, and Nigel decided to take the reputation "head on". Mushy quickly assured him that now "he'd found God", those days were gone. Nigel would "hold him to that" and offered him a contract where 50 wickets satisfied his base salary and each scalp thereafter earned a bonus, with a further premium for the Championship. As Peter Moores would never hesitate to remind Nigel whenever they later bumped into each other: "In 2003 that cost the club a fortune". It was worth every penny. It was not just the god-fearing spinner's contribution on the pitch, but his presence in the dressing-room, "his support for the young players, his sheer enthusiasm for the game." For Peter, it was like "having 12 men in your side".

Nigel is a man without rancour, and he felt no bitterness over his CEO interlude. Even in its immediate aftermath, he still "felt the same sense of elation" he always has done on entering the ground. "It feels as if you're entering history. It's not a beautiful ground. A bit of a hotchpotch really. But it's unique." And he was quietly gratified in 2003 to be invited by the then chairman to the hospitality suites for all three days of the Leicester game when the club clinched their first pennant.

He remains a regular spectator and travels down from the High Weald throughout the year to give of his time as trustee and secretary of the Sussex Cricket Foundation. Fan, player, committed charity volunteer and fleeting head honcho – a Sussex CCC man, through and through.

Michael Simkins

"I always get a frisson of that childhood excitement when I walk into the pavilion, and this was an exquisite sensation, but tinged with nervousness."

The prospect of prompting Michael Simkins' reflections on the County Ground was more than a little daunting. Michael, in his 'day job' the acclaimed actor of stage and small screen, is also an accomplished writer, author of the best-selling *Fatty Batter*. What could he possibly have to say that he hasn't written of already?

Michael modestly describes himself as no more than "a dilettante watercolourist" when it comes to the writing, but he is far from that. Humorous, playful, and reflective, Michael's pitch-perfect evocation of his long and loving relationship with Sussex CCC, is richly rendered in vivid gouache. For anyone who loves county cricket, particularly those whose first fumblings took place in the 1960s, the book resonates with a sustained and poignant clarity. *Fatty Batter* is no less than the cricketing peer of Nick Hornby's *Fever Pitch*. But much funnier.

My concerns prove unfounded. I meet Michael outside a pub in Richmond on a balmy October evening, before Covid-19 struck. He comes straight from rehearsal – Bernard Shaw's *Candida* at the Orange Tree – and he is generous with both his time and his memories. If he touches on tales from Fatty Batter (or its excellent follow-up, *The Last Flannelled Fool*), he is quick to stop himself and apologise. Mostly, he enchants with seemingly fresh-minted reflections.

We explore the role Eaton Road plays as a place of solace; an oasis of timeless calm in which to shelter from life's vicissitudes. Michael doesn't, at first, have many memories of using the ground as a haven, "other than that it is a haven, and I love going there", but then, with masterly timing, recalls one such occasion.

It was late summer 2007 and Michael was directing the touring production of Michael Frayn's *Donkey's Years*. He had been asked to take the helm by Sonia Friedman, then the biggest theatre producer in Britain, and now probably the world.

Directing can be a difficult job, one of trying to coax, bully and enthuse a disparate group of actors, each with their own ideas, into a well-drilled squad. A bit like cricket captaincy, perhaps. Michael got the production on successfully but found himself absolutely wrung out by the experience. He had thought of little else for several weeks. "My wife said she'd never seen me looking so ashen. I was waking up at four in the morning, sweating."

The play opened in Richmond, where it received enthusiastic acclaim. But Michael and the cast knew that it still needed tightening. And so, onto the second week in Brighton, where rehearsals continued each day in an effort to hone the finished product. Eventually, one of the actors urged Michael to take a few days off: "You've done all you can. Time to leave us alone to play it now. You need some time off from us, and we from you. Get some rest." He took the advice without further persuasion.

When he awoke the next day back home in London, his wife asked him what he was going to do with his unexpected freedom. She was worried about him and wanted him to rest up. But without it having crossed his mind until the question was raised, Michael realised that he wanted to be at Hove. "I *needed* to be there. I needed to sit in the sunshine and watch cricket and have a pint of Harvey's and a pasty. And to try and forget the travails of the past few weeks." The fact the play was showing just down the road in Brighton had nothing to do with it. "It wasn't a calculated need. It was visceral."

Day two of the final round of the Championship: Worcestershire the opposition; the pennant still within reach if the home side won, and Surrey played their part against leaders Lancashire at the Oval. "It was one of those lovely mellow September days." As Michael settled down with his first pint to watch Mushy weave his magic in the pellucid light, "I felt the weight easing off my shoulders for the first time in weeks."

They'd just got to lunch when Michael's mobile rang. It was the tour manager. There was a problem. Severe delays on the London to Brighton line meant that one actor, by chance the individual who was playing the very part that Michael had made his own for nine months in the West End, was stuck at Victoria and would miss the sold-out matinee. The conversation was brief and to the point:

> "Where are you, Michael?"
> "Actually, I'm at Hove."
> "I thought you might be."
> "Are you asking me to come along and have a go at the part this afternoon?"
> "Yes, please."
> "I'll be there in twenty minutes."

His second pint and pasty left unfinished. Michael hurried through the Tate Gates and into a taxi. Ninety minutes later, he was on stage in a borrowed costume delivering the part he hadn't played since the run at the Comedy Theatre. But the healing power of Eaton Road, even those couple of snatched hours, had worked its magic. The performance went off without a hitch. "I didn't drop a line." And two days later, in the most thrilling finale to the old competition in years, Sussex clinched the title.

A couple of years ago in chill February, Michael came to give a talk to the Sussex Cricket Society in the pavilion at Eaton Road. I asked him how he felt coming back to his youthful field of dreams in such a capacity: "Nervous" he told me. "I always get a frisson of childhood excitement when I walk into the pavilion, and this was an exquisite sensation. But an exquisite sensation tinged with nervousness."

"As an actor, one of the great things is that you sometimes get to meet your heroes." Michael met Arthur Miller several times and played cricket with Harold Pinter. But the highs of the trade are always laced with the fear of getting found out, the feeling heightened when Michael knows his peers are in the audience; first among them, his wife.

On that grey afternoon at Hove, the room was packed. No Arthur Miller or Harold Pinter. And no wife. But seated in the front row, waiting expectantly, were revered figures from Michael's cricketing youth. Not the professionals, but the still more exacting luminaries of the local club game – people like Tony Doctors and Alan Langridge, people who'd coached Michael when he was a boy. Small wonder that as he kicked off his talk, the imposter syndrome lurked in the wings.

He needn't have worried. His performance went down a storm. Rather than the usual subdued drifting off after such events, the buzz from the audience as they set off home under the darkening sky was akin to that of an excited pavement throng outside a West End theatre after an opening-night triumph.

"Sport is theatre. You should be able to make an entrance, sweeping down the steps straight onto the outfield, just as they did in the old pavilion." The 'new' players' pavilion allows for no such dramatic a flourish, requiring rather the protagonists to dogleg down the steps and onto the pitch from a far-flung corner of the ground.

But none of this dimmed Michael's pleasure when, in the brief flare of fame after the publication of *Fatty Batter*, he led the Harry Baldwin Occasionals onto the field in a charity game. This was the squaring of the circle; a sweet exorcism of the moment, half a century earlier, when at his first net session in the Chalet, Les Lenham had given him back his coaching fee, and gently told him that he was wasting his money. The Baldwins were duly walloped, and Michael got a duck. But it didn't matter. He was out there on the square, out there with the ghosts of his heroes. "With Jim and Kenny, Colin and Alan, John, and Mike and Tony".

Tim Burges

"Don't be embarrassed. If you're going to cry, cry with us."

The Nawab of Pataudi was Tim's first hero. He can still summon with ease his feeling of "Just - Wow!", when he caught sight of a padded-up Tiger standing in front of the large photo of Ranji that held pride of place in the pavilion. "That picture was huge to an eight-year-old". It was almost as if the two of them were about to set off on their princely way down the steps to the field of play.

Born Luton, in 1956, Tim moved down to Lancing three years later when his father took up the job of estates officer at the South Eastern Electricity Board. It was a cricketing family. His uncle on his dad's side was on the Surrey ground staff between 1929 and 1931 and he knew Jack Hobbs, Bert Strudwick and Andy Sandham well. His mother worked as Billy Griffith's personal assistant during the war. Tim still has the letter Billy wrote when Peter and Sheila got engaged in which he reminded the prospective groom what a lucky man he was. Tim has a brother, five years his senior and they played football and cricket in the garden and would go together to both the County Ground and the Goldstone when Tim was still in short trousers.

The Electricity Board headquarters was on the seafront at the end of Grand Avenue and in the holidays, their dad would drop his sons off on Eaton Road before work. Still well before play started, arrangements had been made to allow the two boys into the Long Room to watch their heroes having morning coffee in their civvies. At the end of the day, they had instructions to make their way down to the seafront by 5.30. There were a few times, if Parks was nearing a century, springs to mind, when his father would have to come up and drag them out of the ground. If Parks was still on the cusp, dad would stay with them and they'd all be a little late for tea.

Tim's first match was in 1964, against Cambridge University, and he can remember next to nothing about it. But that summer, two games against Surrey – in the Championship and a Gillette Cup match – are clearer in the memory. Andy Sandham was by then the visitor's scorer. At the Championship game, the family connection led to his uncle's old mate introducing the boys to Ken Barrington – *the* Ken Barrington, of Surrey and *England*. Much more awe-inspiring than being introduced to his mother's old employer Billy Griffith. To an eight-year-old, Mr Griffith "was just some old bloke. Why do I want to meet *him*?" But Kenny, that was different.

166

At the Gillette Cup game, Tim recalls a similar sense of wonder when looking across the sold-out ground to see crowds several deep watching the game from a building-site gap in the villas that lined Palmiera Avenue. The boys got junior membership for Christmas that year and from then, during holidays and at weekends, Tim rarely missed a game. Cavaliers, Championship, Gillette Cup, 2nd X1, benefit matches, celebrity games. "I remember Pat Boone catching Dexter. He seemed shocked at just how hard the ball was."

Once in a while they'd get a lift in with their neighbour, Les Lenham, alongside his great mate Kenny Suttle. Tim was, and still is, an autograph hunter and at the start of the season, he would take a new book down the road and leave it with Les's wife, Val. In the autumn, Les would bring it back with the pages filled.

An Albion fan, Tim's perfect Saturday was the train from Lancing, down to Eaton Road for the morning session, walk to the Goldstone for the match and then back to the ground for the last 20 overs. "What a day!". At that time, when the winter and summer games and those who played them dovetailed rather than overlapped, the Albion players used to come down and watch the cricket after training, and Tim has an assortment of scorecards signed by Seagull legends such as Bobby Smith, Brian Powney, Kit Napier, Jimmy Collins and Dave Sexton.

Tim did his 'A' levels at sixth form college while working part-time at a local timber works. It was at the timber yard that he lost most of the forefinger on his left hand in an accident involving a circular saw. "It didn't hurt at first. Then I got to hospital and the nurse doused it in TCP. Then it did". But once 'A' levels were done, the industrial injury compensation was enough for him to spend the next couple of years travelling to Australia and the States. On a day-off from working on the line at the Epicure Pickle Factory, Tim will always remember standing in the infamous Bay 13 at the MCG for the Boxing Day Test against West Indies as Denis Lillee ran in with the crowd's fervent enjoinder to: "Kill, Kill, Kill". Nor will he forget the mountains of beer cans left on the terrace at the end of play. It was a long way from the County Ground at Hove. Even on a Gillette Cup Day.

Once the money ran out, Tim returned to Lancing with the reluctant realisation that it was time to knuckle down and enter the world of work. He joined flight-simulator engineers Link Miles as a clerk, progressed to Head of Logistics and stayed until retirement.

Since his return from his gap years, Eaton Road has been a constant in Tim's life. As an avid signature hunter as a youngster, he wasn't one to rush out onto the outfield with bat and ball during the breaks. But he took to doing just that with his grandchildren. His sense of pride as he watched his family playing in the kid's match spontaneously shepherded by Richard Montgomerie, Ollie Rayner and Carl Hopkinson in 2007 after the Worcester game finished early with the third pennant decided, is still palpable. As is his sense of relief when, despite Mark Butcher urging him to, "Drop it, drop it" from the deckchairs, he pouched a steeper hit skywards by his grandson.

"The physical closeness between player and spectator is a big part of the magic". With the family, Tim would sit near the new players' pavilion. He remembers a late-season game with his granddaughter who was struggling with her chemistry homework. Knowing Richard Montgomerie had a degree in this very subject, Tim asked him half-jokingly if he wouldn't mind giving Domi a hand. Despite merciless ribbing from Matt Prior, Monty duly came down after lunch and spent 20 minutes going through her work. "The best chemistry lesson she ever had." Whenever he bumped into Tim after that day, Monty would always ask how his granddaughter was getting on.

The most precious memories though, are those spent with his beloved wife, Jeanne. Jeanne loved the game. Once their children had grown, Tim would finish work and meet his wife on the deckchairs in the north-east corner. They'd "just chat, the cricket sometimes incidental", until the shadow of the pavilion reached the square and stumps were drawn.

Jeanne tragically died after a short illness on a Friday in May 2018. In his devastation, the family urged Tim to go to the ground as planned the following day. They knew that Eaton Road was the one place he'd shared with his wife where there was a chance of him carrying his grief with some degree of safety. Sensing they were right; knowing there was nothing else he could do except stare at the walls through the fog of bereavement, Tim did as he was told. Nothing could really assuage the pain, but the kindness of his regular ground companions when he broke the news and warned he might get a bit emotional – "Don't be embarrassed. If you're going to cry, cry with us" – provided at least some salve.

Tim's interest in people and the game retains the freshness of his childhood; small wonder that when he takes his regular morning walk round the ground just after the start of play to greet and chat with long-held acquaintances, he only just makes it back to his seat in time for lunch. He's here for most games and helps out with the museum and the Foundation's Sporting Memories initiative. He loves the place. "It hasn't really changed. Still got the rust spots on the pavilion." And as long as "they keep the grass bank and the deckchairs", he always will. He hopes his new great-granddaughter will share his passion. He has given her a good start. Tim popped into the ground and bought her first junior membership when she was just a day old.

Brenda Lower

"It's my life."

For more than 50 years, whenever Sussex are at home, Brenda Lower has taken up her seat in the pavilion by the steps the players came down. In the early days, it was just Saturdays; later there were Sundays for the John Player, but since she stopped work, she has been an ever-present for pretty well every day's play at Eaton Road. Championship, T20, one-dayers, second XI games, women's matches – you can be sure Brenda will be there. From her 'gold seat', along with a box of spare balls, she holds an unbroken thread that goes back even longer than the half century. Brenda never takes a holiday unless it's to join one of the supporters' trips to an away game. She is almost as much a fixture of the ground as the Harmsworth scoreboard and the pavilion itself.

Born Brighton, 1943, Brenda first went to the County Ground to watch cricket with her father in the late fifties. As it happens, though she had no idea at the time, she'd been on the threshold before, as a nipper. Her dad worked for the machine tool manufacturer CVA in the foundry on Portland Road – "I don't know what he did but he always came home mucky" – and children's Christmas parties would be held either up in Hollingbury or at the Eaton Road assembly plant. After her first visit proper, Brenda and her dad were regulars. They weren't members and would sit wherever, mostly on the south-west terrace: "I remember the rows of upright chairs in front of the benches. Metal with canvas seats".

Though the early Gillette Cup games are the first on-field action Brenda has any memory of, right from the off she loved the atmosphere. As well as accompanying her dad, she often went solo. The only child of elderly parents – "I never knew what it was like to have grandparents" – the County Ground was "somewhere I could go on my own". And it was just a bus-ride from the family home by the Level. She'd catch the train to the old Recreation Ground at Hastings too, and for Saffron's Week would get a nice bed and breakfast.

Brenda went to Fairlight School – "the only school I ever went to" – and when she left at 15 started work as a machinist at a garment factory down the road at Bevendean. "In those days, the firms used to come into the schools to recruit the leavers." It's easy to forget that in the fifties and early sixties, Brighton was no longer just a destination for dirty weekends and racecourse razor boys, but a manufacturing town. Just down from Brenda's factory, on the site of what is now the University of Brighton, stood engineering firm, Allen West, at its height, employer to upwards of 3000 workers; in provincial terms, a giant.

None of her fellow dressmakers were cricket fans but that didn't stop Brenda spending weekends and holidays down at Hove. When the factory closed and she moved to the grocery department at the Co-op on London Road, she got chatting to regular customers the Smallwoods, lynchpins of local club St Peter's. If Sussex were away, she'd go to watch them at Preston Park. But whenever there was play at Eaton Road, that's where she'd be.

The Co-op had closed down and Brenda was working in the wages department at Advance Laundries when she married in 1975. Peter liked cricket, but when he wasn't working as a painter and decorator, he was playing bowls. He'd drop Brenda off at Eaton Road in the morning, head off for the greens and pick her up at close of play. It was on the bowling green that Peter very suddenly passed away. "I would go and watch him when there wasn't any cricket and I remember he came over and said: 'Brenda, I'm not feeling very well', and that was it. It was a terrible shock. But we'd had lovely times together."

With Peter and both parents sadly gone, and the Advance Laundry head office closing, Brenda's seat in the pavilion became her second home in the summer. In winter there are Sussex Cricket Society talks, regular lunches and special events.

One such special event, right in the cold heart of February when the coming season is still but a speck on the horizon, was Brenda's 70th birthday. When she received telephone instruction from the club to ready herself for pick up at 12 noon, she had no idea what was planned. Her delight on arriving in the Long Room to find guests assembled for a lunch in her honour, was unbounded. Friends from the pavilion were there as well as members of the committee and Jim Parks and his wife Jenny and coach Mark Robinson. "Kevin did the cooking. It was just such a special day."

Brenda is much loved at Eaton Road. Children from the days when they were barred from the pavilion unless accompanied by an adult and would just tell the stewards "We're with Brenda", hold a particular fondness for her. But so does everyone else. Players, ground-staff, stewards, fellow supporters, the committee; even visiting umpires. Brenda thinks it was David Constant who first handed her the box of spare balls and asked her to look after them for him. Ever since then, if a ball gets lost or out of shape, it is Brenda who will come onto the outfield with the replacements.

Brenda likes to get to the ground early, first in line for when the gates open at around 9.30. The bus pass is valid from nine, and it's about 20 minutes from her flat on Elm Grove, a stone's throw from the house she grew up in, to Palmiera Square. Perfect. For the first game after lockdown to which spectators were allowed, Brenda couldn't wait for her bus pass to kick in: "I just thought: 'blow it, pay the £2.20 and just get out there'. I like chatting to Sam on the gate anyway."

Once in the ground, Brenda makes her way to the seat she has presided over for so many years and watches the ground slowly filling. She always comes alone with her packed lunch and a cake for tea, but she never stays unaccompanied for long. With her friendliness and willingness to get chatting to anyone, people naturally gravitate towards Brenda. It's the social side that's the main thing. And she loves talking to the players. Tony Greig – "It was such a shock when he split up with his lovely wife Donna" – and Chris Adams and family have a special place in her heart, but there are countless others who dwell there too. Her passion for and loyalty to Sussex are unbridled and when it comes to the ground itself, quite simply: "It's my life."

I met Brenda for our chat on a bench by her regular match-day bus-stop and it was affirming to learn that the club cherishes her almost as much as she does it. During the pandemic, there have been phone-calls from the chairman and Luke Wright and most memorable of all, one from Chris Adams. Given that Chris left Eaton Road over a decade ago, such kindness says much about Chris and the club. It says much, too, about Brenda.

Sam Wheeler

"And what a lovely view it is on a fine summer's day looking down Selbourne Road to the sea."

Sam got his love of his cricket from his father. As a youngster, he would travel down to Hove on the train from Horsham with his mum and dad and they'd set up for the day in the north-east corner close to the nets, fertile ground for the young autograph hunter. He reckons his first matches would have been in the late Fifties when he was nine or ten. He can't remember much about the games, but the players are still clear in the memory. Ian Thomson was his favourite, along with Kenny Suttle, Alan Oakman, Jim Parks, Don Smith and Ted Dexter. And Peter Loader from the Oval: "He dragged his foot in delivery and I was fascinated that he wore steel-toe-capped boots, and you could see the metal poking through the canvas".

Until Sam reached his early teens, the family were regulars at the ground and always there for the August Bank Holiday game against Middlesex and whenever Surrey came to town. And his mum would take Sam and a couple of mates on the train to Arundel to watch the tourists play the Duke of Norfolk's X1. He played a bit too. There was little cricket at his secondary modern, but he turned out for Horsham Colts under the watchful eye of Dr John Dew. Sam says he wasn't much cop with the ball and would always save more runs in the field than came from his bat. An energetic fielder, Sam was a good schoolboy athlete, representing his school in the long jump.

When marriage came along, followed by raising two sons and three daughters, playing and watching took a back seat. But cricket was always Sam's game and when his sons got older and developed a bit of an interest, he'd pick them up after school and take them along to the ground after tea "when it was free to get in". The boys would eagerly offer to carry the players 'coffins' to their cars. Both sons went on to play for local clubs and the grandsons do the same. Sue, Sam's wife of 50 years, came from a sporty family and she too became keen on the game. Sam is a fortunate man: all his family except his eldest still live locally. The eldest moved north, albeit only to Horsham, two doors down from Sam's uncle.

Sam spent over 40 years working in the timber trade. After finishing school at 16, his first job was as an office boy at the yard right next door to the family home. He carried on working on his doorstep until "small town syndrome got to me" and he took the longer commute up to a big timber importer in London, as a sales representative. When the firm re-located to Henfield, Sam, already living in Brighton, was back working in his home county. He stayed at Henfield for 29 years before moving over the border to a yard at Tonbridge, only for the owner to decide to close the business for personal reasons. Redundant in his fifties and with still 10 years to go before the pension kicked in, Sam needed a job.

It was Sue who spotted the posting in the *Friday-Ad* for Albion stewards at the Withdean Stadium. The advert stated that in addition to the football, work might involve duties at the County Ground. Sam was a bit underwhelmed by the prospect of donning the high viz, and almost didn't go along to the interview; but the cricket was a lure and Sue can be very persuasive. He got the job and, sure enough, when the Aussies came to town that first summer, he was called in as a relief pavilion steward alongside well-known Eaton Road fixture, Brian Smith. Half-way through the day, Brian observed: "You're enjoying this aren't you", and suggested he write to the club and see if there were any vacancies. A prompt reply followed, only to tell him that regrettably their roster was currently full. But as luck would have it, a few days later they were short, and Sam got a call asking if he was still available. He most certainly was. They put him on the gate. And there he's stayed there for the past 20 years.

Right from the start, he loved it. He quickly came to terms with the fact that he wasn't going to see much of the games, but reasoned that though he loved cricket, he liked people just as much. It was a great time to join the club; 2002 and with the pennant years in the offing, the whole place was buzzing. "I just felt so privileged to be front of house on the same gate I used to walk through with my mum and dad in the Fifties. And what a lovely view it is on a fine summer's day looking down Selbourne Road to the sea."

Sam has carried on stewarding for the Albion, but there's been winter work at Eaton Road too. Painting, mending deck chairs, generally helping out the maintenance crew. "We repainted the whole pavilion one year, inside and out as well as the Indoor School." That was when he got fresh paint on Monty Panesar's leather jacket. Monty was being taken on a tour of his new club by Mark Robinson and left his jacket hanging within reach of Sam's brush. "At least I think it was mine. I took one for the team anyway." They managed to get rid of most of the paint and Monty was pretty good about it. Either way, the mishap wasn't enough for the club to exclude Sam from official welcoming parties. Soon he was picking up the overseas players from Gatwick and Heathrow. "It's a great honour to be able to help them." On one occasion, when Sam and Sue went to pick up Umar Gul and his wife, they got a taste of fan fervour. Many of the staff at Heathrow have roots in the subcontinent and when they spotted Umar, they flocked to him: "They were even trying to join us in the lift. Quite an experience." In his free time, Sam scores for the Sussex Sharks staff team in their fixtures with local clubs. "Rob Andrew plays and there was one game against Palmers at Hove Rec when 'Dizzy' Gillespie took the field. That was almost surreal."

Sam's not sure how long he'll keep going. He still hums with an energy that belies his years, but his knees are a bit dodgy. And the work takes quite a lot out of you. Observe him on the gate for five minutes and you get tired just watching him: greeting old acquaintances, directing newcomers, keeping an eye out for anyone trying to sneak in without a ticket and making sure (legitimate) cars make their way safely through people milling around just inside the entrance, Sam is always fully on it. No wonder he's still reed thin. But there rarely seems any danger of him snapping.

The Sussex stewards hold dear their well-earned reputation for friendliness. It's not always easy. "After all, it's quite an officious job." But it's one they do their best to do with a cheery wave and a smile. Keeping all the balls in the air got trickier when they took the Tate Gates down and the turnstiles with them. For a time, Sam had to operate a manual barrier – "We used to call it Checkpoint Charlie" – along with everything else. "That was certainly more challenging. As far as I know it was never the plan to get rid of the second pillar or the gates. They had to be removed to let the lorries in when they were building the Shark Stand, but the original idea was to put them back once it was all done." In the end the decision was made to create "a more open vista" by relocating the gates and leaving just one of the pillars in situ. After the Arianna Grande Manchester bombing prompted beefed-up safety measures even at Hove, the loss of the turnstiles was felt yet more acutely by Sam and his colleagues on the front-line.

"All in all, though, it's been the perfect job. I've met so many interesting people – players, Sussex members, regular visitors from other clubs". The vast majority have been as pleased to see Sam as he is them. When it comes to the players, Sam says it would be invidious to single out one of them because they have all been great, "so friendly and polite". Sam's "golden moment" came in 2003 when, with the crucial batting points imminent, the then safety officer told him to leave his post and go and join the throng on the boundary. The next day he was standing on the steps of the Players Pavilion keeping the crowds at bay while Chris Adams held the trophy aloft. There's a photograph of the scene curated for posterity within the pages of the Wisden Almanac. "Last year, a very kind and thoughtful Chris contacted me offering his condolences on the passing of my decade-long gate partner and friend Michael "Gunny" Gunn. It's that sort of club."

Sam is excited by the new developments at the ground and whether he's still wearing his high-viz tabard or taking up his seat in the Shark Stand with Sue and the family, he will welcome the return of the Tate Gates to their rightful place. Life took him away for a time, as it does with many of us, but once he'd found his way back, he's not going anywhere.

Paul Weaver

"Even with the Shark Stand and a few other changes, it's still very recognisable as it was 50 years ago."

Save for his junior membership years in the upper tier of the pavilion, most of Paul's watching at Eaton Road has been from the press-box. Now happily retired as a full-time pressman, Paul has been one of our most respected sports journalists. As well as the definitive story of the magical season when Sussex won their first pennant (written with his co-author Bruce Talbot), he has worked for a virtual full house of national newspapers, including the *News of the World*, the *Daily Mirror*, the *Sunday Telegraph*, *Today*, and the *Guardian*. Paul's writing is distinguished by its dispassionate objectivity, but "though you always try to disguise it", when it comes to cricket, he has always been a Sussex man. After all, "I was a member before I was a journalist."

Paul was born in Dingle, in the Irish Republic, but moved around a lot as a child. Early stations on the way down to the south coast were minor counties, Lincolnshire and Suffolk. Opportunities to watch first-class cricket were rare. He'd first got hooked on the game not through playing or family prompting, but through watching the 1963 England versus West Indies Tests on television. When he was coming up 16 and the family settled in Peacehaven, he was delighted to at last be resident of a first-class county.

He remembers his first match at Hove well. June 1968, Sussex versus Australia. For the rest of that season and beyond he went to every home game as a junior member. "I was absolutely thrilled to be witnessing a proper cricket team and completely oblivious to the fact that we were hopeless and would finish bottom of the Championship." 'Lord Ted' Dexter, making a bit of a comeback that year after his unsuccessful tilt at becoming the Conservative candidate for Cardiff and then crushing his leg attempting to give his petrol-less Jaguar a push, was an early attraction.

After just a term at Tideways in Newhaven, Paul left school with five 'O' levels and was pushed by his parents to join the Inland Revenue. "Their principal impulse seems to have been that once you were in the civil service, you couldn't get sacked. It didn't sound as if they had much confidence in me." University was never considered, "It wasn't a natural option for people of my generation. It was leave school and get a job, really."

Sinecure though it might have been, working for the taxman did little to hold Paul's interest and he had already decided he wanted to become a journalist. "Hoping for a bit of magic dust", he'd written to John Arlott to ask him how he might become a cricket writer. Though a little deflated to learn from his hero that there was no secret key, it wasn't enough to stop him "hanging around the press-box" at Eaton Road, "making a nuisance of myself", albeit in a characteristically "shy kind of way".

The realisation that "you can't be a journalist if you stay blushing in the corner", and his determination to "push himself out there a bit", would pay early dividends. Over the next few years, whenever John Arlott pulled up in his old Mercedes and parked up at the sea-end, he'd give the young would-be journalist a pound note – "quite a lot of money for a teenager" – to phone in his copy to the *Guardian* from the pay-phone in the Sussex Cricketer. "He hated doing it himself as he'd always want to make changes when he was reading through it". At lunch, the famous commentator would come down and relieve the Merc's boot of a couple of bottles of claret and share a glass with young Paul. "He was a great man. Very generous. And he had a real soft spot for Sussex. Loved coming to the ground." It is hard to think of a better apprenticeship.

At just 17, Paul entered a BBC National Short Story Competition. And from 10,000 entries, he won. The now defunct *Brighton and Hove Gazette* did a profile. Paul still cringes at the youthful naivety of his blithe response to the question as to what he planned to do with his future: "Well, I want to write a few film scripts and maybe a few plays for the West End. In between my novels."

Embarrassed though he felt when he came across the cutting when helping his mother clear out her garage 20 years later, the *Gazette* profile nonetheless helped launch Paul's career. While still at the Revenue, he began freelancing on sport for the *Gazette* and the *Argus*, and then, in 1970, became a full-time junior reporter at the *Sussex Express*. There, along with the usual fare of court reports, human interest stories and the like, he filed on Sussex cricket under the by-line 'The 12th Man'. It wasn't long before the 12th Man was Fleet Street bound. For a time, Paul commuted up to the Smoke on the Brighton Belle to the tough school of Reg Hayter's press agency. "A dream job for a 20-year-old."

From there, it was a stint at the *Southend Evening Echo* where he did an English 'A' level at night school and won the Astro-Turf Provincial Newspapers' Sports' Writer of the Year award. This was a prize which came with the not inconsiderable sum of £500. When his mother heard the news, she concluded this meant her son "was the best in Britain". Paul gently pointed out that his was a *provincial* award. Hugh Mcilvanney of the *Observer* and Ian Woolridge of the *Daily Mail* had shared the still more prestigious *national* version. His mum asked how much cash they'd won. As it happens, their joint prize carried the same pecuniary reward as the Astro-Turf trophy. "Well then", his mum pointed out with irrefutable maternal logic, that made Paul worth twice as much as each of his illustrious peers! "Good old mums."

The award triggered a return to Fleet Street and finally to the *Guardian*, home to his press icons, David Lacey, David Foot and John Arlott himself. It was "the job I'd always wanted". The week before I met Paul on a dank November day in the Sussex Cricketer, he had taken his old colleague, David Foot, for lunch to celebrate the West Country cricket laureate's 90th birthday.

Paul retired from the *Guardian* in 2016. There have been no screenplays, West End shows or novels. As yet. But it has been a rich and rewarding professional life and, with typical modesty, he considers himself "very lucky".

Among the players, Snow was his hero – "he had a bit of the rebel about him" – and Dexter and Parks, the players who shine brightest. The Gillette Cup matches – "Cricket's FA Cup when the FA Cup mattered" – and the unforgettable afternoon in 2003 when Sussex finally won the Championship, the games that will forever stay with him.

Now that he has left the press-box, Paul's favourite vantage point is at the top of the ground, "leaning on that blue rail next to the sight screen behind the bowlers' arm where you can see who is spinning or swinging it and before the flats went up, you could look straight down to the sea."

From wherever he watches though, Paul loves the ground. "Even with the Sharks' Stand and a few other changes, it's still very recognisable as it was 50 years ago." 50 Years ago, when John Arlott would pull up in his old Merc, Snowy would swing through the Tate Gates in his bright orange BMW, followed a little later by Tony Greig in his white Jag. And the young Paul would "run up from the bus-stop on Church Road in my civil service suit" to catch the evening session and hang around the press-box "making a nuisance" of himself.

Michael Wilkinson

"What I've always loved about the place is the sense of intimacy. The sense that the cricket is never that far away. You don't get that feeling at the bigger grounds."

Born Brighton, 1950, Michael grew up in a cricketing family. His mother schooled at a convent in East London where one of the nuns was mad about the game, and she played organised matches as a child, unusual for a girl of the era. His father had also been a useful schoolboy cricketer. Six children and his work on the floor in menswear at a local department store put the kibosh on adult participation, but he maintained a life-long love of the game.

Michael's primary school was St Mary Magdalen, just a decent boundary hit from his home on Montpelier Road. After the eleven-plus, it was the bus to Queen's Park and the now defunct Xaverian College for Catholic Boys. There was proper cricket at Xaverian, but Michael played very little; when he did, he was, by his own reckoning, "incompetent"; a truth revisited on the rare occasion he "made up the numbers" for the staff team at the local tech, where he would teach for 39 years.

Lack of athletic prowess, however, did nothing to dim Michael's interest in the game. He has been going to Eaton Road since 1964 when he watched the Australian tourists under a fiery sun from the benches in the south-west corner. It was the match when Ted Dexter's bat sheered-off horizontally, the greater part of it landing at mid-off's feet. In his mind's eye, Michael can still see the parabola described by the sundered timber as clearly as if it were yesterday. Despite getting badly sunburnt, he was hooked. He became a junior member and whenever school and his part-time jobs allowed – as a butcher's boy at the Sainsbury's on Western Road and as a paperboy for ex-Sussex player Alan Oakman at his newsagents on Norfolk Square – he was ever-present. Except for a brief interlude for university in Manchester and regular visits to Old Trafford, so he has remained.

In the early days, before he reached the age of maturity as determined by the Sussex CCC committee and was permitted to cross the threshold of the hallowed pavilion, he would set up shop in the Hencoop by the main scoreboard. Michael loves the way the sun illuminates the green expanse of the outfield, but "coming from Irish stock", if he sits in it for more than a "breath", he comes to resemble a lobster. Ever since being granted entry to the citadel all those years ago, he has taken up his station in the shade of its upper tier.

For the most part, Michael goes to the ground alone. "I've always been someone who can keep myself reasonably entertained with my own company" but sitting in roughly the same seat for 50 years means he has got to know a rich and varied cast among denizens of his chosen residence.

"When I first went to the pavilion in the sixties, it tended to be full of old colonels who seemed to start every conversation with: "When I was in Pune…" Fascinating though tales of the Raj might have been, there was a general militaristic tone emanating from the committee room, which seemed to permeate everything. The impression given that the players were mere hired hands was unavoidable. There was the time when Middlesex were practising in front of the pavilion and a stray ball had the temerity to breach the enclave. One of the old colonels, in the peremptory tones he might have used when addressing his houseboy on the veranda at Pune, barked at Mike Brearley to "watch what he was doing". Michael remembers his quiet pleasure at Brearley's polite rejoinder, featuring a firm reminder of the importance of common courtesy. "For too long it was too much of a gentleman's club. Women weren't allowed in the bar, remember." Nowadays, things have changed for the better and the old pavilion plays host to an overwhelmingly convivial and "civilised community".

But even in the days of the colonels, there was always a richer picture to be found than might have appeared at first glance. "You sit down next to someone and as is the way of things, you get chatting and you learn a lot." Michael remembers when he had just signed up for his doctorate on the socialist ecclesiastic, Archbishop William Temple. He was just pondering the enormity of the task when the gentleman sitting next to him brought out a heavy tome on the very subject of his research. It turned out his new companion was an emeritus professor at Trinity College Dublin, and an expert on Temple. He proceeded to give the grateful new PhD student an inspiring tutorial on the man and his work. "The odds on that must have been thousands to one."

Another *habitue* of Michael's 'nook', was Denis Foreman, with whom he became very friendly. Denis had come to England from the Cape townships at the invitation of Brighton and Hove Albion to play as a forward in the winter game. But in the summer of 1952, he became the first non-white South African to play first-class cricket in England. Cricket was always Denis's first love. Indeed, to the puzzlement of the Albion reception party as he disembarked at Southampton docks, Denis was carrying three cricket bats. "You do realise we're a football club?" asked concerned manager Billy Lane. Billy needn't have worried. Denis made 219 appearances for the Albion at Numbers 10 and 11. And for 15 summers, he turned out in 130 first-class matches for the county. When his professional sporting life ended, Denis became a much-loved PE teacher at Shoreham Grammar. Michael is unsure if his friend ever fully came to terms with his adopted country, but he has no doubt that in the upper reaches of the old pavilion, he felt at home.

And along with ex-players, old school friends, visiting professors and, on rare occasions, his wife Imelda, there have always been the "old Sussex boys". The sun-wizened men with their deep-rooted knowledge of the game; a nuanced and sophisticated understanding that sometimes seemed at odds with their take on the world outside the ground. Witness the "maddest conversation" Michael has ever heard between two such archetypes in the scorching summer of 1976:

> "Here, did you see? 100 degrees it was here yesterday. 100 degrees!"
> "Yeah. That's boiling, that is. Our blood could have boiled in that. We could have boiled."
> "We never had this weather when we were young. You know what this is? This is *continental* weather."
> "Yeah. You're right."
> "No, we never had this before we joined the Common Market."

You learn something new every day. For Michael, a man with a love of learning and an acute ear, Eaton Road holds material as fertile as any library.

The players who have touched Michael most have tended to be the lesser sung. Snow in full flight, and latterly the fluid brilliance and fine cricket brain of Jofra Archer, have enthralled. But the running between the wickets of Mike Griffith and Peter Graves; Terry Gunn standing up behind the stumps to Ian Thomson; the sterling efforts of Jason Lewry and, above all, John Barclay, "as a player and a man", have equal currency.

Michael had a long and rewarding career as a teacher. Until the tail end of it, when the coalition came to power and financial cuts to further education followed thick and fast, he loved it. "It was a privilege to do work that made a difference to people's lives." And when the incessant emailed diktats from panicked managers dancing to Ofsted's discordant tune became intolerable, at weekends and in the holidays, there was always solace to be found at the County Ground.

"There is a sadness at the start of each season when you look around you and realise that seats previously occupied by those you'd got to know, are now empty." Yet the gentle school of the upper tier remains in session. It has been an integral part of Michael's life for over half a century and, though he's reached the point where one occasionally ruminates on such things, and muses that if he were to be cremated "some of my ashes would be scattered there", may there be many seasons still to come.

Laurie Marshall

"Hove is just a very nice way to spend the day. And I love Sussex cricket."

Laurie was nine when war broke out. Cricket was on the edge of family life, his grandfather, a market gardener, was president of Littlehampton CC but his father, a local bank manager, had little interest. Rather, Laurie's boyhood in Bognor Regis was themed not by cricket – he played very rarely at school and when he did, he "was absolutely hopeless" – but by the battle in the skies.

During and beyond the Battle of Britain, Laurie and his friends would spend much of their time with necks crooked and eyes squinting into the sun as they scanned the heavens for dog fights. He remembers the thrill he felt when walking with his mother down his road and a low-flying Spitfire chasing a Messerschmitt 109 passed straight over their heads, "Close enough to see the rivets". When a plane came down, they would scavenge for souvenirs of war. "German crosses and Swastikas were highly sought after." On one occasion, they came upon a crashed Messerschmitt, and when they peered into the cockpit, a dead German pilot. An early lesson in reality.

Laurie could see RAF Tangmere from his bedroom window and can recall the Luftwaffe's bombing raids on the airport with the clarity unique to childhood memory. The first and worst, in August 1940, involved German fighters shepherding gull-winged Junkers '87s (Stukas) and it caused extensive damage. Fourteen ground-staff and six civilians died. But Tangmere remained operational and throughout the war, Hawker Furies, Hurricanes and the Submarine Spitfires of 602 and 616 squadrons, ensured it stayed that way. Laurie felt a sadness that so many German attackers were shot down: "I felt sorry for them. And they were such beautiful planes."

Laurie's first visit to the County Ground was for the 1948 Australians. He remembers clearly travelling on the train from Bognor and then the walk down to the ground. "It was absolutely packed." He can't remember what Bradman did but was entranced by the brilliance of Neil Harvey.

Laurie left Chichester High School for Boys aged 16, and the same year was off to National Service in the station workshops at RAF Sinderby in Lincolnshire. "I had the perfect job – machine tool operator and setter. I never had to go on parade.

Too busy." They would put out stacks of outstanding work on Monday mornings and then hide them away again at the end of the week. If the sergeant wanted them for something or other, they would just gesture apologetically at the piles of metal on their benches.

After National Service, Laurie's love of railways led to him applying for an apprenticeship with every major British locomotive builder. He eventually joined Hudswell Clarke & Co in Leeds, but found the cost of living away from home unsustainable. Reluctantly, he moved back to his childhood bedroom and asked his father to recruit him to Lloyds Bank.

His first posting was to the North Street branch, Brighton, as an office junior. What with the journey from Bognor every day, there was no chance of nipping out early and popping down to Eaton Road for the evening session. Besides, "we were too poor to even go out for lunch". His manager's options were less circumscribed. Both the boss and his assistant were Sussex CCC members and tended not to take customer interviews on afternoons when Sussex were playing at home. Laurie remembers once asking his manager if he was, "Off to the cricket then, sir?" It was only the once.

Laurie was with the bank for 35 years, ending up as Brighton area senior manager. He remembers giving John Barclay a £30,000 unsecured loan to help fund his benefit year. "I didn't hesitate. Well, John Barclay wasn't going to let me down, was he? He's never going to let anyone down."

Having moved to Brighton and the home where he still lives, Laurie became a regular in the front rows of the pavilion's upper tier. He is president of The Pavilion Rooftop Society whose articles of association are succinct: To sit together and open a bottle of wine at exactly 12.00 o'clock. "We just enjoy each other's company." When fully quorate, there are around 15 of them. "They come from all over – Burgess Hill, Seaford, Goring, Wivesfield, Worthing, Hassocks, Horsham, Haywards Heath." Laurie is the only one of their number Brighton-based. "That's why it's called the *County* Ground."

Laurie retired from the bank a little early. "Standards had dropped, and computers were coming in." While not all businesses he supported proved as copper-bottomed as John Barclay, Laurie considers that he was "a good lender", but as algorithms started to replace really getting to know people and their businesses, it was time to go. When he started at North Street, 75 people were working there; by the time he left it was down to 50; now "it's probably around 15".

There is plenty to keep him busy in retirement. Laurie's railway enthusiasm is lifelong. He is an acknowledged expert on Indian Railways and has written several books on the subject. He is also a keen collector of brass locomotive builders' plates from withdrawn engines and has them covering most of the walls of his light and airy 1960s house. There are currently 370 of them from all points of the compass, including India, China, Cuba, the Soviet Union, North and South America and Great Britain. All are lovingly cared for. "It takes about fifteen hours to polish the lot." A bit like painting the Forth Bridge.

In the summer, there's the County Ground. Since his wife's death, Laurie is to be found in his rooftop bailiwick pretty well every day of the Championship. The T20 is a bit noisy but he enjoys the 50-over matches. "The Royal London nicely fills the day."

Laurie loves the ground. He can catch a bus down the road from his house at the top of Dyke Road and be sat among fellow members of the Rooftop Society within 25 minutes. He likes the fact that nothing much has changed, especially the old pavilion. "I remember a game when Peter Roebuck was given out controversially. As he stormed off, he took a swipe at the pavilion gates and some wag called out, 'Hey, steady on, Roebuck, you'll bring the whole thing down.'"

Favourite players have been Tony Greig and 'Lord Ted' Dexter. "He was amazing. Just a forward defensive prod that frequently went for four. An imperious sort of man. Not someone you'd have in your pocket." The Vicar of Bognor, Reverend Snow, was a familiar sight on the streets of Laurie's hometown and his son John, "with his silky run up", is another who stays in the memory. Above all, there is the sentiment shared by so many: "Hove is just a very nice way to spend the day. And I love Sussex cricket."

Laurie Marshall sadly died, June 9th, 2021. He was 91.

Peter Graves

"The harem was absolutely stunning. It included Benazir Bhutto. They looked like princesses…well, they were princesses. 'Only at Hove' we used to say."

At 13, Peter came to cricket relatively late. An only child brought up in a flat just a long throw from the Tate Gates, there was play-ground football and cricket, and his mum would throw him catching practice in their small back garden – "six with your right hand, then six with your left" – but there was little 'proper' cricket at the start. Like most Secondary Moderns, Hove Manor wasn't a cricket school. If it hadn't been for one man, it all might never have happened.

'Basher Bates', the uncle of Sussex quick, Don Bates, "was a man driven by a love of the game" and, against the odds, secured school funds to take a "few likely lads" to the indoor school in the Chalet at Eaton Road. "This was very unusual in those days for a state school." When weather allowed, Basher would march his charges up to Hove Rec to feel the grass beneath their feet. That same year, Peter's uncle enrolled him in Easter nets on the outfield at the Sea End under Rupert Webb, a man with "a gentle way about him". Soon a junior member, Peter would go up to sit on the benches in the south-west corner and absorb the "rich tapestry" of the game. He remembers Don Smith taking Bomber Wells apart. And "with no idea he was an amateur or what that meant", Hubert Doggart with his "strange multi-coloured cap". Peter thought Hubert looked "a bit fat for a sportsman".

'Basher' had seen something in the young Peter on the asphalt; George Cox and Rupert Webb up at the ground, did too. And they went with what they saw. "It wouldn't happen now", Peter reckons. At 15 he was playing for South of England Schools, alongside Alan Knott and future Manchester United centre-half, David Sadler. On leaving school, he joined the ground-staff. There was a lot of repairing deck chairs, carrying the senior players' bags and picking up litter under the eagle-eye of Colonel Grimston, but there was also regular practice and games for the Club and Ground. Not a bad first job for a 16-year-old.

Graves served the county for 15 years. In his first month, he remembers being barked at by his fellow left-hander and erstwhile hero, Don Smith: "Take your hands out of your pockets, Graves". Other than that, he was made welcome and settled easily. By 1965 he had made his first-team debut, picked as a slow left armer and batting at 11. In the changing room before that first game, the skipper, Lord Ted, had no idea who he was. He bowled just five overs and took one wicket. "Stanley Jayasinghe; a long-hop, and he hit it so hard it knocked Les Lenham off his feet taking the catch."

Quickly though, his batting took over. When Sussex beat the West Indies in 1966, it was "the first time I felt fear; realised a ball could kill you", but Peter top-scored and cemented his place in the side. And he remained pretty much an ever-present until 1980 when a finger injury inflicted, not by "Wayne Daniel bowling like lightening at the other end", but the medium pace of "Mike Selvey, of all people", led to his retirement.

Peter's record is impressive: nearly 300 first-class games and over 200 one-dayers, Sussex Player of the Year in 1974, brilliant gully fielder, official MCC standby to the England tourists down under in 74/75 and vice-captain to Tony Greig, who was often absent on Test duty. As regular on-field captain of the side, Peter did much to prepare for John Barclay's Championship challenge in 1981; not least in helping bolster Imran Khan's surprisingly fragile confidence. Imran was "someone with so much natural talent but who just didn't have any belief in himself."

Peter loved it. "We always tried to play positive cricket and enjoy the game. Not all counties were the same. What better way to spend the summer?" The success of Peter's 1978 benefit signalled that his enthusiasm was reciprocated by both supporters and a local garage, Southwick Motors, who sponsored his orange Mitsubishi Colt Celeste. He played with some great players. Of his team-mates, Dexter stands out in terms of class. Javed Miandad, Kepler Wessels and Ken McEwan too. But it's Jim Parks who leaves the most lasting memory. "I remember batting with him and thinking 'Christ, he makes it look so easy.'"

To a lad whose geographic grid had been pinned to the square half mile bordered by Selbourne, Church, Connaught and Eaton roads, getting around the country was a boon rather than a chore, especially once the nation's motorway network extended beyond the M1, and road travel replaced dashing for trains. Norris Rothwell, a keen volunteer, would go on ahead with the kit in his Land Rover and the players would follow under their own steam. Peter, John Spencer and Jim Parks formed a travelling triumvirate. They would plan routes in Jim's white Ford Corsair to allow for dropping in on what were "euphemistically called 'installations'"; their job to check that the newly-launched Stella Artois was "going alright". That way, Jim could touch base with his other job as area rep for Whitbread.

When Norris passed away, chairman and local garage owner, Alan Caffyn, came to the rescue and bought the club a van. Peter became the lead driver with Tony Greig his nominal co-pilot. "We laid a mattress on top of the kit bags in the back and Tony would have a kip most of the way." Once the skipper graduated to his sponsored Jaguar Mark 10, Spud Spencer shared the driving. "You didn't do it because you were getting paid for it. You did it because you loved it. Lucky enough to be playing sport."

And if in the off season you had to find a job, that was alright too. It would prepare you for when the playing career ended. Peter had no trouble finding winter work. In the early years he worked for Corralls, the Coal and Coke Merchants at Turberville Wharf, Southwick. Rupert Webb, by then regional manager for Coralls, engineered openings for Peter and Kenny Suttle, Peter to the dispatch office and Kenny to the weighbridge. Peter progressed quickly to branch manager of the Lancing office, a decent salary and company Ford Anglia. "Life was good at 21."

Later, he would winter in the southern hemisphere as Orange Free State's first overseas professional. The Cape was a long way from the flat in Selbourne Road and learning Afrikaans was "daunting at first", but Peter's openness to new experiences helped him flourish. He enjoyed eight seasons for the state with over 1000 first-class runs and three centuries. More importantly, he also met his future wife and mother to their five children.

Peter admits to not taking much notice of the ground when he was playing. "It was a nice place, and the members were friendly", but first and foremost it was a place of work. "We were oblivious. Like most professional sportsman you lived in a bubble…it's only when you get a bit older that you start to take more of an interest in life in general." But he does remember how the new flats at the Sea End seemed to "change the dynamics of how the ball swung". Before they went up, "the wicket would suddenly appear to turn green at certain times of day and the ball would make little indentations in the pitch. If the tide had come in at six o'clock, why did it change then? There has to be something in it."

While the physical make-up of the ground might not have made much impression, the tone of the place did. Peter never liked the side-on view from the players' balcony and tended to fall asleep while waiting to bat so would stir himself by walking around the ground and chatting to the spectators. A vivid memory is watching Imran Khan's seraglio sunning themselves at the Cromwell Road End. Imran's on-pitch lack of confidence certainly didn't seem to extend off it. "The harem was absolutely stunning. It included Benazir Bhutto. They looked like princesses… well, they were princesses. 'Only at Hove' we used to say."

After retirement, Peter moved north. Not far north, just south of Dyke Road; still within easy walking distance of the ground. He remains a "Hove boy". The social organiser of a group of former players who meet regularly, Peter always keeps a quiet look out for those he suspects might feel most acutely the loss of camaraderie they had as players.

Now well into his eighth decade, Peter could easily pass for 15 years younger. After spells as a ski-tour organiser and as the England rep for an Indian bat manufacturer, he started his own business with a partner and still co-runs it today. And if that wasn't enough to keep him active, nine grandchildren certainly keep him on his toes.

He is a regular at the ground. Walking down there is "a real pleasure, just as it used to be walking down to the Goldstone." He can be found usually at the top end, leaning on the rail near the sightscreen. Sometimes he'll be with an old team-mate; he's got "Snowy out of the house" over the past few years. But whoever he's with, he'll invariably be chatting. "Being a local person, you meet people you know, and they want to talk to you." Considerate man that he is, he rarely refuses.

As time marches on, the spectre of domicile downsizing lurks, and the Hove boy is eyeing a flat overlooking the ground or further south on the seafront. Wherever he ends up, long may he continue to frequent the field that has been part of his life for 60 years and counting.

Frances Low

"What can be better on a bright summer's day than sitting at the County Ground enjoying first-class cricket?"

Frances came to cricket through watching the home Ashes series on the television in the summer of 1961. There was no cricket at St Mary Magdalene's Primary school, nor with the nuns at Our Lady of Lourdes Convent, where Frances went at 11 on a local authority scholarship. There was no particular family interest, either. But something about those grainy black and white images intrigued. By the end of the summer in which Richie Benaud's tourists retained the urn, Frances had figured out for herself how the game worked, even if she was as yet ignorant of the historic significance of the tiny trophy.

Interest piqued, Frances paid her first visit to the County Ground the following year, aged 12, with her mother. They sat on the benches in the south-west corner and the atmosphere as much as anything, had her hooked. For Christmas, she was given junior membership and the next season would regularly spend the day in the Hencoop. Maths was her subject at school, and she shared the game's fascination with figures and taught herself how to score. During term-time, she went mostly alone; a 13-year-old girl on her tod with her scorebook, an early indicator perhaps of Frances's singular self-sufficiency.

In the holidays, friends would sometimes join her, and once Tony Greig made the team, she often found herself surrounded by classmates, "hormones bubbling", to mutually "swoon over" the new blond Adonis. They were all there in the Hencoop when Greig got his first century on his home debut against Lancashire and Brian Statham. "What an occasion!" And there were others from those early years: West Indies in 1963 and 1966, "Hitting flat sixes into the pavilion still bring back a thrill."

After 'A' levels, Frances trained to be a maths teacher. Her first job took her to the Thomas Peacock School at Rye in the far eastern reaches of the county; geographically closer to Canterbury and Kent CCC than Eaton Road. But just as when she had reached 14 and was allowed into the pavilion, Frances had stayed loyal to the Hencoop, so her allegiance to her home county remained solid. In the holidays, she would be down at Eaton Road with her scorebook, and when her next job brought her back to Brighton, she was home for good.

On returning, Frances finally moved on from the Hencoop and took up a seat in the deckchairs in the north-west corner where she soon built up a cadre of new friends. Many of them were women, all were members, and all were increasingly exercised by the dearth of facilities in the pavilion serving their gender.

It was 1975 and second-wave feminism was at its height. Frances "was fired by it. Assertively so." With her friends, Frances decided it was high time the male bastion of the committee room was breached. After all, women formed a significant proportion of the membership. Frances was chosen as their representative, and they all steeled themselves for what they knew would be a long campaign. So it proved.

There were few places where the bulwarks of chauvinism were more firmly entrenched than the Sussex CCC committee room. For starters, the rules had to be changed as only male club members could stand. It took them three full years to win that battle. "Hurrah!" But it was not over yet. The first tilt at committee election fell short, but Frances is not the type to give up easily. At the second attempt, she was voted in comfortably. The first woman in the club's history to join the committee.

"At first it was difficult". There certainly weren't any copies of *Spare Rib* or The *Female Eunuch* lying around the Long Room, and she would "bridle at the assumption" that she was invariably assumed to be, "the cleaner, one of the catering staff or just there to sort out the flowers."

But she remained undaunted, and before long, her competence and commitment made it clear to all that she had a valued place at the table. She played a key role in awakening the club to the need to develop its commercial activities and was instrumental in setting up the first club shop. She enjoyed it, travelling to the out-grounds with their caravan, and she became sufficiently established to comfortably survive the pruning of the committee from 20 to 12; though even then, she "remained excluded from playing matters which were sorted by the secretary and a small inner male caucus."

In all, Frances served for 18 years. By the end, the whole tenor had changed markedly for the better. With the demands of her work as head of maths at Roedean School, she was unable to give as much of her time as she felt was needed and she left shortly before the Tony Pigott purge. "The time for a more professional approach had come."

Frances lives a full life. She is official scorer for her local team, Rottingdean CC; the venerable ground (first recorded match: 1802) on the edge of the Downs and just up the road from her home. It was from here that the legendary biggest hit in the history of cricket was made when a batsman scored 67 off a single shot. Seventy odd years before boundaries were introduced, the ball hit was down one slope only for a fielder to throw it in so wildly that it disappeared down the other side and required nearly the whole team throwing in relays, to return it to the wicket-keeper. Though there have been no such thorny score-book challenges for Frances, her role nonetheless takes up a lot of time.

But she still gets down to the County Ground for pretty well every Championship game. She sits now in the upper deck of the pavilion, and though she comes alone, her husband having little interest in the game, she enjoys the company of fellow members, some of whom she has known since primary school days. She often bumps into Michael Wilkinson, "We used to go round to his house after school when we were at St Mary Magdalene's. His mother always gave us fantastic teas with wonderful cake."

It is this sense of continuity that forms a big part of the allure: "The peace and quiet of the County Championship is wonderful. You can almost see all those legendary Sussex cricketers of old batting or bowling once again." Who says there is no houseroom for the poetic in the soul of the mathematician?

Holly Colvin

"While I was playing there was talk of moving to out of town. I'm really glad that didn't happen. It would have lost a lot of its charm."

Holly speaks to me via Zoom from Dubai, where she has spent the last five years as Women's Cricket Manager for the ICC; the lead on pretty well everything women's cricket from governance and regulation, to organising international tournaments, drawing up the global calendar, and developing and resourcing women's and girl's cricket in associate nations from Argentina to Zambia. It's a bigger stage than Eaton Road, but Holly remembers her beginnings with a fondness palpable even across our stuttering internet connection.

Her earliest ground memories are of County trials in the indoor school, but they remain hazy. More vivid are those of the club's annual pre-season photo, when the whole the playing squad, from the professionals to the boys' and girls' under-11's, would be herded onto the outfield in the spring sunshine. "You'd rock up in your whites and it'd take ages trying to fit everyone in. My mum has got a selection from Under 11's and it's fascinating to see how we all changed." She remembers too her first match as a spectator in 2004 for the first ever 20-over International, when England Women played New Zealand. "One of the New Zealanders was running sprints on the outfield before the game. The Beep Test was big back then and we were all sat together chorusing the sound effects. Really stupid!". The 'all' Holly refers to, were her Sussex Girls' team-mates; when it came to playing the game, she spent most of her time with the boys. In those embryonic days for both academies and women's cricket, the Sussex Academy comprised: "Just me and Sarah Taylor and about ten 15-to-18-year-old lads."

Less than a year after that inaugural T20 and aged just 15, Holly had been plucked from the neophyte ranks and was stepping out onto the Hove outfield to make her England debut. In a Test match against the Australians. It was an almost surreal initiation. Holly had been summoned to the nets the day before the game to help the England team prepare to face to Shelley Nitschke, the world's leading left-arm spinner. She travelled home that evening nursing little more than the solid but small satisfaction of having got Charlotte Edwards out. Nothing prepared her for what came next.

She still remembers the confused look on her mum's face that evening when she handed Holly the phone. "They asked whether I was free for the next four days. I first assumed they wanted me to help organising the drinks or something." Dumbfounded doesn't cover it when told they wanted her to actually play. In the event, the short notice worked in her favour. "I'd barely played for the Sussex first team, and I had absolutely no idea who I was up against. I just bowled the ball." And she did so with immediate success, taking 3-67 in the visitor's first innings.

Holly went onto to enjoy a hugely successful career with Sussex, the Braves and England. There were five Tests, 72 ODIs and 50 T20s for the national side with 173 international wickets. She was a key member of England's World Cup winning side in 2009, taking nine wickets at 18 and was the leading wicket-taker in the inaugural World Twenty20 the same year. For the generation who followed her at the County Ground, Holly was an inspiration. One of these, Georgia Adams, told me: "I can never understand why Holly doesn't crop up on those lists they do of the top England players of all time. For us she was a hero. Such a great bowler."

And she loved playing at Hove. "We started playing one game a year there and it was a real privilege. We usually played on one side of the square and the short boundary added another nuance and challenge. A lot of people don't like bowling up the hill, but I liked it. I had quite a good record there." In List A matches alone, 23 wickets at 10.52 and best bowling of 7-3; 'quite good' is perhaps being overly modest.

In terms of her future career, there was one event in particular that had perhaps as much impact as playing the game. When Holly was with the Academy, there was a personal development strand to the learning, led by Kate Green, "a wonderful lady". Kate charged her young tyros with running a community project and they all plumped for hosting a charity cricket match. "That project was amazing. We ended up speaking to everyone back-of-house – the Head Chef, the facilities manager, the cleaners, the stewards – the people who are absolutely crucial to running the business. Rather than just turning up for training and then going home, it made you feel part of the club. For me, that was a real turning point."

Holly used this formative experience in her successful interview for the ICC and has drawn on it ever since. She has loved her time in Dubai – "It's like marmite but I'm a believer that things are what you make of them" – but when I speak to her, she is waiting for quarantine to be lifted so she can move to Birmingham to take up her next challenge: running the cricket competition at the 2022 Commonwealth Games; "an opportunity too good to be missed". Everything about Holly suggests she will grab it with both hands. From helping to organise a charity game for army veterans at Eaton Road, to the first ever Women's T20 Tournament at the Games, it would be no surprise if she follows up doing the same at the 2028 Olympics.

But wherever Holly ends up, Hove will always have a special place in her heart. "I really do like the ground. There was talk of moving to out of town. I'm really glad that didn't happen. It would have lost a lot of its charm. Nowadays, there's a bit of 'stadium' to it, but it's still got that intimate, relaxed, kind of family feel."

Don McCrickard

"I won't tell anyone, if you don't."

Born in London in 1936, Don grew up in Burgess Hill where his parents ran a general store. He schooled locally and then, after the Eleven Plus, moved on to Hove Grammar. Jim Parks, a fellow 'train boy', was in the fifth year when Don started; future Sussex quick Don Bates, whose uncle 'Basher' Bates taught PT at the school, was a year behind Jim.

Don's father was a "cricket and football addict". Working in the shop ruled out joint trips to matches, but he would take a break to hurl a tennis ball against the garden wall for his young son to take the return catches. Don played both football and cricket with distinction. In winter, he turned out for Brighton Boys and Haywards Heath FC in the old Metropolitan League, where Jim Parks was a team-mate. In summer, he started out as a scorer for Burgess Hill, but was playing men's cricket by his early teens.

Don's first visit to the County Ground was alone. Monday, 7 June 1948. A school day. And day two of Sussex v Australia, 'The Invincibles'. Don didn't let on he was planning to play truant; his dad assumed the teachers were being enlightened in giving the boys the day off to watch the great Don Bradman and his son wasn't about to tell him otherwise. When Don entered the ground from the Cromwell Road End, "It was heaving". He set himself up with his pack lunch and a cushion and leant against the heavy roller parked by the main scoreboard. No sooner had he settled in than who should walk by with that unmistakable sergeant-major gait, but 'Basher' Bates. Basher glanced down briefly and without breaking stride, said from the side of his mouth, "I won't tell anyone, if you don't", before continuing his march round the ground.

Bradman secured his century, and then Don watched enthralled as the 18-year-old Neil Harvey elegantly dismembered the Sussex attack before Ray Lindwall skittled the home side in their second innings. All over in two days. When he got home, Don reported to his dad that he hadn't been that impressed with Bradman; "I thought he looked a bit sluggish on his feet". But he was full of the young left hander. Harvey's batting was one thing, his fielding something else. "The enchantment of watching him swooping over the outfield and then that hard flat throw right over the stumps, has always stayed with me." That first game "whetted the appetite".

By his late teens, Don's own game had progressed with school and local club. In 1954, he joined the Sussex ground staff. He would travel down by train or bicycle until he bought his first car – £10 for an old Austin 10 (gravity fed). With fingers firmly crossed, he'd urge the old motor up Clayton Hill, before gliding down to Eaton Road. "I remember getting my first pay packet from Jim Langridge in a brown envelope, £3 10 shillings. I'd have done it for nothing." But he earned it, stacking and repairing the iconic blue and white deckchairs, painting and erasing white lines, clearing up litter and mending the nets. Along with half-a-dozen or so other "lusty youths", there was a lot of pushing the same heavy roller he'd pitched camp against on that first visit in 1948. It was even heavier than it looked.

There was professional coaching too. Ted James told him that as a bowler he was a 'one-trick pony' and taught him the yorker and the in-swinger. There were games against local sides for the Club and Ground and bowling in the nets to the likes of David Sheppard and Hubert Doggart. "We were cannon-fodder really."

This first taste prompted dreams of becoming a professional player, but Don's father firmly deterred him. It wouldn't make much sense to be looking for his first 'real job' in his thirties. He went off to university. In summer breaks he would continue to bowl in the nets to the pros. He remembers a young Ted Dexter practising his driving and hitting Don and his fellow foot soldiers from the top of the ground in the north-east corner down to the distant boundary in the far south-west, "The ball never leaving the ground".

Don reflects fondly on his couple of seasons on the ground staff. There was at the time "a certain edginess among some of the pros who resented the amateurs swanning down from university in June and taking their place in the side." That didn't affect Don. He was a local boy, and anyway unlikely to usurp anyone's spot in the first team. It was pretty well the "perfect summer job". But his father's advice to "get yourself an education", would prove to be spot on.

Don's early career took him to the United States and later Australia, where he played club cricket for St Kilda where he remembers being almost brought to tears by his fruitless efforts to get past Bill Lawry's broad bat. He returned to the UK into a full-blown recession and "unable to get a proper job", resorted to management consultancy. One assignment led to him becoming the first non-American CEO of Amex UK. "Before they invited me to New York to offer the job, they warned me that the new European headquarters would not be in London. They asked if I knew of a town called Brighton". He did indeed.

Don was nervous at first about justifying the huge expenditure the new building represented; sufficiently concerned to insist the architects ensured the top floor was constructed so as to allow it to be converted into flats, in the event he failed to "get enough passengers on the ship". He needn't have worried. In short order, the building variously described as the Wedding Cake and something out of *Thunderbirds*, played host to 3000 staff. The biggest employer in Brighton.

Don wanted his new domain to be at the heart of the town, no fly-by-night multinational satellite, but a permanent provider of local livelihoods. The gleaming headquarters was a long way from the general stores in Burgess Hill, but he remained a Sussex boy at heart, after all. And what better way to forge community links than through teaming up with Sussex CCC and Brighton and Hove Albion? The fly in the ointment to this aspiration was that the chairman of American Express, Jim Robinson, was American and knew next to nothing about 'soccer' and absolutely nothing whatsoever of cricket. Don was determined though to get his blessing. And when Robinson flew over to check out the new headquarters, Don arranged a lunch at *English's*, to meet Tony Greig and Mike Bamber, chairman at the Goldstone. Jim Robinson's travelling companion was none other than Jack Nicklaus, over for his annual visit to attend Wimbledon and play the Open. Don had worked with Jack for some years, hosting the great champion's ambassadorial role with Amex. It struck him that a little help from the world's best golfer might go a long way. A quiet chat before lunch swiftly secured the Golden Bear's moral support.

Lunch didn't start well. The head man from New York was "screwing up his nose at the idea of an Amex/Sussex/Albion enterprise" right through the main course. But when right on cue, Jack interjected with: "I don't know why you're not grabbing this with both hands, Jim", the tide turned. By the time they reached the brandy and cigars, Don had secured a pledge of $50,000 each for Sussex CCC and the Albion, equivalent to half a million in today's prices. Alas, a few weeks later, news of Kerry Packer's controversial circus broke, with Sussex's own blond Adonis the ringmaster. Amex's New York PR people killed the project. They knew nothing of cricket, either.

Despite that hiccup, 40 years later Amex in Edward Steet remains the biggest private sector employer in the city. The original building has gone, but the city breathed a sigh of relief when the decision was made to build a new headquarters on the same site. The house that Don built remains. And the Albion have the Amex stadium.

With American Express European headquarters firmly established, Don moved on to a long career as an international banker and government advisor, including a stint as a personal consigliere to Margaret Thatcher. Latterly, he served as the financier George Soros's Senior London Non-Executive Director. He finally retired in 2018, aged 82.

One of the founders and vice presidents of the Sussex Cricket Foundation, Don can be found in his gold seat in the pavilion on most Championship days, and though "I'm a cricket purist", he enjoys the T20 nights too. On Championship afternoons, gazing across to where he first set up camp beside the main scoreboard that June day in 1948, he can almost see the ghost of Neil Harvey prowling the outfield. Sometimes, it feels as if he has never been away.

John Spencer

"I just loved the place. Loved going. Still do."

John 'Spud' Spencer is a Brighton Boy, "through and through". Raised in his early years just a 10-minute walk from the County Ground, he put down his first roots in the game on a more prosaic patch of green. The family home at Cissbury Road was just a gentle lob to the 'keeper from what is now BHASVIC field. Little more than a toddler, John would hang around watching the older boys playing and then join in. It wasn't a cricketing family. John's father was more for encouraging schoolwork. He'd left the Navy in his late thirties and, having been made to finish school at 14 by a father "who didn't believe in education", he lacked qualifications and found it difficult to find a fulfilling job. Little surprise then that the one message he drummed into his three boys was to do their best and get their qualifications. "Once you've got them, they can't take that away from you."

At seven, the family moved to Preston Drove and though the Jesuits might have deemed it too late, under the expert eye of Mr White at Balfour Juniors, John started playing the game properly. John remembers his first game at Eaton Road clearly. July 1959, when his friend Raj Sukra's dad took them to watch Sussex play India. They sat on the boundary on the in the south-west corner and played their own version of the game, with a lolly stick and penny. A couple of the players came over to chat – "I can't remember who. Probably Les Lenham. He was always chatty." And though he "wasn't that excited by what was going on out in the middle", John just "loved the day".

He was given junior membership for Christmas and for the next six seasons, he went along to the ground all the time. Sometimes, straight after lessons finished, Mr White would take him on the back of his motor-bike – "no helmet, of course" – but usually it was "Shanks's pony". Except during Saffrons' Week when, aged 10 that first year, John would catch the train to Eastbourne accompanied only by his tomato sandwiches – "always tomato sandwiches, sliced white bread" – and watch all six days.

At the County Ground, like most at that age, it was more about playing stump cricket with a tennis ball, than watching. At lunch, they'd race to nab the one available net at the north end. If another mob got there first, no matter. There was the outfield with the litter bins for stumps and then behind the main scoreboard during play. Unless Parks or Dexter was batting, in which case they would cluster on the boundary to watch their heroes.

Then there was the Tizer Challenge. "We all used to bring a bottle and the winner was the one who finished it by the end of play but started it last. One lad used to hold out and guzzle it down in about two minutes just before stumps. Went thirsty the whole day!", marvels John, not a man to defer slaking a thirst a moment longer than absolutely necessary.

By the time John moved onto what was then Brighton, Hove and Sussex Grammar School for Boys, his own cricket was progressing apace. Mr White had taught him the out-swinger and now his new PT teacher, Mr Smith (Mike Smith, later football manager of Hull City, Wales, and Egypt) taught him the off-cutter. "Shedloads of wickets" followed. "I reckon my average was never more than five or six. I hated being hit for runs. Hated it."

At 15, John was playing for Brighton Boys and was invited on a tour of the Midlands. He turned down the offer at first, knowing that money was tight at home but that if he asked, his dad would find the cash somehow. It was then the headmaster called John into his office and shared a letter from the tour organisers with the news that John had declined the invitation. "He asked me straight out if the reason was financial. When I admitted it was, the school funded the trip". John got his customary bumper haul of wickets and was selected for England Under 15s on the back of it.

He played his first few games for the county seconds at the end of the 1968 season just as he finished his upper-sixth year. The Brighton Old Grammarians umpire, Maurice Farncombe, was a Sussex committee member and had been infuriated that while there had been eight Sussex boys selected for England Schools, the county second team was still made up of club players aged 40 plus and the odd first teamer returning from injury. "If it hadn't been for Maurice, I might not have got a chance."

John remembers playing against Surrey seconds at Eastbourne at the end of that summer with his parents in attendance. He can still see his dad waving a bit of paper with his 'A' level results from the boundary edge. "I asked the skipper if I could run off and check them. I'd done rather well." Though he doesn't recall the cricketing stats when we meet, the record also shows he picked up four wickets for 30 in the second innings.

At the end of that season, John had a year off while waiting for a university place, and Sussex asked him to join the staff on a one-year contract. "Five pounds a week. Thirty bob for Mum, and the rest for me. Just 18 years old. Happy days."

His debut first-class match came the following year, June 1969 v Cambridge University (his imminent destination) at Hove. He bowled well (seven for 64 in the game) and was selected for the next fixture against Gloucestershire. Allan Jones, then a bit of a tearaway, missed out, and angrily declared: "You've only been selected because you've got blue eyes and fucking blond hair!" John, who indeed had both, quickly replied: "It might help if you didn't call the captain a ******* **** ". John and Allan, who had a long career at Somerset and Middlesex before becoming a respected umpire, are now firm friends.

John travelled down to the Gloucester game with Tony and Mike Buss. They stopped on the way at a Berni Inn for steak and chips. John, who had rarely eaten out in a restaurant before, asked the waiter for a double portion of chips. Surprised by the unusual request, the waiter came back bearing an overflowing plate and a challenging look which seemed to say: "Let's see you finish that lot, then." They were wolfed down without touching the sides. "You must like potatoes", observed Tony Buss, "we'll have to call you Spud."

At the end of that 'gap' year on the staff, Spud went up to Cambridge and Sussex put him on a three-year retainer at £200 a year. "That was the modern equivalent of 2,000 pints of beer. With a full grant, I felt as rich as Croesus." While at university he played a number of games for Sussex in the John Player Sunday League, travelling down on the train on the morning of the match and then back at the end of the day. On graduation, he became a full-time professional cricketer.

John is modest about his abilities as an opening bowler. He describes himself as "a donkey", his job to humbly plough a line and length so that more luminous talents like John Snow, Imran Khan and Garth Le Roux might reap the harvest. Unlike some, Spud does not carry his stats in the memory (except like many bowlers, his batting highlights), but his figures give the lie to his own assessment. A stalwart of the club over 12 seasons, he played 215 first-class matches with 554 wickets at 26.39, along with 192 list A games and 228 wickets at 23. Sussex Cricketer of the Year in 1975, and proud holder of a Gillette Cup Winner's medal, he was much more than mere beast of burden.

And he loved it all. Until the end. The end was another tale of casual execution. John was "effectively sacked" at the start of his benefit year; a benefit which he'd willingly agreed to share financially with the club at the behest of the chairman; the same chairman who had so crassly signalled the end of Kenny Suttle's career, and who proceeded to do his best to cheat John out of a proportion of what he was owed.

Despite the fact that he was wise to such shenanigans, and managed to secure what was rightfully his, it wasn't how John had wanted to finish with the club he'd supported since he was 10 and was so proud to play for. For the next three years, as he embarked on his new career as a teacher, he never went near the County Ground. "I didn't even check the scores in the paper." But time heals; and after Chairman Harrison had moved on, John found he couldn't keep away, "I just loved the place. Loved going there. Still do."

The Gillette Cup final victory over Lancashire in 1978 is John's highlight as a player, but as a supporter, the first County Championship in 2003 comes close. John wasn't at the ground on that magical September day. He'd already committed to taking one of his school's sports teams to an away fixture. Calling in sick or getting someone else to take on the duty, isn't Spud's way, but he still remembers his deep elation as he listened on the minibus radio to the moment Murray Goodwin pulled Phil DeFreitas for *that* four through mid-wicket.

Now retired from teaching, John still coaches local young cricketers and is a regular at Eaton Road. If he's meeting up with old friends Peter Graves or John Snow, he takes his seat in the pavilion; if he's on his own, likely as not you'll find him perched right at the top of the new Sharks Stand, with its "fantastic view". And he's always very happy to talk about Sussex cricket. I first met Spud in the Black Lion at Patcham in the middle of winter. "You'll recognise me, I'll be the only one wearing shorts", and since then he has always been generous with his time and memories. The fair hair and blue eyes combo that so got Allan Jones's goat all those years ago are unfaded by time. And yes, he always wears shorts.

Jon Filby

"I'd sussed out the place was special when I was 11. It grabbed me then and even though I went away, the power of feeling when I returned was just immense."

Born Eastbourne, 1959, Jon's father was an Anglican curate and until his dad secured his first parish as a fully-fledged vicar, the family moved about a bit. Cricket was a family passion. Though the Reverend Filby regularly put in 70-hour weeks ministering to his flock, he managed throughout his life to make time for the game and once he'd settled in at Bishop Hannington Memorial Church, Hove, he wasted no time taking out membership at the County Ground. Jon's mother too, was keen. Her father, an eminent economics professor, attended at least one day of every home Ashes series between 1921 and 2005, including travelling back from Hitler's Germany in 1938, just in time to see Len Hutton complete his triple century at the Oval. Family lore has it that when Jon was still in nappies, he would toddle about endlessly repeating the mantra: "Mummy church, Daddy cricket."

Jon's father took his eldest son for his first visit to the ground at an early-season Championship game versus Gloucestershire in 1971. After that initiation, armed with junior membership, Jon would set off from Holmes Avenue with his three younger brothers in tow. They'd leave their sandwiches and bottles of diluted lemon squash on the grass in front of the Hencoop (they knew it as the Cowshed) and then got on with the main business of the day: not watching the game but playing it.

The Filby brood would invariably meet up with friends, and they were always six to ten strong. Plenty for competitive matches out on the outfield during intervals, and straight onto the road behind the main scoreboard once play restarted. "All you needed was a bat and a tennis ball. The world was our oyster." Keen autograph hunters, there were pauses in the narrative when they would inveigle their way into the pavilion at strategic moments, books at the ready. Jon reckons he got Tony Greig around 150 times, and even the reputationally less obliging John Snow at least 60 or 70.

They went to pretty well every game. Second XI, young cricketers, whatever was on. But never on Sundays. Jon's father was evangelical and, "Sundays were for church and…church basically." Jon was less than happy at school and couldn't wait for the long summer holidays when they'd be down there "literally every day."

When Tony Greig was batting or bowling some actual watching started to weave its way into the day. When Tony wasn't involved, they'd sit on the boundary and take the mickey out of the opposition. Among the home side, the Kiwi, AEW Parsons was their favourite. They dubbed their base camp the 'Austin Parsons Stand', stringing up a large home-made banner to proclaim the fact.

Jon remembers a Derbyshire game when the decidedly well-upholstered Phil Sharpe had just joined from Yorkshire and they spent a whole session chanting their version of the then ubiquitous jingle for Lego's new toy, the Weeble. "Weebles wobble but they don't fall down" was the catchphrase for the egg-shaped plastic figures. The Filby posse ruthlessly piped the incessant refrain: "Sharpey wobbles, but he don't fall down." Again, and again, and again. In their shrill unbroken voices. "We probably weren't quite as funny as we thought at the time." But it was true about the Weebles, they never fell down. And nor did Phil. A great slip-fielder, he'd pluck nicks an inch off the turf, but you'd never catch him diving. If the ball went beyond the immediate compass of his crouch, it was Alan Ward's to gather down at third-man.

And it was the big paceman who came to the rescue when Jon's four-year-old brother looked to have come a serious cropper down on the south-east terrace. Bill was clambering alone over the near derelict concrete and wooden benches in what's now Cow Corner, when a metal stanchion toppled over and pinned him to the ground. Jon was trying in vain to lift the thing off his youngest charge, when Alan Ward sprinted 40 yards from fine-leg and freed the child with ease. Bill was right as rain and spent the rest of the day happily scampering about as if nothing had happened, but Alan still took the trouble to run over at the start of the tea interval to make sure everything was okay.

"We were in our own little world. We couldn't have been safer. It felt as if we were at home." And apart from the odd potentially fatal accident, the sense of security was unassailable. The only other brush with danger Jon recalls, was a Sussex v Northants game where the gang had been joshing the opposition all morning so vociferously that at the lunch interval, they were handed a letter. Beneath the printed header marking David Steele's Benefit Year was a hand-written dispatch from the away team addressed: "To the Ill-Mannered Members of the Paul Parker Stand" (Jon & Co's latest stand name) and containing an invitation to "bring your mouths" to the dressing-room at end of play and "explain yourselves".

As group leaders, Jon and his mate, Ingram Losner, duly made their way as instructed to the away team door. To their now respectful knocking, the door opened abruptly, and Ingram was grabbed by the scruff of the neck and yanked into the inner sanctum in the vice-like grip of Geordie hard man, Peter Willey. Somehow Ingram managed to convince the visitors that "We weren't football hooligans; we were just cricket fanatics" and it all ended amicably. Jon still has the letter.

Aged around 15 or 16, the concentration of days at the ground thinned when Jon started playing for a local club. Then came university, where he didn't play at all. He'd follow Sussex scores religiously and went along to Grace Road when they were at Leicester and made it to the Lord's final in 1978. "That was the first time I got drunk. Cricket has always been tied up with rites of passage." After university came unemployment, work, marriage, two children and playing weekends for Barns Green. Visits to Eaton Road were rare. "But I always knew it was there."

At the turn of the century, Jon was Head of Performance and Development at London Underground. He would bring individual staff to the ground for their performance reviews. It was a setting where he felt secure and happy, and it seemed to allow his appraisees to feel the same; a context away from the office, where, if needed, difficult conversations could play out and future follow-up was framed within a safe green space – "You remember when we talked at Hove…?"

In 2003 a major work reorganisation led to Jon negotiating the terms of his own redundancy. After the crucial meeting, he was given a couple of days "to go away and think things over". It was the first day of the Championship game against Leicestershire when Sussex would clinch the pennant. He sat with his father in the same pavilion seats they had taken on that first day in 1971. While they talked things through, Mushy weaved his magic and Murray Goodwin laid the foundations for his record-breaking innings. "That's the great thing about cricket. If you know the game, you know when to watch and when to carry on the conversation." That personally seminal day, marked Jon's return to his boyhood playground. "I'd sussed out the place was special when I was 11. It grabbed me then and even though I went away, the power of feeling when I returned was just immense."

For a time after London Underground, Jon worked as an independent consultant, but increasingly found he was organising assignments around attendance at Sussex fixtures rather than the other way round. He would have lunch in the Dexter dining room for a tenner "and feel like a king".

Affable and interested, Jon is a broad church. He has the knack of finding common ground with almost anyone and the natural inclination to do so. To no surprise, he soon built up a large constituency of regular companions from all corners of the ground. "It's the people that really make it what it is. You meet people from all walks of life, and you know just because they're there, they share a love of the game. And the ground. And many of the same values." Though he didn't realise it at the time, Jon has reflected that of the six or seven lasting university friendships forged at a time when the game didn't play much of a role in their lives, all were with 'cricket people'.

At Hove, he rekindled friendships with some of those he'd played with on the outfield as a boy, as well as the great and the good from the pavilion. He got to know Sussex coach, Mark Robinson, and did some professional work with the team. He started travelling to away games and before long remembers saying to himself: "I really love this place. Sod it. Sod the money. I'm going to be here as much as I can."

He's followed that enjoinder-to-self to the letter. Long-standing committee member, chair of the Foundation and of the Museum, Jon goes to every day of every fixture, home and away. Sometimes he's with his son or daughter; sometimes with his still-keen octogenarian mum; most times alone, though he never stays that way. Even in winter, he finds himself driving down to Hove from his home in Surrey as many as four times a week. His partner, Ali, is still working; she too loves cricket and "she knows this is a happy place for me".

"What I love most is the wall. It was the first thing they built when they moved up from Brunswick and it's still there. There is such a sense of place. If you go over and sit on the east-side and look to the west, it's basically the same view as it was in 1872. It just hasn't changed." A haven, reassuringly constant in a changing world but where different perspectives can always be found.

"You can sit wherever you want. And each time you move it's like you're able to start afresh. If you're not feeling so good and want a quiet moment you go and sit on top of the Gilligan Stand; if you want to concentrate on the game, there's the Shark Stand and if you want people, then there's everywhere else."

Paul Parker

"The weather was glorious with that beautiful September light; the angle of the sun creating the shadow of the pavilion gradually working its way across the outfield towards the wicket."

Born 1956, Bulawayo, in what was then Rhodesia, Paul spent his childhood in the capital, Salisbury (now Harare). His journalist father was imprisoned when he refused to bow to pressure from prime minister Ian Smith to reveal a source. Released on appeal, he was nonetheless forced to leave the country.

For a 10-year-old, the month-long voyage from Cape Town to Southampton was all "incredibly exciting". Even disembarking on a freezing grey February day, was garnished with the magic of Paul's first sight of snow. The family settled in Horsham.

After the Eleven Plus, Paul was off to the local grammar. The headmaster at Collyers, Derek Slynn, was a cricket lover and the school pitches were good ones. Paul's development was so seamless as to seem inevitable. Cricket had "just been part of my upbringing pretty well since birth". He was playing for the school first XI by 14, and soon for Sussex Schools. It rankles a little that Collyers never played the private schools and so missed the chance to play Christ's Hospital First XI, just two miles down the road. At weekends, he played men's cricket for Horsham and later Three Bridges. It was a "natural progression" to Sussex Young Cricketers and by his upper sixth year, he was playing the odd game for the County second X1. "None of this was planned in any way. I didn't feel any sense of: 'Now I've made it.' It had just become what I was going to do."

While waiting to go up to Cambridge after 'A' levels, Paul was given a year's contract with the county at £17.50 a week. On those wages, there was no way he could afford to rent in Brighton, so he carried on living at home. All his cash went on train fares or petrol money for his mate, John Denman, who, when he was playing in the same side, would give him a lift. Once Paul got his provisional licence, John would let him take the wheel and they'd go the back way, through Poynings, over the Downs and swoop down to Eaton Road with the sea stretching out before them as they crested Devil's Dyke.

That year on the staff holds other bright-lit spots of time. There was the moment, milling around waiting to set off for an away game with the Under 25s, when he watched John Snow coming down the hill at Barry Richards and letting loose an "absolute beauty that came back between bat and pad and clean bowled the best batsman in the world neck and crop; Barry looked up at Snowy and gave him the thumbs up before walking off. It was a private moment in a public arena between two champions. That's a memory that stays."

And "Hove was always a special place" with that "beautiful light, so clear, sometimes almost too clear" and it "had an integrated feel". The *Sussex Cricketer* was a big part of the players' lives, and he remembers Joyce the barmaid introducing him to the delicious, red-fleshed apples from the trees up by the nets. For his first game he was 12th man in a friendly against the New Zealand tourists and came on and ran out Geoff Howarth. To mark the event, a bottle of bubbly was presented by the sponsors at the end of play. Paul remembers getting off an empty train at Faygate after the game and tramping the mile and a half home across the fields in the gloaming, proudly clutching his prize.

But overall, that first year as a pro was frustrating. Sussex had a squad of 25 contracted professionals in 1975 and Paul was often 12th man for the seconds. He remembers mostly a lot of hanging around and says now that he "should have seen the writing on the wall in terms of the lack of intellectual stimulation", and wishes he'd used the time better to learn languages. Paul's reputation among his playing peers is unequivocally that of being a "good bloke and a good team man", totally without airs and graces and "always first to get his round in". But there is no doubt that he has always had a restlessly enquiring mind. As a youngster, he taught himself leg spin because he considered it a lost art and wanted to revive it. Flaws in his batting technique he worked through himself. As a Latin teacher, post-cricket, he taught himself Spanish which he speaks with precision, and today in retirement, he is learning Russian "to keep the brain going". Small wonder that at the end of that first year, he remembers thinking to himself: "If that was professional cricket, I wanted nothing more to do with it."

It might well have turned out that way. Paul played for the university throughout his degree, but in his first year, that long hot summer of 1976, he had a dire run of form and was on the verge of being dropped before rediscovering himself against Essex at Fenners with a double century in the second innings. And from there his destiny was pretty much sealed. In late June when he arrived at Lord's for the Varsity match, Paul had played "something like 29 days out of 30", and with his two sets of whites festering in his kit bag, was looking forward to nothing more than a well-earned rest. It was at lunch on the final day when he received the phone call from Sussex with instruction to be ready at end of play to travel up to Leeds for the following day's county game. And that was that.

Paul went on to play 289 first-class matches for the county between 1976 and 1991. Over 15,000 runs and 37 centuries together with 288 one-day games, including top-score on that great day in 1986 when the soft southerners beat the hard men of Lancashire in the NatWest final. There was a single Test appearance at the Oval in the final match of Botham's Ashes. "It came at the wrong time, just as my form fell away." Four-time Sussex Cricketer of the Year and captain for four seasons, he was also a brilliant fielder; the undisputed heir to Derek Randall and David Gower in the covers and considered almost an all-rounder on the back of it. Mike Brearley thought him to be the "best in the world". Fielding was just "something I've always done. Never ever thought about it. It came very naturally, and I just did it." And he has always kept himself fit.

As a captain, Paul is modest about his achievements, and on paper, results tell that the pennant fluttered on a very distant horizon throughout his tenure. But it should be remembered that the post-Imran and Le Roux era was an especially taxing one. Urgent rebuilding work was required at a time when there was precious little material to work with. Paul's response was to think laterally and bring spin to a ground whose history hitherto had been characterised largely by its absence. Ian Salisbury was recruited from the Lord's ground-staff and Andy Clarke from the local amateur league.

Having decided on the strategy and realising that both he and the county knew next to nothing about how to work with the back-of-the-hand brigade, Paul wrote to Richie Benaud to ask him for his insights. Richie replied that he'd be "delighted to help" and duly travelled down to Hove "at his own expense, to give two hours of his time in the outdoor nets. It was a pretty special thing for him to do."

Perhaps Paul's proudest moment as skipper, was opening the bowling with both leg spinners in a Sunday League match at Old Trafford. More common though such a move might be in today's short-form game, it was sufficiently unheard of then to warrant a headline on the back pages of the *Times*. "It would have worked too, if Andy Clarke hadn't dropped a relatively simple caught and bowled off Wasim Akram at the start of his innings."

By any measure, Paul Parker had a very good county career, and was considered unlucky to have played just the one Test. But "success is a double-edged sword. It's great when it's going well but tough when it isn't." And there were tough times. The loss of form and technique the season after his Test debut and the way in which he left Sussex, were two of them. "They wanted me to step down from the captaincy and I told them they'd have to sack me because", he tells me with appropriate self-mockery, "my work here is not done."

But despite the low points and the general lack of mental stretch it was nonetheless a period of his life that remains rich and rewarding in the memory and, as he says: "Everything is an experience you can learn from."

He recalls his last game at Eaton Road with fondness. He'd scored a century opening the batting in a thrilling tied game with arch-rivals Kent in his penultimate match and began his final appearance on a bit of a high. The weather was glorious with "that beautiful September light, the angle of the sun creating the shadow of the pavilion gradually working its way across the outfield towards the wicket." He stationed himself at short-leg and remembers his delight in taking two sharp catches off one of his spin proteges, Brad Donelan. And Sussex won.

At the end of the match, he was interviewed on the outfield by the local media while holding his young daughter in his arms. When asked if he had any regrets, he replied with concise emphasis: "I'm looking forward, not back".

As for firing up the synapses, Paul has certainly made up for any time lost carrying the drinks. After our chat in a café on Tonbridge High Street, he walks me round the old castle walls, and with easy fluency, gives me a succinct but comprehensive history of the place. And while it's Russian at the moment, all bets are off against a still stiffer challenge next. Arabic perhaps, or Chinese.

Hayden Brunsdon

"Every time you go there you get a sense of belonging. And a sense of history."

Born in 1966, Hayden grew up in Suffolk, "right in the sticks". He was a natural cricketer. Though there were no organised games at school, he was spotted by a PE teacher bowling fast on a rough-cut strip and encouraged to join a local club. Pretty quickly, he was in the men's side, taking wickets and getting a trial for the county.

When adolescence hit, cricket fell away, and the guitar took over. He was soon playing with semi-pro bands from the local area with bandmates 10 years his senior. From there, with his own group, success came early. Sessions on the BBC's Andy Kershaw Show, and a tour of the UK at aged just 19. The moment driving home from the pub down a single lane back-road in his 1971 Rover V8 3500 and hearing his self-penned single playing on national radio, remains a golden-hued memory.

By his early twenties, the limelight had dimmed, and as his peers partnered up and his girlfriend moved out of their shared caravan, he decided that his day-job valeting cars at a local garage was not something his hero, Keith Richards, would be caught dead in. It was time to leave the country lanes and hit the streets: he moved to Brighton with a bandmate.

"Brighton was the big city to me." His new domestic circumstances added to the urban edge. Driven down by a workmate with the back seat full of his music gear, the police were making enquiries at the flat where they were to stay as he pulled up at the door. His bandmate's younger brother proved to be a person of continual interest to the local constabulary. "It was quite exciting at first. but I always knew it wasn't really me."

It was an unforgiving spring that year. Hayden was forced to sell his guitars and deliver leaflets round still alien city streets. It all seemed a long way from the soft greenery, the "cow parsley on the verges and the blackthorn blossom in the hedgerows", of home.

He first chanced upon the County Ground on a cold day in April 1991 on his leaflet-round. "I had no idea it was there. Cricket might as well have been another country at that time, but I remember stopping by the Tate Gates and I could hear what sounded like bat on ball."

Walking through the gates was like coming upon "a lost city in a clearing in the jungle." Then the outfield came into view, and "there was this green field with white figures on it". It seemed almost unreal, "like a dream". The ground was completely empty of spectators, and as he settled into one of the plastic seats on the south-west terrace, he was totally alone. He stayed for three hours and allowed flashbacks from his boyhood to drift through him as he half-watched the creaking early-season goings on. "It was magical. Like an oasis. Something to hold onto"; its potency enough to put aside any thoughts of giving up 'city life' and returning to the sticks.

After leafleting came a number of casual agency jobs including delivery driver, care worker and cleaner. Then he found the kitchen, and began a 25-year career in catering, latterly as a senior head chef. Tough though it was, until his hips gave out and a new fast food obsessed managerial regime laid its dead hand on his hard-won fiefdom, he enjoyed the cooking. It was creative, and the gallery of characters who people an industrial canteen, proved more 'rock n' roll' than the new generation of 'musos' he'd half-heartedly had dealings with since he moved to the coast. And working early shifts meant he was usually done by mid-afternoon and could always catch at least the post-tea session at Eaton Road.

With the ground to himself, watching the next generation making their way, second X1 games were and remain a favourite. Hayden goes mostly alone. You need a bit of solitude after a hard day in the kitchen. Sometimes he's there with friends who, like him, live half a mile from the ground. A couple of cold beers from the fridge, the cricket forms the backdrop, but the easy inconsequential chat is where the action plays out.

There are also times when it is good to be part of a crowd. There was the first jam-packed Twenty20 on a chilly June evening under the floodlights. Dancing girls, fireworks, very loud music through tinny speakers. A whole-hearted, but somehow reassuringly homespun attempt to bring razzamatazz and glamour to the old ground. Ahead of him in the queue at the burger bar, fresh off the float on which they'd paraded round the ground in the innings break, was one of the 'Shark Girls'. Goose-fleshed and shivering in an outfit clearly not designed for the cold, she informed the harassed chef that she was a vegetarian. Did he have anything for her? He was afraid he didn't. The best he could do was chicken, would that do? It would. Hayden found himself nodding in professional approval.

He became a member, a significant moment. "For a start, it was the first time in my life I could afford such a thing. It marked a change, gave me a feeling of solidity. I belonged to something established." He remembers one Saturday that year sitting among a sparse crowd, watching the West Indies tourists ambling through a 50-over game. It was a hot day, but there were thunderstorms brewing and, when they came, he hightailed it home like everybody else. But later the sky cleared, and when Ceefax told him that play had resumed, he hurried back. "It was great realising that with my new badge, I could pop in and out whenever I wanted." He returned to a ground bereft of spectators in time to watch Chris Gayle and Shiv Chanderpaul smacking the ball to all parts. "I remember Luke Wright's first over cost just four, the next three 57."

Especially during the Championship-winning years, there were days at the Cromwell Road End with the deckchairs and benches pretty well filled with regulars and the after-work crowd. "We'd stay until they'd all gone home and just sit and gaze out across the empty outfield until dusk fell." Then down to the Sussex Cricketer for a last pint and an early night in readiness for the five o'clock alarm the following day. "A perfect evening."

The ground still retains much of the magic of that first day on the blue seats, the bag heavy with undelivered leaflets at his feet. "Every time you go there you get a sense of belonging. And a sense of history." Not only the public history of past players and generations of spectators, but also your own personal history. Hayden's got his guitars back now and plays them like the ringing of a bell, but Eaton Road will always play host to "some of the best days of my life".

Leigh Latham

"Hove is just unique. There's some sort of special feel about it. It's hard to explain to people who don't go there what it is. But it's there."

Leigh reckons he would have been six or seven for his first visit to the County Ground. He went with his brother David who is 10 years older, and they sat in the top-deck of the pavilion. He can't remember who was playing or the exact year – "It would have been the late sixties" – but, despite the sparse crowd and overcast skies, he can remember being "massively excited". And he knows Tony Greig and John Snow were playing because his brother, "knowing Snowy to be a bit peppery" badgered his sibling into approaching the man once dubbed 'Hostile Son of a Vicar' by the *Brighton Argus*, for an autograph. Snowy signed without demur and while Leigh can't say he "caught the bug" at that first game, "It had sowed a seed in me."

At one time, before he lost the lot, Leigh's father Mick, was in the money. He and Leigh's uncle owned and ran a factory first located at Shoreham and then Newhaven, making blow-moulded plastics. With plastics now recognised as the world's bane, "It's a bit like being a drug dealer from today's perspective", laughs Leigh now. But in those less environmentally aware times, Mick was a respected local businessman; and an avid cricket lover: ideal club-committee material. Mick duly took up a key role on the Player's Welfare sub-committee. "Pre-Packer the players weren't earning much and needed work in the winter. Unless you were Ted. It was still all a bit Gentleman and Players then." For those without 'independent means', Mick would use his network of contacts to find off-season work in a range of local firms as well as down at his own factory in Newhaven. David remembers Denis Foreman and Don Bates as two of several temporarily joining the 'drug trade'.

After that first day, Leigh's visits were occasional. He was too busy playing the game for one thing. Part of the final year of Brighton and Hove and Sussex Grammar School for Boys before it morphed into the Sixth Form College, Leigh was in the first team by the fifth year. He left school after O Levels and started work at was then the South Downs Bus Company in the computer department, "basically data input into a machine the size of a room". It was then his visits to the ground became more frequent. Though he was playing for the bus company staff team, over the hill at league side Clayton on a Saturday and for Hove Oddfellows on a Sunday, there was still time to pop into Eaton Road with workmates or old school friends on a fairly regular basis.

Leigh remembers going more often in the silver spoon year of 1981, but it was really from the early nineties, when he became a member, that he "started going religiously". By then Leigh and David had started their own business based just down the road from the ground at Medina Place and "whenever work was bit quiet you could just nip up for a session" to sit in his then favoured spot at the top of the Gilligan Stand.

In 1995 when the business folded, Leigh did the knowledge and became a Brighton taxi-driver. "Like most cabbies I said I'd only do it for three or four years and then find something else." More than 25 years later, albeit now 'jockeying' part-time on someone else's cab, he's still at it. "I pretty quickly realised that for a cricket fan, it was the perfect job. I wasn't going to be rich, but I was going to have a lot of fun."

And fun he has certainly had. The nineties had its highlights; like all of us who were there, he'll never forget the Cheltenham and Gloucester semi-final against Glamorgan – "I had the biggest bet I'd ever had on a cricket match and before Neil Lenham and Alan Wells took after Viv Richards, I nearly threw the ticket away". And as for the final, even with the Warwickshire fans incessantly chanting: "You'll not see nothing like the Mighty Din" to the tune of the Mighty Quinn, and despite the gut-wrenching outcome, it was still a fantastic day.

The Noughties were the glory years, and while Leigh lost his father at the start of the decade, his son Sean was soon old enough to embrace the Latham family love of the game. "I took him to his first match when he was five and he loved it. In the 2000s, I'd take him and a couple of his mates who liked cricket. I'd plot up and they'd spend the whole day in the nets, only coming to see me when they wanted to eat. They were my favourite days ever." But there have been many which have come close.

"You could tell something was happening the season before the first Championship. That game against Surrey when Mushy was playing for them and we had to avoid defeat to stay up and Murray got a 100, sticks in the memory. I remember Robin Martin-Jenkins saying when facing Mushy that the sound was like hearing a swarm of angry wasps. When he first joined us some of the lads weren't too sure about it…".

In 2003, Leigh didn't miss a home game and in September, when it was theoretically possible that Sussex could win the championship at Old Trafford, he travelled up to Manchester, just in case. He went with a mate from Clayton, Andy Beal, straight off the night shift on the cabs. "I finished at 4.00 in the morning, and we drove straight up, parked up behind the Statham Stand and had a kip in the car." Leigh was absolutely bushed and grateful for a rain delayed start. He and Andy emerged "still knackered and probably smelling horrible" as the imminent start of play was announced. On the way to their seats, they bumped into Jason Lewry, on his way to getting into his match gear. Leigh had had a banner made up with the Sussex crest bearing the legend: "Mushy's Gonna Get You". Jason loved it and took it up to the changing room where the whole team signed it with Mushy's signature writ large. The fact that the magician didn't get the Red Rose on that occasion, and Sussex were thrashed by an innings, didn't matter. The prospect of the pennant being raised at home beckoned.

"When Murray hit that four, I remember just sitting there and bawling my eyes out. I don't know where it came from… thinking about my old man…".

Later in the *Cricketers*, any eye-water was beer-fuelled tears of pure joy. And as for the Friday: "It was riotous. Phil Tufnell came down to the *Cricketers* with his radio show and there was so much singing he had to relocate to a caravan; we all went out and were rocking the thing to put him off ". Leigh has loads of great photos – with the players, 10-year-old Sean, his champagne-soaked Mushy banner and the whole elated melee. To top things off, for the first and only time, Leigh successfully appealed a parking fine on the shaky grounds that "there was nowhere else to park". In the days before such things were 'contracted out', perhaps the local council assessor, was a Sussex fan.

After that first pennant, Leigh and his mates would go to more away games. The banner – "The best 70 quid I ever spent "– had them recognised and they got to know the players. Leigh remembers in the 2006 season going up to Trent Bridge with a bunch of mates for all three days and the players inviting them round to where they were staying: "I remember James Kirtley standing on a table, singing the 'Wild Rover'.

While the glory years might have faded, and while Sean, now busy with work as a P.E teacher at the Aldridge Academy and playing for local club Poynings, no longer joins his dad, Leigh's allegiance to club and ground has never wavered. He goes to T20s for a drink and a get together with mates, but it's the first-class game that has the most resonance. "I still get excited for the Championship games, even though it seems to be falling down the pecking order. I fear for it really, but for me, it'll always be the Championship."

218

Leigh, a well-liked and respected luminary of local club cricket for over 40 years, still plays the game. Sometimes he takes the field with Sean in the Poynings front-side, but with the eyes going a bit and the shoulder feeling its 58 years, more often in the seconds. He wants to keep playing as long as he can, but when the time comes to finally hang up the boots, it won't be the end of cricket, it'll just mean more time down at Hove.

We meet for our chat at the Velodrome at Preston Park, and as we gaze across the outfield where, at different times, we both watched our sons playing for local club St Matthias in pairs cricket, we try and work out just what it is about Eaton Road. We both agree on the link between past and present; that pretty well every time we go there, percolating memories of great days will bubble up unbidden. But as Leigh says, it's also simpler than that: "I love just being able to turn up, sit wherever you want and watch the game I love." Leigh is usually to be found on the deckchairs in the north-east corner, or sometimes in the Shark Stand – "You have to pay a king's ransom to sit at the top of the Gilligan Stand now" – but wherever he sits, for him: "Hove is just unique. There's some sort of special feel about it. It's hard to explain to people who don't go there what it is. But it's there."

Alec Keith

"I know cricket followers have got a reputation for being a bit stick-in-the-mud, but it never seemed that way at Hove."

Alec is a County Ground irregular. He's never been by himself, and he's never been a member. He describes himself unashamedly, as a fair-weather supporter. Fair weather in the literal, rather than metaphorical sense. In contrast to his 'all-weathers' allegiance to Craven Cottage and Fulham FC, Alec's visits to Eaton Road have been invariably bathed in summer sun.

Over the years, he reckons he's probably gone on average a couple of times a season. There have been periods of his life when it's been more frequent, but these are offset by whole seasons when he hasn't been at all. But he's followed this dilettante pattern for more than half a century. In aggregate some way short of the 10,000 hours Malcom Gladwell deems necessary to acquire mastery but, except on rare occasions when the weather forecast lied, it has been a practice uninterrupted by rain breaks and bad light.

He first went to the ground in the late sixties when he was seven or eight with his father. They sat at the top of the Gilligan Stand and though he can't remember any specifics, "It was just lovely. I was so excited that first time". From then, until adolescence brought teenage distractions, father and son would travel down from Haywards Heath for three or four days a year. "It was always meaningless Championship games but that didn't matter. I was with my dad, he loved cricket, I loved cricket. Sitting in the sun, coke and crisps and all those cakes from that tea-room in the Chalet. Not a care in the world. I'd keep the score on those scorecards they printed out, but I don't remember much about the games. I just remember really loving it. Just loving watching boring County cricket."

From his late teens until his early thirties, visits to the ground were sporadic at best. None of his mates were into cricket, he'd stopped playing the game himself, was playing football reasonably seriously and then bringing up a young family. But he was kept fully abreast of goings on just down the road from the family home on Wilbury Avenue, by his next-door neighbour, Laetitia Stapleton, vivid chronicler of all things Sussex CCC. Laetitia and her husband, always referred to as 'The Captain', were "Lovely neighbours. Posh but lovely. I remember one evening getting a phone call and being asked if I wouldn't mind popping over to help with an urgent task.

When I got there, it turned out they needed a bottle of champagne opening and were struggling with the cork."

In the late 80s and for much of the next decade, attendance markedly increased. Through a colleague and friend from work, Alec hooked up with a band of regular watchers. These were the Beer Years, cakes and Coca-Cola replaced by prodigious quantities of lager. "I can remember loading up the rucksack of a morning and working out how many cans I needed. I'd reckon eight, and then add two more just in case, but we'd finished them by the tea interval, and then it'd be buying more from in the ground before staggering down to *The Sussex Cricketer* at end of play."

There was a fair bit of boisterousness, and the banter was lively. Sussex-by-the-Sea got belted out with gusto as well as good-natured barracking of the opposition. They'd sit usually in the row of seats at the bottom of the main scoreboard – "there was a bar actually in the scoreboard then" – but sometimes ended up in the upper tier of the pavilion. "I've no idea how we got in there." There was one match when the posse would bellow the repeated refrain: "Siddown" whenever anyone got up from their seat during the over. "But we did it with humour and somehow got away with it. As soon as one of us made a move there would be a chorus of "Siddown" from everyone around us. All these 80-year-olds caught up in the moment and chuckling away. I know cricket followers have got a reputation for being a bit stick-in-the-mud, but it never seemed that way at Hove."

The highlight of that era was definitely the 1993 Nat West semi-final against Glamorgan. "Such a great day. The Glamorgan fans were just fantastic. When he got his match-winning hundred, we dubbed Alan Wells 'Lord Wells of Newhaven' and then Viv Richards came down the pub after the game. I have such fond memories of those days. Getting drunk and sitting in the sun with your mates and being silly at a cricket match. What could be better?"

Since those halcyon days, work pressures have meant a return to once or twice a season. Alec rushed up from the office with a mate just in time to see Murray Goodwin's points-sealing boundary in 2003 and he arranges annual unofficial works outings where up to 20 of them will take up residence in the north-east corner in easy reach of 'Sid's Shack'. The drinking is more restrained nowadays, but not by much and it's always "a proper day out".

Asked for his favourite section of the ground, Alec plumps for the pub garden: "I've spent hours in that pub garden. You always feel part of the ground when you're sat there. There's the Chalet and you can see the back of the Gilligan Stand where I used to sit with my dad which brings back lovely memories". Coke and crisps, laughter and lager, it's always been 'cakes and ale' at the County Ground for Alec Keith. Cakes and Ale and sunshine. Though the pub garden and the Chalet are no more, long may it stay that way.

Rob Steen

"The sense of it being unchanged; the smell of the sea; the sea fret; the deckchairs, the floodlights; the fact that it's in the heart of Brighton and Hove."

Rob is another who first came to cricket watching the 1966 England v West Indies series on television. He is London born and bred and his formative county cricket years were spent at Lord's watching Middlesex. But the family would come down to Hove in the summer to stay at his grandfather's flat just up from the sea on The Drive, and the County Ground became a regular boyhood stamping ground. Rob's father had no interest in team sports, but his grandfather did. For a time, the official ringside doctor at Bethnal Green's York Hall as well as long-suffering GP for The Small Faces, it was the grandfather who sat his 8-year-old grandson down in front of the telly to watch the Windies and in 1969 took him to his first game at Eaton Road. Rob can remember nothing of this initiation apart from the fact that Jim Parks was playing and The Who's *Pinball Wizard* had just reached the Top 10. Music is Rob's first love, but sport, especially cricket, comes a close second and has informed his professional life.

Rob Steen is an award-winning sports journalist who has worked for, among others, the *Guardian*, the *Independent*, the *Sunday Times*, *Sunday Telegraph*, *Sydney Morning Herald*, *Melbourne Age*, *India Today* and *Cricinfo*, as well as authoring more than a dozen books on sport. He has twice been shortlisted for the William Hill Sports Book of the Year award and was the winner of both the Cricket Society Literary Award and the 2005 EU Journalism Award (UK section) 'for diversity, against discrimination'. With such a track record, I was a little intimidated before meeting Rob for the first time; this somehow made more acute by him designating "outside the press-box" for our rendezvous at the County Ground. My fears proved entirely unfounded.

I am punctual almost to a fault, but Rob is already waiting for me when I arrive early for our appointment. He is dressed in shorts, faded New York Yankees baseball cap and a somewhat garish t-shirt featuring the American singer-songwriter, multi-instrumentalist and revered producer, Todd Rundgren. The t-shirt puts me at my ease, suggesting that here was a man not only free from sartorial vanity, but one still fired by the youthful spirit of fandom.

It transpired that the hat is a red herring: Rob is in fact a Mets fan; he picked up the

Yankees titfer when sent to cover the post-9/11 World Series. But the t-shirt does not lie. Rob is warm and approachable. Recently retired as a university senior lecturer in journalism, he makes no mention of his awards and when prompted to reflect on his considerable journalistic success, attributes it either to luck or the support of others. He has just spent the afternoon catching up with Mike Selvey, who, along with David Hopps, had championed the young freelancer at the *Guardian*; others such as David Foot and Frank Keating are thanked for their encouragement in absentia.

It is the August home game against Middlesex; a fixture which holds memories for both of us of a time when bank-holiday crowds would throng the ground. Today, as we sit on the blue seats in the temporary T20 stand next to the main scoreboard, we are the only occupants. Even in the pavilion, empty seats predominate as Sussex easily knock off the post-tea runs needed to secure a comfortable three-day victory. The match done and dusted, we sit in the warm sun in a near empty ground. A couple of small boys with tennis ball and bat are playing with an earnestness that, like the bank-holiday crowds, seems an echo of a distant past. Just once they hit their ball into the stand and forage for it beneath our seats, but otherwise we are undisturbed. Only the seagulls, the rumble of the roller, the gentle ticking over of the mower and the wind off the sea accompany Rob's sparkling reflections. We talk of music, boxing, baseball, cricket, cabbages and kings. And Eaton Road.

"What I love about it is the intimacy. The fact you can walk round the ground in about 10 minutes and the cricket is always close. I have lovely memories of the press box and having lunch in the pavilion with colleagues. The sense of it being unchanged; the smell of the sea; the sea fret; the deckchairs, the floodlights and the fact that it's in the heart of Brighton and Hove."

Rob came down "on a busman's holiday" for the Leicester game in 2003 when he realised the pennant was in the offing. "I just felt I had to be there." When teaching at the university he would always arrange a day at the ground with his students to get an insight into all aspects of running a club. "Mark Robinson was a brilliant and informative host."

But the memory which shines brightest was his day on the deckchairs in the north-west corner in the company of the Reverend David Sheppard and "his delightful wife Grace". We gaze across the outfield to the now empty enclave and the look in Rob's eyes and the wonder in his voice tell that he has been transported back to that hot August Bank holiday in 1998 when he was working on his book *This Sporting Life: Cricket*. Sheppard was a hero – "the early fight against apartheid, the work done with the disadvantaged in Liverpool" – and he didn't disappoint. "That afternoon is probably the most memorable experience of my professional life. I have met quite a lot of famous people in my work – Botham, Dexter from cricket spring to mind – but no-one has had such a powerful presence, a charisma, as David Sheppard."

Rob's written account of this encounter is a must read. I feel blessed to have him re-live it with such immediacy and fervour 20 years later. As we finally make our familiar way back to Hove station for Rob to catch the train home to Lewes, the evocation stays with me. It is there, even when the conversation turns to music – I am ever grateful to Rob for introducing me to Laura Nyro – and it has stayed with me ever since; a jewel stitched into the weft and weave of shared memory which for me and many others goes into forming the emotional fabric of the ground. Whenever you find yourself gazing across the outfield to the pavilion, the past links arms with the present. Sometimes, if the light's right, there's an imagined future too.

Clare Rogers

"What's as entertaining as the game, is listening to the people talking about it."

Clare's first ever cricket match was on Boxing Day in 1956 at Cape Town. Aged just five, she went with her father, who though "apparently pretty useless as a player, loved scoring and the statistics. We had a lovely day". Her next attendance, over 20 years later in the summer of 1978, was at the County Ground, Hove.

I met Clare on a cold November morning during the pandemic lock-down. It was her second day of retirement from her role as an administrator in the School of Global Studies at Sussex University, and she was looking forward to the next stage of her life with enthusiasm. We sat on a bench in a local park, and as well as sharing her Bulgarian 'Rothmans' cigarettes, Clare outlined her journey to Eaton Road in evocative detail; a narrative laced with self-deprecatory humour and an infectious, smoky chuckle.

An only child, Clare was born in Umtali (now Mutare), in what was then Rhodesia. Her parents, second generation South Africans, were "buccaneering types" and without any background in agriculture, they had moved to Zimbabwe to start a farm. The homestead was miles from anywhere, and though it had running water, there was no electricity. They started out "in a very poor way". It was hard graft, though Clare remembers her father's work-rate noticeably slowing whenever the Tests were on the radio.

Aged five, Clare went to the village school, "about 12 miles up a dusty track", as a border. At 10, she was off to school in Harare. From there came university in the capital, and then the *Bulawayo Chronicle* as a trainee reporter.

A confluence of events led to Clare moving to England. "There was a civil war on, but I can't say that affected me much." What did affect her, was her parents selling up the farm and setting sail across the Atlantic in the boat her father had built. "And they didn't invite me. No reason why they would have, but at the same time my then beloved found another, and I was sacked from my job at the paper." Why? "Because I was no good. I had writer's block. Not ideal for a journalist!" All things considered it seemed the right time to make a fresh start.

Clare's first flat when she got to Hove, backed onto the western edge of the ground.

She could hear the sounds of play drifting over the communal garden, but she never ventured in until, "as one does", she met a man on a bus. It turned out Stanley worked at the same place she did, ITT Creed, up in Hollingbury. Stanley had been a Sussex member since the fifties, and he persuaded Clare to come and join him at the next match, a disastrous Benson & Hedges game where the home county were bowled out for 68. They sat in the pavilion that truncated day, because Stanley thought it would be nicer for Clare, but for the next game, they decamped to Stan's home patch in the north-west corner.

So began a long and rewarding friendship. For the next 20 odd years, Clare and Stan would be in the deckchairs at every home game. They would travel to the out-grounds, too. Clare knew nothing of the nuts-and-bolts, let alone the subtleties of the game, but under Stan's gentle tutelage, and with the *Playfair Annual* and the *Cricketer's Who's Who* as her textbooks, she now considers herself "reasonably au fait".

But right from the off, it was the atmosphere of the place that held her. And the people: "For me, the stewards have always been heroes. And there was Fred with his calls of "Argus, Argus", and Keith with his raffle tickets."

Stan had previously watched alone, but once Clare joined him, they built up a cohort of companions. "We were among friends." There was Tony, a retired investment adviser for Midland Bank who'd been detailed to count the cash from the Great Train Robbery – "they were locked in over three days". There was Jim from Worthing, Gillian who came down from Tunbridge Wells and with whom Clare "smoked a lot", and "a glorious chap called Gordon who would place a line of biscuits along the advertising hoardings so our friendly sparrow would drop in and say hello."

After the Benson and Hedges debacle, that first year was a great one for Sussex in which they won the Gillette Cup. Great players too – Javed Miandad and the god-like Imran Khan with the "gorgeous voice", who Clare watched entranced one day as he practised advanced yoga on the boundary while the rest of the team did their desultory limbering up in front of the pavilion.

The highlight of Stan and Clare's day was the first scheduled break in play. Stan had been in the habit of bringing along nothing more than a flask and his ham and Ryvita sandwiches – "a very sober affair" – but with Clare on the scene, luncheon became a ritual event. One of them would do the main course, and the other a pudding. The puddings became the thing. "They got more and more elaborate – roulades, creamy cakes, trifles. All washed down with a bottle of red wine. It was 'our thing.'" After lunch, Clare would have a snooze in the sun.

When Stanley died 10 years ago, Clare asked the club if perhaps she might bury her dear friend's ashes on the outfield. "They could not have been more helpful." On a crystal-clear November day, "about 12 of us sat in a semi-circle in front of the pavilion steps". The chairman, Hugh Griffiths, had had a neat hole dug in readiness. Stan's ashes were interred and, "we each got up and said something in his memory. It was a lovely moment."

Though "sometimes you can be closer to a friend than to a partner", Stan's passing did not pause Clare's visits to the ground. And the circle was nicely closed for a while when she was joined on the deckchairs by her parents. When they had set sail from Cape Town, the plan had been to drop anchor somewhere in the South Pacific. They made the Caribbean, but no further. In part, this was due to them being suspected of piracy, and while Clare says, "that wouldn't have bothered them too much", Robert Mugabe winning the civil war and plundering all their money, did. They settled in the Virgin Isles, where her father, in his sixties, forged a new livelihood as a sailing instructor, before finally moving to Hangleton to live out their days.

ITT Creed made telex machines, and when these became 'old tech', they closed down. Clare worked for a time for Bupa, until they moved to Manchester and "kindly made me redundant", when she decided to train as a teacher. It was "a disaster. I was too old." A short interlude at a lawyers' office as a bookkeeper followed. "Another disaster. The computer would not do what I had hoped it would." Clare thought she might never work again, but then her temp agency sent her to the university for a short-term appointment. She stayed for 20 years. She loved it. And they clearly loved her. As an administrator, you see more of the students than do the lecturers, and Clare made many friends. "Among the students from India and Pakistan and the Caribbean, cricket has an immediate currency." Through an alumnus from Pakistan, she has visited the troubled country many times. She was more than a little nervous the first time, just after Benazir Bhutto had been assassinated, but assurances from her friend, and the lure of "just being in the same country as Imran", persuaded her.

Clare takes with her into retirement "so many invitations; some from places I had to look up". Once the pandemic is over, along with reprising her regular visits to Zimbabwe, she fully intends to take them up. But when she's not flying off to distant lands, she will be down at Eaton Road. A life member, Clare is looking forward to the retirement luxury of being able to attend all four days of a Championship game. "I shall savour each one." She'll be at the T20 nights too. "They are a good thing to take people to; people who don't normally go to the cricket." And she likes seeing the fathers with their young sons.

Clare has now graduated to the pavilion, where she sits with Brenda and her coterie, and enjoys listening to the murmured chatter of the cognoscenti. One of life's appreciators, I reckon Clare will always find something to amuse and engage her. And to give her joy.

Spinghar Shinwari

"When I first saw the nets, I'd never seen a proper ground before. I'd never seen anything like it. The lights and everything. My heart just came out. When you play shots indoors it makes a really nice sound. You feel that happiness inside."

"Cricket is like light", says Spinghar Shinwari, or 'Spin' as he is known in his new home. It was the glare of the strip-lights at the indoor school that illuminated Spin's first visit to the County Ground. On a dark mid-winter night, he went with his then team, Worthing CC, for pre-season nets. It had been a long journey.

Spin was born and raised in Haska Mena Dihalba, a small village in Nangarhar Province, Afghanistan. His father never came home from work in uniform, and it was never spoken of openly, but everyone knew he was an officer in the Afghan Army.

The elders of Spin's Shinwari tribe had signed a pact against the Taliban and the village was nominally in government hands. But "you never knew who was supporting who" says Spin. What you did know, was that the Taliban were up there; up in the 'White Mountain' that loomed above the village and from which Spinghar was given his name.

He was never allowed to leave the house alone; his grandmother would always accompany him, even when playing endless cricket games with local boys in the brick works or the village cemetery. "I grew up with cricket. There was no TV, but I had a radio and I used to buy cassettes with commentaries of Afghan games." His grandmother told him later that he would always go to bed with his cricket bat when he was small.

Spin's second passion was the English language. He took every opportunity to practice with the American soldiers who took up sporadic residence in the village. He remembers standing on a stool in front of the blackboard, teaching his peers. School took place under a large tree and when the rain came, they were sent home.

It was a Friday, a holy day, when Spin's life changed forever. As usual, he was to accompany his father to Mosque; as usual he was late, washing himself in readiness while his mother chivvied him to get a move on. Tired of waiting, his father had gone on ahead and Spin was hurrying to catch up when he heard shots ring out.

Running blindly towards where the guns had sounded, he found his father lying still on the red earth. Spin holds a memory of his father reaching up and placing his hand on his oldest son's forehead, before everything went black.

He came round in a hospital bed, with his uncle at his side. He was uninjured and had apparently passed out from shock. To begin with his uncle told him his father had survived, but once they had moved to a neighbouring village the truth emerged. Spin's life and that of his uncle's family who harboured him, were now in immediate danger. "Everyone knew I was my father's son." It later transpired the Taliban had received reports of the young boy talking with the Americans. Letters had been sent, ordering the family to leave the village.

Spin spent just one night at his uncle's home. At the crack of dawn, he began the odyssey that would end with his arrival in the UK. "I had no idea where I was going." The journey would take 16 months.

Spin doesn't know exactly when he was born, but reckons he was around 14 when his uncle handed him over in the provincial capital Jalalabad to what would be the first of a succession of agents. From Jalalabad, it was through Pakistan, Iran and Turkey. Spin never carried cash and still has no idea how much the journey cost. Everything was arranged by his uncle back in Afghanistan. "Mostly we travelled in cars or lorries. Sometimes it was on the back of a motorbike. When we got to the mountains, we went on foot." Sometimes the drivers knew they were hidden in the trailer; sometimes they didn't. There was an ever-mutating cast of fellow travellers, some friendly, some threatening. Spin, who'd had no chance to say goodbye to his family or attend his father's funeral, was hungry and exhausted most of the time and admits to being "scared the whole way".

It took three attempts to cross from Turkey to Greece. The agents gave each of the travellers a knife with instruction to puncture their inflatable raft when they got close to the shore, if coastguards were in sight. The theory was that if they started sinking, they'd be saved from drowning. Everyone knew that too often the water was deeper than it looked, and if the coastguards arrived at all, they arrived too late. Fortunately, Spin's knife was unused. On its third foray, his boat got close enough to the shoreline at Samos to wade to the beach and make a break for the trees. Many made it. Spin held back to help a young mother with her two children. "It's a great feeling when you help someone else." He was arrested and taken to a holding camp where the new arrivals were asked if any of them spoke English. Spin put his hand up and was landed with the role of unofficial liaison officer and told he couldn't leave until someone arrived who could take his place. It was two months before his journey restarted.

The stress never eased, but there were interludes of kindness. In the hills above Athens, they came upon an isolated farmstead. The old couple who lived there looked after Spin and his fellow travellers, like long lost sons for several days. The couple didn't want them to leave but paid for a taxi to where they were to wait for the next lorry.

There were further hurdles on the way to Dunkirk. More than once, Spin refused to get into the back of a freezer truck, fearing he would die if he did so. And then there was a rough Channel crossing in the back of another truck. Finally, the lorry doors were flung open and a man he didn't know barked "Afghan" and pulled him out before he had a chance to gather his belongings. For the first time, Spin hadn't been handed a mobile phone with a number to ring to arrange the next leg of the journey. As the truck pulled away, he realised he must have reached the end of what the agents always called, "your mission". He was alone, in a lay-by on a dual carriageway. It was raining and cold and he was wearing only one shoe. He was shivering uncontrollably and in tears when the police came. An officer fetched a bottle of water from the back of the squad car. Then she hugged him and told him he was safe.

While he sought asylum, Spin spent his first year in Worthing; in a hostel at first, and then with a foster family where he didn't leave his room for a month, except to go to the bathroom. But gradually, with the help of his social worker and his sponsor, the woman he calls "mother", he took the first steps into his new alien world.

And one sun-kissed late-summer Sunday afternoon, he was taken for a drive. They came upon a green field with white figures on it. He pleaded with his 'mother' to stop the car and ran straight out onto the pitch and begged to join in. "I felt joy for the first time since I'd arrived". Though he was gently told he couldn't play right then as they were in the middle of a match, the team promised to contact him. Soon he was playing for Worthing every weekend. Once he'd overcome his initial fear of the hard ball, he began to feel more at home.

Spin very rarely goes to the County Ground as a spectator. He's too busy playing for one thing, and then there's the cost of admission. But he remembers his first experience as one of the highlights of his life. On 1 August 2018, Afghan leg-spin hero Rashid Khan was playing for Sussex against Gloucestershire in the Vitality Blast. The Sussex Cricket Foundation had provided free tickets to the sizeable Afghan community in Brighton and Hove. Here was the chance to welcome the number one T20 bowler in the world to Eaton Road. On a clear summer night, at least 80 of Spin's compatriots were joyfully gathered in a designated area at the top of the ground. For Afghan refugees, "Cricket is the thing that gives us the most happiness. It unites us."

Sussex lost the match, but Spin's fellow native son of Nangarhar Province did not let them down. Rashid got the best figures of the night with two for 14 off his four overs. After the game, they were all invited out onto the pitch to meet their idol. "He's a really nice man. Very modest. He gave me his batting gloves. I still talk to him on social media."

Spin now lives in Brighton in a long-term hostel for vulnerable young people. It is a safe space. He has his own room. Though he no longer sleeps with his bat, he has a cricket ball on the end of a long length of elastic, fixed to the ceiling. He is grateful "beyond words" for the welcome he has received in England, and while memories of his village, of his birth mother and his brothers, remain wounds which will never fully heal, cricket does more than anything to build protective tissue.

The County Ground is a big part of his life. Or at least the Indoor School is. Spin plays now for a local league team – their player of the year in 2019 – and as well as team practice in winter, he is up at the nets with smaller groups throughout the season. "I just love the place." He loves the rifle-crack of the ball echoing off the ceiling. He loves the fact he can give full rein to his preferred batting style – smacking the ball as hard as possible – without having to go searching for it behind stacks of bricks or gravestones. And while he's still waiting for a scout in the indoor school's viewing gallery to fulfil his dream of playing professionally, there's no Taliban up there in the White Mountain, watching his every move.

John Barclay

"Whenever I go there, it still feels like my second home."

For over a decade from 1975, I lived far from Eaton Road and so missed most of John Barclay's playing career. I must have seen him at Hove before then, but I can't say I remember it. Perhaps Snow and Greig and Jim Parks still shone too bright in my adolescent gaze for me to pay him any heed. Later, in July 1985, when I knew more about him, I caught a day of Sussex versus Warwickshire, but he was near the end by then, no longer opening the batting. The captain's asterisk on my scorecard had him coming in at number nine, and with Imran and Colin Wells hitting unbeaten centuries and the home team declaring, he didn't bat.

Throughout my time away, I always kept in touch with Sussex cricket. Indeed, despite what I always told myself was a temporary absence from my home county, walking down to the newsagents to pick up the paper and see how Sussex were doing, took precedence even over the day's first cigarette and mug of instant coffee.

In the winter of 1981, my foreign travel hitherto limited to a daytrip to Dieppe, I moved to Madrid. No more insipid granules from a jar, the start of my day was now fuelled by strong espresso in a crowded bar, watching workers shout at each other in a language that might as well have been double-Dutch as they downed shots of brandy, presumably to ward off a biting cold I had neither anticipated nor packed for.

As well as a warm coat, I missed my morning trips to the newsagent but soon chanced upon the British Council Library and would go there every day in my lunch break to catch up on the scores, albeit with a two-day delay.

For a Sussex boy in a strange land, even before 'Botham's Ashes' ignited at Headingly, the summer of 1981 was a particularly good one. My home county was on the up. Unbeaten in May, by early June, Alan Ross told of an optimistic tenor where 'John Barclay seems to have got a new spirit going in the county'. There was talk of 'an invigorating approach to captaincy', along with some 'quixotic' declarations. In June at Tunbridge Wells, they lost what looked from Madrid like a thriller, but then thrashed Lancashire and beat Glamorgan. As the temperature rose on the streets of my new home to the scorching levels I had expected from the off, they beat the Sri Lankans at Hastings, and were unbeaten until the final match of July.

What was going on? This wasn't the Championship team I'd suffered with pretty much since my first game in 1966. In addition to going well in the Sunday League, there was a real chance of the elusive pennant. It seemed the 'invigorating approach to captaincy' was having an effect. How did he do it? How, I asked myself, did this young old Etonian with the odd middle name and relatively modest on field contribution, manage to get a team made up of hardened pros at the end of their careers, alongside the usual caucus of younger players unlikely to be lost to Test duty, to play like this? Admittedly, he had an international-class pair of opening bowlers, but as Sussex supporters too young to have seen Maurice Tate knew from experience, it wasn't easy to get international opening bowlers to bust a gut for the county.

Of course, similar questions were posited that year about the captain of the Test team, but as far as I was concerned, it was John Troutbeck Barclay who reached me first, even if always a couple of days late. And if it hadn't been for that lbw decision at Trent Bridge…….

At the tail end of the eighties, my self-imposed exile over, I settled just a five-minute walk from the Cromwell Road End and the County Ground became once more a regular haunt. Little had changed at the ground, save for a load more sponsor logos plastered about than I remembered, but I had a lot of catching up to do.

When I quizzed friends as to what I'd missed while away, Imran and Le Roux featured heavily, as did Paul Parker and Colin Wells and the Gillette and Nat West triumphs of 1978 and 1986. But time and again, the name John Barclay came up. Almost universally, he was credited with the team's resurgence after the bleak years of the early seventies. He'd achieved something that even the blond Adonis had failed to do – moulded a team greater than the sum of its parts and one which played the game with evident enjoyment to boot. Older companions compared him to David Sheppard, "not as a player of course. But as a captain and as a man." My contemporaries too, all seemed to hold him with nothing but affection and respect; sentiments echoed by those I've spoken to more recently who played under him. Answers to the question I had first asked myself in the British Council reading room, were starting to emerge. Then I read his books and it all became clear.

I started with *Lost in the Long Grass*, with its sketches of those the author has known through cricket. The observations and assessments are often acute, but always deftly delivered and always rooted in a bedrock of generosity. I then moved onto the *The Appeal of the Championship*. I'd waited, partly because I wanted to defer the pleasure of being taken back to the British Council Library. It didn't disappoint. Even though you know the ending, you are somehow kept in suspense through the sheer energy of the writing. And on its penultimate page, you get Ian Gould's succinct summary of his skipper's approach: 'Basically, you always knew what you wanted to do but just waited until the actual suggestion came from someone else.' Read any book on leadership by academics, and they will tell you that knowing what to do, resisting the temptation to do it yourself, and still getting it done, is what distinguishes leaders from managers. The gurus will take several volumes coming up with this; weighty tomes where you will have to wade through a thicket of 'empowerments', 'ownerships' and 'team-generated solutions' just to get to what 'Gunner' Gould said in 20 words. Save yourself the time.

Life Beyond the Airing Cupboard followed, and the picture became complete. It is simply a wonderful book. You get the cricket, you get the man, and you get both evoked in finely judged prose; a prose seasoned with a judicious sprinkling of self-deprecatory humour but which is never allowed to overwhelm the integrity of the main ingredients – love, loss, depression, self-doubt, success, failure, joy, people – the stuff of life. Most of all, people. What emerges from John Barclay's always readable pages is of a man with a deep and serious liking for people; a commitment to learning about and reaching an understanding of his fellow man. And where his fellow man remains beyond comprehension, a suspension of judgement. If Mike Brearley has a degree in people, John warrants an honorary doctorate.

I met John in the year before the pandemic broke, on a July morning at Arundel. I remember that the day before, overhead conditions were grey and the atmosphere muggy. Perfect for swing-bowling but less than elevating. That night it rained, and I woke to a cloudless blue sky and bright sunshine; the kind of day where the pathetic fallacy seems neither fallacy nor pathetic, and you can't help but feel optimistic.

At the Castle Ground, I found my way to John's office over a damp carpet of pine needles steaming gently in the mid-summer heat. I was given coffee and biscuits and we sat and chatted in the village hall-like pavilion. The muffled hum of the chain mower grooming the outfield puttered away in the background. I couldn't have asked for a more perfect setting.

Or a more perfect chat. We talked of Sussex cricket and its headquarters. John relived for me anecdotes from his books – the bus-rides from Patcham in the snow to the dimly lit Chalet and the patient tutelage of Terry Gunn; the naked cavorting on the rain drenched outfield after events in Nottingham meant the county would fall just short of their first pennant; Peter Eaton's lair in the crypt below the committee room where the museum now sits, and where Ian Gould would hang out among ground-keeping paraphernalia, overflowing ashtrays and copies of *Men Only, Mayfair* and *Parade*.

He told me of his love for the ground. He went to his first game in 1962 with his godparents. "It was a beautiful day and David Sheppard got 109." Ever since, it's been an enduring part of his life. "It's not a beautiful ground. Quaint more than beautiful, but with the pavilion and the scoreboard it retains a timelessness. Whenever I go there, it still feels like my second home."

We talked too of John's work, then soon to come to an end with his retirement, leading the Arundel Castle Cricket Foundation, and the inspirational impact of cricket and nature on under-privileged young people. And we talked more generally. John spoke of the importance of kindness: a kindness that needn't cloud a clear and sometimes critical eye, but which always balances the negative and the positive in favour of the latter. He read aloud an extract from Lost in the Long Grass on Lord MacLaurin, where he felt he had come closest to breaching that principle (he hadn't), and he talked about writing.

In keeping with Gunner's assessment of his captaincy, it is no surprise that John considers *Team Mates*, where his primary role was mustering contributions from others rather than doing it all himself, to be the book he's most proud of. The good news for his readers is that there may be more to come. This time a story: "Nothing to do with cricket. At the moment I've got too many ideas and can't decide which would work, but I'm very keen on not being too fixed on the outcome. Just enjoy the process, love doing it and if you sell a couple, great but just have fun. It's nice to put the words together."

All the encounters I have been privileged to have as a result of helping put this book together, have been life-affirming in one way or another, but none more so than that on that perfect July day. I left Arundel with a new signed copy of the revised edition of *The Appeal of the Championship*, a charming water colour by John's wife Renira, replacing its less evocative original front cover. I drove home along the coast road with the sun still high in the sky and the pathetic fallacy firmly intact. And whenever I think back to it, even in the darkest of times, it stays that way.

Georgia Adams

"I have such fond memories. It was just the best playground ever."

I meet Georgia at the cricket school at the Brighton Aldridge Community Academy, where she is coach and centre manager. BACA lies at the edge of the Moulsecoomb estate, according to the latest national Index of Multiple Deprivation, one of the 10% most deprived in the UK. The cricket school, like the rest of the buildings on the old Falmer School site, is relatively new, immaculately curated with the support of Sussex CCC, and the academy Georgia helps run is one of the very few state schools to appear in *The Cricketer's* Top 100 schools.

Georgia has "always loved Hove because of that family feel". For Georgia of course, that 'family feel' is given a particularly personal heft as her childhood involved going with her mum to watch her dad play. Though "my earliest memories are of the old squash courts when I was five or six, just whacking a ball around with Tom Moores", mostly, it was playing cricket on the outfield. "I'd be out there every break in play with Tom and Natalie Moores and Murray Goodwin's and Mark Robinson's kids, running about and fielding and batting and just causing havoc. It was a free for all. We definitely got told off a few times by the stewards for breaking into the nets. I have such fond memories. It was just the best playground ever." And when even childhood energy needed a refuel, it was a short hop to the Wag Shack where the family, along with Candice Davis and Tarsha Goodwin, had set up camp at the start of the day. No wonder the weekends when Sussex were away left a big hole.

Georgia vividly remembers the first pennant in 2003, because it was signalled by her cricket-mad headteacher bursting into her maths lesson with his arms raised in triumph shouting, "They done it, they've only gone and done it!" By the follow-ups in 2005 and 2007, she was an informed watcher of the game. She remembers driving in with her mum and them all hoping dad was still batting when they got there. Sam on the gate would always give them an update as they pulled into the ground – "quite often it was to tell us he was already out" – but whether Chris was at the crease or not, "I became absorbed in men's cricket. I didn't realise that women could actually play proper cricket until I was about 11 or 12."

Indeed, until Clare Connor spotted Georgia playing on the outfield and suggested to Chris that he send her along to Sussex trials, she had never played with a hard ball or worn pads. Her dad never pushed her. His own father had been very focussed on his son's career, but Chris's approach and that of Peter Moores, perhaps realising that Tom and Georgia were safely "obsessed by the game", seemed to be: "Just let them go. They'll find their own way." And they did.

Georgia's career progressed quickly. She made her debut for the county at 16, captained the side at just 21, scoring a century to mark the occasion, and is still the youngest to play 100 games for Sussex Women. "I remember my first senior game at Hove. It was a T20. I scored 40-odd (actually 58, top score) but the best thing about it was a few members coming down to watch us. We were so used to playing in empty fields, it was simply great to have familiar faces there. I always used to love going round the ground as a kid and chatting to people like Brenda."

After finishing school, Georgia was off to Loughborough University and the England Academy. From playing on the outfield at Eaton Road, it looked as though the pathway to the national team would be clear and untroubled. But then came what might have been a terminal roadblock: at the end of her degree, she was summarily dropped from the England programme. She is open and honest about the impact of this set-back: "I'd kind of thought it might happen and I could understand their thinking" but when she received the phone call, it was brutal. "Everything for the last four years had been focussed on getting into the England team. It was just England, England, England and suddenly it seemed it was game over. I was at a crossroads, thinking about giving up and getting a nine to five job away from the game."

The coaching opportunity at BACA came to her rescue, and she threw herself into it. Georgia loves coaching, but she still wanted to play and "very conscious of how privileged I was", she didn't allow herself to languish in the doldrums. "I challenged myself" and took every opportunity to get into the nets at Falmer, and a couple of times a week worked seriously on her batting with her father.

In 2020, with the pandemic raging, the '100' was cancelled and the women had nothing to fall back on. "People were losing their jobs. I felt so very lucky to be on the coaching path." But as lock-down eased, Georgia's determination to pick herself up after the England disappointment, was rewarded. Following a zoom call between the ECB and "about 200 very unhappy women cricketers", the governing body brought forward its plans for a regional structure and to her surprise and delight – "Though I still felt really bad for all those who hadn't been so lucky" – Georgia was one of the 41 to be awarded a retainer contract. When the Rachel

Heyhoe-Flint Trophy was belatedly allowed to go ahead in the bubble, she was once again sailing before the wind. Captaining the Southern Vipers at the Ageas Bowl, Georgia hit an unbeaten 154, averaged over 80 for the series and led her team unbeaten to the trophy. An emphatic resurrection. It couldn't have happened to a nicer person.

As I set off for home, there is a spring in my step. The spanking 'new' school building stretches in a gentle curve against the horizon; a glass palace, glinting in the high-noon sun. In the foreground, the outfield is pristine. From higher up on the hill, the vital sound of kids at break-time drifts down to pitch level where, beneath the youthful whoops and hollers, the determined hum of the roller, cries of "Catch it!" join the soundtrack. It's all a long way from the days when Stanmer Secondary Modern and Westlain Grammar shared the same patch, and pictures of police-horses deployed to break up daily skirmishes between "local schoolboys", would regularly feature in my local paper. Now, large banners announcing Ofsted's judgement of the school as being 'A Good Provider' supply the printed visuals. Say what you like about academisation, there's little doubt that at least at BACA, where philanthropy rather than profit is the driver, it's working.

Approaching the station at Falmer, I pass two 'youths' and catch a snatch of their conversation. In accents more Coldean than cut-glass, they are talking cricket. An hour spent with the self and socially aware and still cricket-obsessed Georgia Adams, is more than enough to foster hope for the future; that ear-wigged soundbite supercharges it.

Von Krumm Publishing – Titles

Before the Lights Went Out – The 1912 Triangular Tournament
-Patrick Ferriday-
Sold Out

Masterly Batting – 100 Great Test Centuries
-Patrick Ferriday, Dave Wilson & Many Others-
Sold Out (Available as ebook)

Frith's Encounters
-David Frith-
Sold Out

Supreme Bowling – 100 Great Test Performances
-Patrick Ferriday, Dave Wilson & Many Others-
£15 (Available as ebook)

'Stoddy': England's Finest Sportsman
-David Frith-
Sold Out (Signed Limited Edition at £40)

Unnatural Selection
-Trevor Woolley-
£15

In Tandem – Cricket's Great Pace Pairs
-Patrick Ferriday-
£15

Hobbsy – A Life in Cricket
-Rob Kelly-
£15 (Signed Limited Edition £50)

Wilfred Rhodes – The Triumphal Arch
-Patrick Ferriday-
£25 (Signed Limited Edition with CD £75)

Field of Dreams – 150 Years at The County Ground, Hove
-Patrick Ferriday & James Mettyear-
£17

Forthcoming Title

The Headley Family
-John Flatley-
£18 – June 2022

All available post free at www.vonkrummpublishing.co.uk